1985

THE AMERICAN
RADICAL PRESS

1880-1960

THE AMERICAN RADICAL PRESS

1880-1960

Edited with an Introduction by
Joseph R. Conlin

Volume II

GREENWOOD PRESS

WESTPORT, CONNECTICUT • LONDON, ENGLAND

Library of Congress Cataloging in Publication Data
Main entry under title:

The American radical press, 1880-1960.

Essays on various periodicals, many having been
written as introductions for Greenwood Press' Radical
reprint series.
Includes bibliographical references.
1. Socialism—Periodicals—History. 2. Communism—
Periodicals—History. 3. Radicalism—Periodicals—
History. 4. Labor and laboring classes—United States
—Periodicals—History. I. Conlin, Joseph Robert, ed.
HX1.A49   335'.00973   72-9825
ISBN 0-8371-6625-X

Library of Congress Catalog Card Number: 72-9825

ISBN: 0-8371-6625-X Set
ISBN: 0-8371-7283-7 Vol. II

First published in 1974
Second printing 1977

Greenwood Press, Inc.
51 Riverside Avenue, Westport, Connecticut 06880

Manufactured in the United States of America

CONTENTS

THE AMERICAN
RADICAL PRESS

1880-1960

Part Eight

ANARCHIST PUBLICATIONS

AS in all the advanced industrial nations, socialism rather than anarchism has dominated American radical history. As in England, for example, American anarchists in the twentieth century have wandered about on the fringes of the Left, held in amusement or contempt by their Socialist fellows. Historically, the anarchists have frequently been neglected. This is unfortunate, for nineteenth-century anarchists had a great deal to do with stimulating and channeling the discontent that was to comprise the Socialist and Communist movements of the present century. The United States produced thinkers such as Benjamin Tucker and Emma Goldman who rank far higher among world anarchists than does any American Socialist within international socialism. And, in the 1960s, with the emergence of a "new radicalism" owing more to a quest for individual identity than to economic deprivation, a sort of anarchism actually came to dominate the American Left.

Still, "The Anarchist" has been most important in recent history in a passive role, as a symbol for antiradicals of social danger. Since the time of the Haymarket Affair of 1886, political cartoonists reliably depicted a tatty, bearded, sinister, *foreign* figure grasping a spherical black bomb as representation of the political menace presented America by the offscourings of Europe. It was a symbol which was the lineal forebear of "The Bolshevik" (who was graphically portrayed in much the same way), the "subversive" of the McCarthy days, the "outside agitator" of the Civil Rights Movement of the 1960s, the "long-haired hippie," even the durable "Jew." It was a convenient and concrete point of focus for vaguely understood social disturbances. But "The Anarchist" did not reflect the movement exemplified by Tucker and Goldman any better than these other symbols reflected the phenomena of their times.

"The Anarchist" was chiefly in vogue during the late nineteenth and early twentieth centuries. This was the age of anarchist terrorism in Europe, and incidents in the United States periodically revived and gave credence to an American spectre: the Haymarket Affair; Alexander Berkman's attack on Henry Clay Frick; Czolgosz's murder of President McKinley; an abortive attempt to dynamite the offices of Morgan and Company in 1920; and, of course, the Sacco-Vanzetti Case and the Spanish Civil War. But even during this period, American anarchism never presented the threat to the capitalist order of the Socialist party or the Industrial Workers of the World, or even of the Communist party of the USA. Anarchism was an esoteric sect that produced many saints but few catechumens. Even in the major incidents of American anarchist history, most of them—Haymarket, Sacco-Vanzetti, Spain—showed anarchists in a passive, persecuted role, *objects* around which other radicals and liberals rallied for purposes and ideals quite unrelated to the anarchist gospel. The legacy of the anarchists proved so fragile that when a reflexively anarchist "New Left" emerged in the 1960s, only a few of the older New Leftists—men like Staughton Lynd and David Dellinger, who were not completely comfortable in "The Movement"—were cognizant of the American anarchist tradition and sought to educate the new radicals to it.

Liberty

BOSTON AND NEW YORK, 1881-1908

HERBERT G. GUTMAN

IN January 1908, a severe fire ended Benjamin R. Tucker's career as a publisher. It destroyed his entire stock of publications and manuscripts, as well as nearly all of his publishing plates. A few months later, Tucker, then fifty-four, published the final issue of *Liberty*. In spite of occasional irregularities and even suspensions, the anarchist magazine had appeared since August 1881. Tucker's friends tried raising money to help him but did not gather sufficient funds to keep the journal alive and its editor in New York City. With a female friend and their newly born child, Tucker quit the United States to live in France. An annuity from his mother's estate allowed him some regular income and encouraged renewed publishing ambitions. "It is my intention," *Liberty*'s few readers learned from its editor in the last issue (April 1908), "to close up my business next summer, and, before January 1, 1909, go to Europe, there to publish *Liberty* (still mainly for America, of course) and such books and pamphlets as my remaining means enable me to print. In Europe the cost of living and of publishing is hardly more than half as much as here." Tucker never resumed putting out *Liberty*, and he never returned to the United States. Born six years before the American Civil War started, he died an expatriate some months after the Munich Pact was signed and in the year that saw the beginning of World War II.

Except in a few histories of American anarchism (such as Eunice M. Schuster's *Native American Anarchism*, James Martin's *Men Against the State*, and Charles Madison's essays in *Critics and Crusaders*), Tucker has been almost entirely neglected by historians of American radical thought and social movements. Part of this results from the fact that historians have given excessive attention to Socialist radicals and few others. Among the anarchists, for example, only Emma Goldman and those who participated in the Haymarket Affair have found historians to weave them into a larger radical fabric. Other anarchist theorists and propagandists remain buried in their polemical journals and await the probing historian who will relate their significance to the larger meaning of their times.

Tucker himself was partly to blame for his own subsequent neglect. He worked hard as editor of *Liberty* and did much else to spread anarchist literature, but he never published a systematic work of his own. In 1893, he penned *Instead of a Book By a Man Too Busy To Write One*. It was just what its title suggested. A devoted admirer admitted that it was no more than a collection "culled from his writings in his periodical, *Liberty*" and a "closely printed volume of nearly 500 pages . . . composed of questions and criticisms by his correspondents and by writers in other periodicals, all answered . . . in that keen, clear-cut style that was the delight of his adherents and the despair of his opponents." *Instead of a Book* went out of print in 1908, and even its original publication was somewhat unusual. Tucker agreed to publish it only after disciples had ordered 600 advance copies. In 1926, Vanguard Press published *Individual Liberty: Selections from the Writings of Benjamin Tucker*, a selective collection of essays mostly from *Liberty* edited by "C.L.S.," a close friend of Tucker who had helped edit and frequently contributed to *Liberty*. C.L.S. greatly admired Tucker, as his introductory words made clear:

> Mr. Tucker is an educated and cultured man. His literary style is both fluent and elegant, his statements concise and accurate, his arguments logical and convincing, and his replies terse and yet courteous. This reader is never at a loss to know what he means. There is not a word too much or too little. Every sentence is rounded and complete—not a redundant syllable or a missing punctuation mark. What he writes is a joy to read, even when the reader is himself the victim of his withering sarcasm or caustic satire.

C.L.S. celebrated his mentor as a significant American exponent of individualist anarchism.

Few others since that time have shown such devotion or even ordinary concern for Tucker and his ideas. Between 1926 and 1966, only specialists on anarchism and disciples paid him attention. More recently, however, collections of anarchist writings have displayed renewed interest in the man and his work. Staughton Lynd's collection, *Nonviolence in America: A Documentary History* (Indianapolis, 1966), includes portions of Tucker's 1890 Salem, Massachusetts, address, "The Relation of the State to the Individual." *Patterns of Anarchy: A Collection of Writings on the Anarchist Tradition* (New York, 1966), edited by Leonard I. Krimmerman and Lewis Perry, contains a typical Tucker thrust against the dangers of "State Socialism" as well the editors' brief reminder that Tucker "wrote with gritty lucidity on a vast range of subjects. . . ."

Hardly enough is yet known to assess Tucker's precise influence and importance, and readers of *Liberty* can judge the quality of Tucker's mind and arguments for themselves in the pages that follow. Here I shall give brief attention to the man who edited the magazine, to the milieu that produced him, and to the problem of assessing anarchist and nonviolent philosophy and doctrine in Gilded Age and Progressive America.

A belated byproduct of the New England Renaissance, Benjamin Tucker nevertheless differed from the pre-Civil War generation of radicals and reformers. Tucker's outlook was early shaped by both native American and European anarchist and other radical critics of early industrial society. Pierre Proudhon was as important to Tucker as was Josiah Warren, and it is of interest to note that Tucker mixed the critical writings of a major French adversary of Karl Marx with those of a direct descendant of a patriot hero in the American Revolution.

An only child, Tucker was born in South Dartmouth, Massachusetts, in 1854, to a Quaker father who first outfitted whaling ships and later ran a New Bedford grocery store. A Unitarian mother, herself the daughter of "a pronounced admirer of Thomas Paine," made for an unusual household by even reformist New England standards. (Both parents, incidentally, later dissociated themselves from Tucker's mature anarchist outlook.) Not much is known about Tucker's childhood, but admirers hinted at prodigal capacities. "At two years," C.L.S. insisted, "Tucker was reading English fluently and at four gleefully discovered that the Episcopal Prayer Book had misquoted the Bible." This seems exaggerated, but Charles Madison tells that Tucker became "a daily devourer of the *New York Tribune* from the age of twelve." The New Bedford Lyceum helped broaden his learning, as did a local Unitarian minister. In 1870, he graduated from the Friends' Academy and then with some hesitation (and much pressure from his parents) spent two or three years at the Massachusetts Institute of Technology. In ways unknown and for reasons unclear, Tucker found a lecture by pioneer anarchist Josiah Warren and contact with Colonel William B. Greene, the American disciple of Proudhon, more meaningful than formal college training. One strain of Gilded-Age American radicalism (a small but significant and little studied strain) had found a ready convert. Tucker later remembered:

> I . . . cherished a choice collection of chaotic and contradictory convictions, which did not begin to clear until I reached the age of eighteen, when a lucky combination of influences transformed me into the consistent anarchist that I have remained until this day. In the meantime, I had been an atheist, a materialist, an evolutionist, a free trader, a champion of the legal eight-hour day, a woman suffragist, an enemy of marriage, and a believer in sexual freedom.

Just how this all came about is not clear, but the young Tucker associated himself with the New England Labor Reform League, a brief venture that brought together some former abolitionists, labor reformers, advocates of women's rights, disciples of Proudhon, utopian Socialists, currency reformers, and others who were discontented and drawn to radical gestures or philosophies. Efforts by Massachusetts town authorities to suppress her right to lecture on "The Principles of Social Freedom" brought Victoria Woodhull, the arch symbol of radical sexual doctrine, to Tucker's attention. The young man helped her win the right to speak, and soon after, when she visited Boston, "she invited him to call on her and promptly seduced him," according to Madison's account. A trip to New York City renewed "his intimacy with Victoria." So did his father's insistence that he study abroad. Victoria and her family went with Tucker, and they all remained together for a short time.

Tucker did not wed Victoria Woodhull, but in these years he married the thought of the American Warren to that of the Frenchman Proudhon. Settled in Boston in the mid-1870s, he translated from the French Proudhon's *What Is Property?*, helped edit Ezra H. Heywood's short-lived *The Word* (Heywood went to prison for publishing material about birth control), and founded the equally ephemeral *Radical Review*, which printed the writings of important New England radicals such as Lysander

Spooner and Stephen Pearl Andrews, as well as acute and angry commentary about such contemporary social crises as the great railroad strikes and "riots" of 1877. But, like Heywood's *Word*, it had few readers and a still briefer life. Tucker's anarchism did not deter the editors of the *Boston Daily Globe* from hiring him in 1878 as an editorial writer. "Although," Madison notes, "he refused to write on any topic that might compromise his anarchistic principles," Tucker remained with the *Globe* for eleven years. During that time, he started *Liberty* (August 1881), and he continued to edit and publish it after moving to New York City in 1892 to take an editorial position on *The Engineering Magazine*. Tucker and *Liberty* remained in the great metropolis until the 1908 fire.

Tucker gave most of his time to editing and publishing *Liberty*, but there was more to his productive American years than just this work. Twice in the late 1880s and early 1890s, he started literary magazines: *The Transatlantic* and *Five Stories a Week*. Neither got off the ground. Started in 1900, the Tucker Publishing Company lasted less than a year. *Liberty* itself was hardly a mass publication. Madison estimates that its circulation "never exceeded six hundred subscribers." Tucker's importance as a conveyor of international avant-garde literature and anarchist and libertarian books and pamphlets, however, extended far beyond the publication of *Liberty* and other magazines. Madison summarizes some of his work for us:

> He translated and published Felix Pyat's *The Rag Picker of Paris*, Claude Tellier's *My Uncle Benjamin*, Zola's *Money* and *Modern Marriage*, Octave Mirabeau's *A Chambermaid's Diary* and Alexandre Arsene's *The Thirty-Six Trades of the State*. He also translated and published French versions of Bakunin's *God and the State*, Chernishevsky's *What Is to Be Done?* and Tolstoy's *Kreutzer Sonata*. In addition, he issued many books and pamphlets by American and English libertarians, such as Stephen Pearl Andrews's *The Science of Society*, William B. Greene's *Mutual Banking*, Lysander Spooner's *Free Political Institutions*, Shaw's *The Quintessence of Ibsenism* and *The Sanity of Art*, and Oscar Wilde's *The Ballad of Reading Gaol*. One of his last ventures was to bring out an English translation of Paul Eltzbacher's *Anarchism*.

Just how widely these and other books and pamphlets circulated and who read them remain to be studied, but their mere issuance suggests a sensitivity and critical mind that deserve the attention of readers preparing to pore over the pages of *Liberty*. That magazine's editor was rot an insular and parochial nineteenth-century American radical.

Tucker's mixture of Warren and Proudhon and his profession of a version of philosophical anarchism that insisted that ''all the affairs of men should be managed by individuals or voluntary associations'' fill the pages of *Liberty* and infuse its content time and again. How Tucker developed these insights together with their strengths and weaknesses will be discovered by individual readers and need not be summarized for them, but certain points should be made. Much of the economic ''theory'' that filled the magazine is antiquated and often tedious and repetitive. Nevertheless, much else is less dated and still retains a freshness. Tucker's bitter quarrels with the ''State Socialists'' reveal a keen sensitivity to the dangers of centralized power and bureaucracy. His regular defense of voluntary associations as a key organizing principle in his stateless society retains contemporary relevance. So, too, do his attacks on ''military discipline'' and the use of ''force'' as a means of repression or as a way of social improvement, as well as his arguments for ''passive resistance'' as a form of organized protest and as an instrument for collective betterment.

The pages of *Liberty* have important historical value beyond what they tell about American anarchist thoughts and Tucker and his philosophy. Incisive comments on matters of public interest such as the Irish Land League, the Haymarket Affair, and the Homestead Lockout, to cite a few examples, fill its pages. So do the recurrent polemics between anarchists, between Tucker and his Socialist critics, and between Tucker and the significant conservative theorists of his time. Hardly a friend, George Bernard Shaw found reason to compliment Tucker for his toughness as a combatant. ''An examination of any number of this Journal will show,'' Shaw observed, ''that as a candid, clear-headed and courageous demonstration of Individualist Anarchism by purely intellectual methods, Mr. Tucker may safely be accepted as one of the most capable spokesmen of his party.''

There is yet a more important reason to study the pages of *Liberty*. No one can argue that it had a large following or affected significant popular movements. It always had just a small and probably quite select following. But its significance cannot be assessed in mere quantitative terms.

Except for dramatic events like the Haymarket Affair and national figures like Emma Goldman, little is yet actually known about native American anarchism in Gilded-Age and Progressive America. In his introduction to *Nonviolence in America: A Documentary History*, Staughton Lynd quickly passes over the decades that separated the nonviolent abolitionists from the pacifists of World War I. "Nonviolence," Lynd writes, "was quiescent for a generation after 1861, just as it had been after 1776. . . . Anarchism formed an important connecting link between nineteenth and twentieth-century nonviolence in America." Just how these links worked themselves out remains the subject of detailed study of isolated men and women, odd journals, and scattered local "movements" between 1860 and 1910.

Rochester, New York, 1969

Alarm

CHICAGO AND NEW YORK,

1884-1889

HERBERT G. GUTMAN

CHICAGO readers picked up their first issue of *Alarm* on October 4, 1884. Its founding editor was Albert R. Parsons. Less than two years later, in May 1886, when Parsons was still in hiding and had not yet voluntarily surrendered himself for trial to the Chicago police, *Alarm* was suppressed and suspended publication. Earlier that year, it had claimed 3,000 readers and was one of five Chicago newspapers published by supporters of the International Working People's Association. *Alarm* was that group's only English-language newspaper. The German *Arbeiter-Zeitung* appeared on weekdays, and the same Chicago anarchosyndicalists also published two German weeklies, *Vorbote* and *Fackel*, and a bohemian weekly, *Boudoucnost*. On November 5, 1887, just a week before Parsons and three German comrades were hanged by the state of Illinois after a trial that followed the famous bomb explosion in Chicago's Haymarket Square on May 4, 1886, *Alarm* resumed publication. Its editor was Dyer D. Lum, a close associate of Parsons. A son of New England abolitionist radicalism and a fervent philosophical anarchist, Lum was to pen the most authoritative and widely read defense of voluntarist trade union philosophy in the 1890s (a pamphlet entitled *The Philosophy of Trades-Unionism*), but between 1887 and 1889 he gave of himself mostly to sustain the dead Parsons' paper. His efforts faltered. *Alarm* was published until April 22, 1888, suspended until June 16 of that year, and finally died in February 1889.

Alarm and its first editor both lived a short time, but their importance for understanding nineteenth-century American radicalism does not depend on their length of survival. Both were central figures in the explosive drama that rocked Gilded Age America in 1886 and 1887 and is subsumed in cold prose by the phrase "the Haymarket Affair." A full understanding of the events that led to that crisis requires a careful study of *Alarm*. Since most students of American social history and American radicalism know the outlines of that episode from reading standard textbooks and histories of radicalism or the labor movement, there is no good reason to summarize the event in this brief article. Readers without background or with just sketchy knowledge of the Haymarket Affair should put aside this volume and read Henry David, *The History of the Haymarket Affair: A Study in the American Social-Revolutionary and Labor Movements* (New York, 1936). That exhaustive study places *Alarm* in a precise and meaningful historical context, dwells at length on the objective social conditions that gave rise to radical social and labor movements in the early 1880s, dissects the philosophical and social bases of contemporary anarchist and Socialist thought, carefully examines the immediate context that led to the bombing, devastatingly analyzes the biased legal procedures that resulted in the conviction and execution of Parsons and his associates, and evaluates the impact of these events on the labor and radical movements. In sum, it remains a superior study and is essential reading for those who want fully to understand *Alarm* and the movement that it represented.

Rather than summarize David's study (and there is little else of value in the secondary literature), it is more useful to examine part of the career of Albert Parsons. Others, including Lum, Parsons' wife Lucy, Lizzie M. Holmes (who wrote under the pseudonym May Hintley and also used her maiden name, Lizzie M. Swank), William Holmes, and C. S. Griffin, contributed to *Alarm* and are central to its story. They, too, deserve mention.

Those convicted with Parsons were either immigrant Americans or the children of immigrants. The most impressive among them, August Spies, had come from central Germany and was the son of a minor government official. Michael Schwab, Adolph Fischer, Louis Lingg, and George Engel (the oldest) also were German immigrants. Schwab, Fischer, and Lingg were artisans: a bookbinder, compositor, and a carpenter, respectively. A tinsmith as a youth but the owner of a "fairly successful yeast business" when arrested, Oscar Neebe was born in New York City of German parents. Samuel Fielden was not a German. Descended from a family of Lancashire handloom weavers, he had grown up in the aftermath of Chartist agitation and had been a lay Methodist preacher before migrating to America in 1868. At the time of his arrest, he owned a team of horses and hauled stone to make his way.

Parsons differed significantly from these seven men. From the nation's earliest days, his family had been at the very center of the American experience. The Parsons family left England and landed at Narragansett Bay in 1632. More than a century later, an ancestor preached in the Great Awakening with Jonathan Edwards, and his son, Major General Samuel Parsons, helped organize the Connecticut Committee of Correspondence, served with George Washington in New Jersey, and directed the military defense of Connecticut. Later, he served as a judge in the Northwest Territory. Not much is known about Albert Parsons' father. Born in Maine, he quit New England in 1830 to settle in Montgomery, Alabama, where he established a shoe and leather factory. "He was a Universalist in religion," the son later wrote, "and held the highest office in the temperance movement of Louisiana and Alabama." Albert hardly knew his parents. He was born in 1848: his father died less than two years later; his mother three years afterwards. An older brother who edited the *Telegraph* in Tyler, Texas, became his guardian, and young Albert lived for a time on a Texas ranch and then on a farm before moving to Galveston to stay with his sister. Not yet twelve years of age, he was indentured for seven years as an apprentice printer on the *Galveston Daily News*—"transformed," he explained, "from a frontier boy into a city civilian." The Civil War caused him to enlist in the "Lone Star Grays," then in an artillery company, and finally in a cavalry brigade headed by his brother. He saw much service with the "McInoly scouts." He was only eighteen when the war ended.

Parsons later described his early postwar experiences: "I traded a good mule, all the property I possessed, for forty acres of corn in the field standing ready for harvest, to a refugee who desired to flee the country. I hired and paid wages (the first they had ever received) to a number of ex-slaves, and together we reaped the harvest." The proceeds allowed him to attend a Waco, Texas, "university" for six months, and then he settled in as a typesetter. In 1868, he founded and edited the *Waco Spectator*. That newspaper supported the Radical Republicans, and both it and its editor "incurred the hatred and contumely of many of my former army comrades, neighbors, and the Klu [*sic*] Klux Klan." The *Spectator* had a short life, and in 1869 Parsons took work as a traveling correspondent and agent for the *Houston Daily Telegraph*. On business in northwestern Texas, he met and later married a woman of Spanish-Indian descent, Lucy Eldine Gonzalez. Before his marriage, he entered fully if briefly into radical state politics. Just twenty-one, he served the Grant administration as assistant assessor and then as chief deputy collector of the U.S. Internal Revenue Bureau. For a time, he was Republican secretary of the Texas State Senate and headed a state militia company. He quit radical politics in 1873, traveled to the north and west as representative of the *Texas Agriculturalist*, and finally decided in 1873 to settle with his wife in Chicago.

Parsons' career as a "scalawag" has not yet been carefully studied. Just as little is known of it as of his Chicago years and those particular experiences that quickly directed this reconstructed southern "rebel" to trade unionism, socialism, and finally anarchism. But a letter he penned in the Cook County Prison, a few days before his execution in November 1887, reflected on these Reconstruction experiences in significant ways. Perhaps he idealized these earlier days or read a new meaning into them, but "scalawag" recollections are so scant that these deserve our attention. Parsons said an 1868 congressional "campaign document" converted him to radicalism:

> I took up, I espoused the cause of those . . . then powerless to defend themselves or reward their friends. For this I was branded a Benedict Arnold—a traitor—by the whole community, save here and there a timorous Republican and a multitude of ignorant but devoted blacks. Young men, with whom I had played as a boy, my old army comrades, with whom I had slept under the same blanket in war campaigns, cut me short.

Parsons remembered the bitter racial conflict in radical Texas and especially the difficult election campaigns:

> Only one who lived amid these scenes can understand the bitterness and hostility which was provoked by the efforts of the blacks to exercise their political freedom. Out of it grew kuklux klans and a feeling of reprisal among the blacks. . . . During the political campaigns, [I] was not permitted shelter and lodging in a white

man's house in my travels over a large extent of territory. . . . On horseback, over prairie, or through the swamps of the Brazos River, accompanied generally by one or two intelligent colored men, we traveled. At noontime or nightfall, our fare was only such as could be had in the rude and poverty-stricken huts of the colored. I ate at their table with them, and slept in the same room, as the huts rarely had but one room. This was a degree of self-degradation in the eyes of the whites which rendered me odious.

A political meeting in Marlin, a small town forty-five miles from Waco, particularly remained fresh in his memory. In that town's courthouse, about one thousand Negroes (some of them women) from the town and the farms nearby and a small but hostile number of whites heard Parsons speak. His words enraged these whites, but the blacks protected him. Parsons remembered much from that time:

They [the Negroes] came, some of them from long distances, on horseback, mules, in ox or horse wagons, and on foot. . . . Dressed in every conceivable garb, some with and some without shoes, some with "Sunday" clothes, others in patched and tattered workday garb, a few with head wrapped in striped bandanas, but most with hats. When the meeting was called to order they removed their hats, disclosing an immense number with hair tied up or curled round strips of corn-shucks. . . . I told them they now no longer had to call any man "master"; they could work for themselves. I exhorted them not to be intimidated; that the United States Government was their friend and protector. I told them to be men. . . . At the close of this meeting, colored men gathered around me, thanking me, etc., and one old, intelligent man, whose hair was as white as the full-blown cotton in the fields, fell upon his knees, and clasping me in his arms, with upturned face streaming with tears, said: "Bless God that I should ever live to see this day. I never thought a white man could be so good and kind to us poor colored folks." I rode out of town that afternoon and stopped with old "Uncle Monday," a famous Baptist preacher, 80 years of age. I can never forget the heartfelt hospitality of this simple-hearted, naturally intelligent old man. At such meetings as these, the new-born manhood was aroused and they [the Negroes] were stirred with new sensations of independence and self-respect. . . .

Not all of Parsons' Texas radical experiences brought such satisfaction. A Waco banker, angry that Parsons had helped Shep Mullens, a Waco blacksmith and a Negro, win election to the State Legislature, cut a two-inch gash in Parsons' temple with a five-pound piece of broken iron cogwheel. Another time, Parsons led twenty-five state militia from Austin to Bell County to protect "the poor blacks in the exercise of their elective franchise." When he wrote this letter, Parsons was a condemned man. He reflected critically on his radical southern years: "I then believed that the colored people were truly freemen, and that they only needed courage to assert it. But I did not then understand or know that economic dependence, *i.e.*, industrial servitude, made political liberty impossible. I did not know, nor did the blacks, [that] they had been merely emancipated from chattel to wage servitude." Nevertheless, Parsons hardly regretted his Reconstruction efforts. He even idealized the Republican party and wrote of the freed blacks and himself: "The Republican party was to them essentially a labor party, since all the wealth and power of the community was arrayed against these poor wage-workers—these *proleteriat*. I engaged in this work with the ardor and disinterestedness of an apostle." Four days after he penned these words, Albert Parsons hung from the gallows.

This introduction ends just as Albert Parsons arrived in Chicago in 1873 to take a job as a "sub" printer on the *Chicago Inter-Ocean*, before a more permanent place opened on the *Chicago Times*. Soon upon arrival, Parsons joined Typographical Union Number 16. Between 1876 and his death eleven years later, Parsons was the dominant English-speaking trade unionist and labor radical in Chicago. Only a part of his time was given over to editing *Alarm*. The full record of his Chicago years has yet to be adequately analyzed, but there are many clues in David's book, in an autobiography that Parsons sketched while in prison and that appeared in the Chicago *Knights of Labor*, October 16 and 23, 1886, and in the pages of *Alarm*. I have called attention to his pre-Chicago years because historians have neglected them, and for an even more important reason. All too frequently the historians of Gilded-Age American radicalism ignore those native Americans who participated and helped shape these movements. ''American conditions'' are emphasized in explaining the rise and fall of radical movements and sects. But these ''conditions'' serve as a mere backdrop. What it was in the ''American experience''—the American social structure and the popular ideology of Republican America—that made radicals of countless native-born Americans has not yet been fully studied. We actually know little about those bred under ''model'' American conditions who were attracted to Socialist and anarchist movements. Albert Parsons' southern experiences were unique among Gilded-Age radicalism. But there were others with American experiences who became radicals and gave much to radical movements. Lucy Parsons came from the Southwest. Dyer Lum grew up among New England abolitionists. The black Socialist, Peter Clark, was a Cincinnati schoolteacher. Eugene V. Debs grew to manhood in an Indiana small town. There is no need to continue this list, but there is reason to emphasize a single point. What did these diverse native Americans and others like them bring from their American experiences to the late nineteenth-century radical movements? Conversely, what in their American experiences drew them to radical movements? The pages of *Alarm* consistently complain of the injustices felt by workers in the early 1880s. The rhetoric that gives form to these complaints was often shaped by an awareness of European anarchist and Socialist doctrines. But there is frequent ''Jeffersonian rhetoric'' in these pages, too, and the republication of *Alarm* makes it possible to begin to reconstruct the American component that contributed so significantly to late nineteenth-century radical and reform movements.

Rochester, New York, 1969

The Rebel

BOSTON, 1895-1896

ROBERT D. MARCUS

THE expression "anarchist communism" has a strange ring to modern ears. Since 1917 anarchism and communism have stood for diametrically opposed tendencies: the one libertarian, antibureaucratic, and individual; the other coercive, oligarchical, and collective. What is today called communism, the anarchists who published *The Rebel* called state socialism and mightily opposed it. They used the word communism with something of its root meaning in the idea of a commune. The classic American statement of anarchist communism, the *Pittsburgh Manifesto of the International Working People's Association*, enunciated in 1883, called for "regulation of all public affairs by free contracts between . . . autonomous (independent) communes and associations, resting on a federalistic basis." Men in this tradition were anarchists in that they believed that coercive laws were unnecessary to maintain human communities. They were communists in their belief that in a world without laws all goods would be held in common and distributed according to need within small, autonomous natural communities—a doctrine sometimes called free communism. Their anarchism distinguished them from Socialists since they opposed all—not simply class—government. Their communism distinguished them from individualist anarchists: the native American tradition of Josiah Warren and Benjamin Tucker, which argued that without laws individuals would possess their own goods and perhaps even their own means of production.

Anarchist communism was a product of the 1870s and probably owes its immediate origin to the famous Paris Commune of 1871. It was formalized as a body of doctrines, given body and depth, as well as popularized and made at least partly respectable by an amazing man, the

387

celebrated Russian anarchist prince, Peter Kropotkin. Johann Most, an exiled German revolutionary, brought the doctrine to the United States, where it had some slight impact on the labor movement in the mid-1880s. A group of Chicago radicals combined Most's anarchist ideas with an interest in trade union organization to form a native American variant of anarchosyndicalism. But this Chicago school, whose leaders were August Spies and Albert R. Parsons, was thoroughly snuffed out in the aftermath of the Haymarket bombing. American anarchism acquired a martyrology and a shrine at Waldheim Cemetery in Chicago, but at the cost of a reputation for terrorism and a broken movement.

After 1887 anarchist communism in America was confined to small groups of Russian Jewish, German, and other immigrants until the mid-1890s, when anarchist propaganda in English—of which *The Rebel* is representative—again emerged as a late-blooming and somewhat pallid offshoot of British anarchism. The movement had flourished in England for a brief period in the 1880s and early 1890s. Newspapers in German, Yiddish, and English appeared in London. Literary rebels moved on the edge of anarchist groups (as would happen in America thirty years later), producing at least two major works of literary anarchism: William Morris' *News from Nowhere* and Oscar Wilde's *The Soul of Man Under Socialism*. But by 1893, interest was waning as radical energies poured into the emerging Labour party and anarchism dwindled into an unimportant sect. England's loss proved America's gain, as English anarchists turned to the United States for new worlds to propagandize.

The history of *The Rebel* almost too neatly symbolizes English-language propaganda for anarchist communism in America. Four men—Harry Kelly, Charles W. Mowbray, James Robb, and N. H. Berman—founded the journal. Kelly, a printer by trade, was of that rarest breed—a native born, English-speaking anarchist communist. Few comrades could have made the offer to Emma Goldman that he did in 1919—that marriage to him would protect her from deportation. Mowbray, by profession a tailor, had been active in English circles in the 1880s, and had settled in Boston after an American lecture tour in 1894. Robb was a tailor as well. N. H. Berman was a Russian Jewish immigrant and a printer.

These backgrounds—Russian Jews, English immigrants, tailors, and printers—summarized the fragile sources of anarchist support. Kelly was the unusual and probably the indispensable element. He had traveled to London, "the Mecca of the revolutionists" as he later described it, and was eager to start an American journal to advance the ideas emanating from the Kropotkin circle. Money for the first issue—$70—was raised by holding a raffle in which the prize was a tailor-made suit. Mowbray and Kelly peddled the raffle tickets among the Boston unions and bought material for the suit out of the funds raised. Robb contributed his tailoring skills to the enterprise by sewing the prize suit. Berman, according to Kelly's later recollections, was "editor and compositor and the writer, publisher and pressman."

Writing years later in another short-lived anarchist journal, *Revolt*, Kelly summarized the course and accomplishments of *The Rebel*:

> From a literary standpoint the publication was pretty fair, from a typographical one it has never been surpassed by any anarchist publication. Issued monthly, first with eight pages and cover and then twelve pages and cover it cost about $80 an issue. We issued six numbers in eight months and then it passed into history and with it our dream of reviving it.
>
> From the ashes of the "Rebel" arose a small four page leaflet which we intended to publish weekly or bi-monthly. Someone suggested we call it the "Match" and we did. Only two numbers appeared and then the "Match" went out.

This hardly glorious career illustrates the difficulties facing English-language anarchist agitation. Mowbray, commenting on the travails of his 1895 lecture tour, noted that "since the death of our comrades in 1887 it has been almost dangerous to call oneself an Anarchist and the holding of meetings in English has been almost impossible." In Chicago, the police had forbidden Mowbray to continue a speech in which he had talked of "battling on Bunker Hill under the red flag, not the Stars and Stripes, but the glorious red flag of triumph." The meeting nearly eventuated in a riot. Only the presence of mind of the bandmaster prevented a full-scale disaster. He distracted the crowd by striking up the Marseillaise, "which was taken up by every man on the grounds until there was one great chorus."

Such rhetoric was frightening to middle-class American society, not only because of the particular stresses of the depression-ridden mid-1890s, but because in the American mind anarchism had become indissolubly linked to acts of terrorism. The Haymarket bombing and Alexander Berkman's attempted assassination of Henry Clay Frick in 1892 were laid to the account of American anarchists. In addition, Americans were aware of the lengthening list of European assassinations and attempted assassinations which they thought of as the work of the "Black International." Every anarchist speaker who called for the destruction of government raised a cry in the press that he was inciting assassins. Most anarchist journals, therefore, spent a good deal of space refuting the charge that in calling for the overthrow of the state they were advocating the "propaganda of the deed."

In this, *The Rebel* was exceptional. Nothing of Mowbray's rhetoric in his speeches crept into their columns. (Although Mowbray was listed on the masthead as editor, according to Harry Kelly he actually contributed but "one or two short articles.") The journal neither condoned nor denounced violence. In fact, in its short life *The Rebel* never so much as reached the subject of the means by which the social revolution would be achieved.

While the question of means has generally been the historical weakness of anarchism, *The Rebel* is particularly pallid in its rebelliousness, which suggests either the immaturity of English-language anarchism in this period or its desire to avoid the stigma attached to the foreign-language anarchists. Probably there was a bit of both. Emma Goldman was apparently unimpressed with Mowbray's intellectual gifts. Kelly was inexperienced: he described himself years later as at the time "young and foolish," possessing only "ideals and an unlimited amount of nervous vitality." Berman, who was so modest that he refused to allow his name to appear in the journal, was hardly a forceful editor. As a result, the journal was heavily dependent on outside sources: reprints of works by Kropotkin, reports of anarchist activities in Europe, editorials from English anarchist journals, announcements of activities in Boston and elsewhere. *The Rebel* had neither a movement to support nor an editorial line—except the negative one of opposing political activity. It never served to propagandize even a small public. By preaching a thoroughly radical doctrine in the most timid possible fashion, it missed almost its entire prospective audience. To discover what small importance it *did* have in the history of American anarchism, we must turn to other considerations.

Emma Goldman in her autobiography refers to the ''renaissance . . . in anarchist ranks . . . especially among American adherents'' in the mid-1890s. English-language anarchists were active in New York; Philadelphia; Portland, Oregon; and Boston. Merlino's *Solidarity* appeared sporadically in New York; Voltairine de Cleyre's ''Ladies Liberal League'' provided a bridge between the traditional American individualist anarchism and the newer anarchist communism; in Portland, a Mennonite family, the Isaaks, combined with a few native Americans to publish the *Firebrand*—which became *Free Society*. But in many ways the Boston group was, at least immediately, the most important because of Harry Kelly's contacts with the English movements. Mowbray and, more important, John Turner, whom Kelly brought over in 1896, proved the bridge between English-speaking and foreign-language anarchists that had been previously lacking. ''John Turner's coming to America,'' writes Emma Goldman, ''gave me an opportunity to test my ability to speak in English, as I often had to preside at his meetings.'' People were learning more than languages; they were beginning to experience the comradeship toward which their ideals pointed. Soon after *The Rebel*'s demise, Kelly was actively working for Berkman's release from prison. Emma Goldman became more and more comfortable speaking in English and began to emerge as the major figure of American anarchism.

This bringing together of English-speaking and immigrant anarchists, to which ''The Rebel Group'' rather than the journal they published made a significant contribution, was the first necessary step toward the creation of the more vivid and interesting anarchist movement which blossomed in the early twentieth century. The one remaining element to give it major cultural importance—a penumbra of liberal sympathizers and advanced literati—would come then. The mass base to make it a significant force in social politics never came at all—unless in the student movements of the 1960s, whose activists knew nothing and cared nothing for their indeed remote ancestors.

Stony Brook, New York, 1968

Mother Earth Bulletin
NEW YORK, 1906-1918

RICHARD DRINNON

IN later years Emma Goldman always said that her life really began in August 1889, when she moved to New York, met Johann Most, editor of the inflammatory paper *Freiheit*, and Alexander Berkman, a young emigré Russian revolutionist, and joined them in the anarchist movement. But the two previous decades had readied her for this moment.

Born in Kovno, Russia, in 1869, Emma was the first child of the marriage of Abraham and Taube Bienowitch Goldman. Her mother, who had two children by a previous marriage, looked upon her infant daughter as an additional burden. Her father never forgave Emma her sex, so desperately had he wanted a son. After her family, torn by dissension and dogged by economic failure, moved to Königsberg, Emma attended *Realschule* for several years and successfully passed her *Gymnasium* examinations. She was denied admittance, however, when her religious instructor refused her a certificate of good character—Emma apparently lacked from the beginning all capacity for the meek smile which turns away authoritarian wrath. With the way to further formal schooling blocked, Emma worked in a cousin's glove factory in St. Petersburg, read widely in the radical literature of the day, and adopted the free-spirited Vera Pavlovna, heroine of Chernyshevsky's *What Is to Be Done?*, as a model for her own life.

In 1885, gladly escaping her father's demands that she submit to an arranged marriage, she emigrated to America with her half-sister, Helena Zodokoff. In Rochester she found work in a ''model'' clothing factory at two dollars and fifty cents a week. Soon she became a critic of the capitalistic motives which prompted German Jews, like her employer, to welcome their Eastern European brethren to Rochester only to exploit them in their factories and shops. In early 1887, she married Jacob Kersner, a fellow factory worker and naturalized citizen, and was shocked to discover that he was impotent. The impossible alliance ended, after an initial separation and a reconciliation, in divorce.

There was thus a necessary beginning to her life as an associate of Most and Berkman and for her role as one of America's outstanding rebels. She was a daughter of the rich ethical demands of the prophetic strain in Judaism, a product of brutal Russian anti-Semitism, a graduate of the radical milieu in St. Petersburg, and a disillusioned observer of the gap between ideality and reality in the United States. She was irresistibly drawn to the anarchism of Peter Kropotkin, the creative Russian scientist and social philosopher, for his theory promised to replace authoritarian social hierarchies, the coercive political state, and supernaturalistic religion by a society of equals, a polity of small organic organizations in free cooperation with each other, and a warm humanism rooted in a concern for decency and justice in this world.

During the Homestead labor conflict of 1893, Emma Goldman helped her comrade Berkman prepare to kill Henry Clay Frick and regretted that a lack of funds prevented her from being at his side when the attempt was made. Though Frick survived, Berkman disappeared for fourteen years behind the gates of Pennsylvania's Western Penitentiary. In 1893 Emma herself began a one-year term on Blackwell's Island, convicted of advising a Union Square audience of unemployed men that "it was their sacred right" to take bread if they were starving and their demands for food were not answered. But in the next few years her ideas on violence gradually changed and she came to reject the fallacy that great ends justify any means. By 1901, when McKinley was shot by Leon Czolgosz, a demented young man, she could sympathize both with the pathetic assassin and with the stricken president. And notwithstanding the most energetic efforts of the authorities, no evidence was ever unearthed to establish her complicity—aside from a few chance remarks on another occasion when Czolgosz had heard her talk only once, and then she had vigorously maintained that anarchism and violence had no necessary connection.

In the opening decades of the new century, Emma Goldman threw herself into a wide range of activities. Perhaps the most accomplished, magnetic speaker in American history, she crisscrossed the country lecturing on anarchism, the new drama, the revolt of women, and birth control. Subject to stubborn and sometimes brutal police and vigilante attempts to censor her remarks or to silence her completely, she joyfully waged countless free-speech fights along lines later followed by the Industrial Workers of the World. Her activities aroused the concern of radicals and liberals over threats to freedom of expression. Roger Baldwin, whose professional interest in civil liberties dated from the influence of her lectures, hardly overstated the case when he later observed: "For the cause of free speech in the United States Emma Goldman fought battles unmatched by the labors of any organization." And in these struggles her magazine, *Mother Earth*, was an indispensable weapon.

Out buggy-riding one February day in 1906, Emma Goldman saw traces of green in the dark fields which called to her mind the image of life germinating in the womb of Mother Earth. She immediately determined to name her proposed monthly *Mother Earth*, for the title "rang in my ears like an old forgotten strain." It was a singularly apt choice. The forgotten strain led directly to Chernyshevsky and Kropotkin on the one hand, and to Jefferson on the other. Indirectly it led back to Locke and beyond to the writer of Psalm 115, who held that the earth belongs "to the children of men." In *Mother Earth* Emma's overriding economic concern was precisely to remake the earth, in Jefferson's words, "a commonstock for man to labour and live on." The happily chosen title also invoked ancient mother-goddesses of fertility to act as witnesses to the original purity and innocence of the procreative urge and to the need for freedom in sexual relations. The title suggested her purpose of combating the obscene approach to sex of the Anthony Comstocks—curious men whose lives were devoted to public interference with private relations.

Mother Earth appeared regularly from 1906 to August 1917, when postal authorities barred it from the mails; the *Mother Earth Bulletin*, its successor, commenced publication in October 1917, but the following May, post office officials declared it, too, unmailable. The first issue was dated March 1906. It contained an article on the fundamentals of anarchism, a report of labor politics in Britain, an attack on nationalism, an appeal for support for Big Bill Haywood and others who had been arrested for the murder of the former governor of Idaho, an article by Emma on feminism, the translation of a poem by Gorky, a review of Ibsen's *Letters*, and an opening blast against censorship. This pattern was generally followed in subsequent issues. A special issue in October 1906, which sympathetically reconsidered the case of Leon Czolgosz, caused some liberal readers to withdraw their support in shocked anger, but *Mother Earth* remained afloat and continued its independent course.

In an effort to help her comrade regain his feet, Emma turned over the editorship to Alexander Berkman shortly after his release from prison. As editor from 1908 to 1915, Berkman contributed substantially to the measure of success enjoyed by the magazine. Already a writer of some power, he went on to develop a simple, forceful style and considerable discrimination as an editor.

Over the years *Mother Earth* played a significant role in American radicalism. It acted as a rallying center for isolated individuals, as an outlet for their ideas and feelings, and as a source of support for them in their difficulties. Its influence was felt beyond the immediate circle of its readers, who numbered from 3,500 to perhaps almost 10,000 at one point. C. E. Scott Wood, the distinguished poet and lawyer, justly dubbed *Mother Earth* a "gadfly" which stung the "mammoth" by soliciting aid for the victims of Lawrence, Paterson, Calumet, Ludlow, for Arturo Giovannitti and Joe Ettor, Matthew Schmidt and David Caplan, Becky Edelson and Margaret Sanger. Very likely the magazine influenced liberals to think more radically on a number of civil rights issues. And, not least, it sounded a radical note in the animated discussion of the day on the relationship of the sexes.

Mother Earth also had some importance as a medium of the arts. Frequently its pages carried translations or reprints from translations of the writings of Tolstoi, Dostoevsky, Gorky; borrowings from Thoreau, Whitman, Emerson; stories by Floyd Dell, Ben Hecht, Sadakichi Hartman, Maxwell Bodenheim; and poems by Scott Wood, Lola Ridge, Arturo Giovannitti, Bayard Boyesen, Joaquin Miller. There were a number of critical studies and reviews of current works. Finally, on occasion, the covers were designed by artists. An obvious cover (December 1907), for instance, was done for Emma by the French artist Grandquan: a portly, supremely satisfied figure in a top hat—labeled, in case there were any so dull as to misunderstand, "Capital"—was placed before a chained Mother Earth and given a revolver and a paper marked "Law" to keep back the horny-handed workers. On a quite different level were the drawings of Robert Minor, Berkman's friend who had a genius for trenchant radical cartoons. Perhaps the best of his covers for *Mother Earth*—Minor also drew for the *Masses*—was that of May 1915, which showed a very limber, very big-mouthed Billy Sunday doing a tango with a very distressed-looking Jesus, whom Sunday had taken down from the cross for this dubious purpose.

Yet, in spite of all this, *Mother Earth* fell short of fulfilling the avant-garde role Emma had planned for it. Little or nothing was done to encourage experiments in style. All the various literary enthusiasms—the imagism, symbolism, futurism which tumbled through the pages of Margaret Anderson's *Little Review*—bypassed Emma's magazine. Even more importantly, not one young writer or poet of importance was first published in *Mother Earth*.

Perhaps more than anything else, *Mother Earth* lacked a sense of humor. Although there were occasional bright patches of satire contributed by Scott Wood and bits of biting sarcasm from the pens of the publisher or editor, the reader was weighed down by the deep Russian seriousness of its pages. No one seemed to have any ability to laugh at himself or his opponents—the causes were too sacred and the issues too momentous for that. Emma and Berkman could never rise to the satire, gaiety, and impertinence (or sink to the frequent prankishness and irresponsibility) of the *Masses* editors. The July 1913 *Masses* cover by John Sloan, for instance, captioned "The Return from Toil" and showing six laughing prostitutes strolling jauntily down the street, would have been out of place on *Mother Earth*. Involving broken lives and pointing to deeper social evils, prostitution deserved a more solemn, serious treatment—or so Emma and Berkman might have argued. Thus, *Mother Earth* had no great appeal to the laughing rebels who clustered around the old *Masses*. As Max Eastman has recalled, even George Bellows, who "threatened sometimes to leave us for Emma Goldman's paper[,] . . . could never quite carry out his threat." Despite the generous admixture of anarchism in his thought and art, Bellows must have been repelled by the anarchist publication's lack of humor. Such humor may well have been a precondition for any real fusion of social and artistic rebellion.

Well aware of her magazine's shortcomings, Emma tried a number of times to account for them. She argued that a number of radical writers had been alienated by the issue which was devoted to a consideration of Czolgosz and his act. But long after that issue was forgotten, the situation had not changed. Then she suggested that the magazine's weaknesses were "partly because of the scarcity of brave spirits, partly because those who are brave cannot always write," but mainly because "those who are brave and can write are compelled to write for money." Her argument had a measure of validity, for supporting *Mother Earth* brought no financial returns and many professional hazards. But the fact remained that other radical literary magazines had no money and still received active support from writers and artists. Although the *Masses* was on record as favoring the revolution, artists were not frightened away.

A large part of the explanation for *Mother Earth*'s relative lack of literary and artistic importance was to be found in its editor and publisher. Berkman's interests were almost completely devoted to political and economic struggles—strikes, demonstrations, the problem of political prisoners. The magazine naturally reflected his interests. Although Emma had other intentions, she, too, was preoccupied with political and social questions. Inevitably, the main courses in *Mother Earth* were politics, economics, and social studies, with literature, poetry, and drawings thrown in for dessert. A successful little magazine of the arts required someone who was a professional writer, poet, critic, or, at the very least, someone like Margaret Anderson, who read poetry with the feeling that it was her religion.

Thus, contrary to what Emma Goldman had hoped, her magazine did little to encourage "the young strivings in the various art forms in America." Yet one must add that *Mother Earth* could hardly have been all things to all radicals—it was something to be a distinguished gadfly.

Emma's activities as a lecturer, editor, and publisher led the *Nation* to insist in 1922 that the name of Emma Goldman be on any list of "the twelve greatest living women." Government officials had long had a quite different view. In 1908, they deprived her of her citizenship by denaturalizing the missing Jacob Kersner. It was decided not to make her a party to the court proceedings against Kersner, for that, as Secretary of Commerce and Labor Oscar S. Straus confidentially wrote the attorney general, "would too obviously indicate that the ultimate design . . . is not to vindicate the naturalization law, but to reach an individual. . . ." In June 1917, she and Berkman were arrested for their leadership of the opposition to conscription and sentenced to two years in prison. After her release from Jefferson City Penitentiary in September 1919, immigration officials, with the energetic aid of J. Edgar Hoover, took advantage of wartime legislation to order her deported to Russia. Three days before

Christmas 1919, Emma Goldman and Alexander Berkman, along with 247 other victims of the postwar Red Scare, sailed back past the Statue of Liberty aboard the transport *Buford*.

Two years later she expatriated herself from Russia. An early supporter of the Bolsheviki, she had soon discovered their suppression of all political dissent. From Sweden and later Germany she lashed out at the emergent totalitarianism in newspaper articles and in her book *My Disillusionment in Russia* (1923). Her sharpest attacks were aimed at the egregious myopia of the liberals and radicals who cried out against the suppression of civil rights in the West and remained silent about much worse in Russia. In 1925, to obtain British citizenship, she married James Colton, a Welsh collier. Fearful of economic dependence, she sought to establish herself through her lectures and royalties from her autobiography, *Living My Life* (1931). When she was not touring England or Canada, she lived in Saint-Tropez, France, where friends had helped her buy a small cottage. In 1934, she was granted a ninety-day stay in the United States, but her visit made her return to exile more of a torment than ever. In 1936, Berkman, seriously ill and despondent over his forced inactivity, committed suicide. Emma Goldman was saved from utter despair over his death by an urgent request from Barcelona that she come to help combat Franco and aid in advancing the social revolution. Apart from three visits to Catalonia during the Spanish Civil War, she stayed in London to enlist understanding and support for her Iberian comrades. In 1939, she went to Canada to raise money for the lost cause. As she had wished, she went out fighting: in February 1940, she suffered a stroke, and on May 14, 1940 she died. Now merely a dead "undesirable alien," United States officials allowed her body to be returned for burial in Chicago's Waldheim Cemetery, near the graves of the Haymarket martyrs.

When "Red Emma" was in her twenties, reporter Nellie Bly was surprised to discover that she was attractive, "with a saucy turned-up nose and very expressive blue-gray eyes . . . [brown hair] falling loosely over her forehead, full lips, strong white teeth, a mild, pleasant voice, with a fetching accent." Four decades later English novelist Ethel Mannin saw her as "short thickset scowling elderly woman with grey hair and thick glasses." Throughout her life, Emma Goldman had an extraordinary capacity for close, lasting friendships, though she could be imperious and, on occasion, insensitive to the feelings of others. Offering an invaluable counterstatement to the pragmatic faith of Progressives and Socialists in the omnicompetent state, she fought for the spiritual freedom of the individual at a time when the organizational walls were closing in. When she died, radicals had almost unanimously rejected her message, but she was, in the words of novelist Evelyn Scott, "the future they will, paradoxically, hark back to in time."

Lewisburg, Pennsylvania, 1968

Blast

SAN FRANCISCO, 1916-1917

RICHARD DRINNON

ALMOST to a man eulogists of success and victims of a professional obsession with power, historians have ignored the editor and publisher of *Blast*. It is a shame. True, he did not ram a canal through an isthmus or wage a war to make ty world safe, but for all that he was a remarkable and, in some ways, a more admirable figure than those who did.

Alexander Berkman was a rebel from a very early age. Born in Vilna, Russia, in 1870 or 1871, he commenced school in St. Petersburg after his prosperous Jewish father had moved his business to the capital. The virtual civil war within Russian society was as close and as fascinating as the streets outside. One day when he was eleven, for example, his recitation of his geography lesson was interrupted by explosions nearby. The Czar, the excited students soon learned, had been assassinated. The youth went to bed that night enchanted by the words: "Will of the People—tyrant removed—Free Russia. . . ." And his notes for a projected autobiography, which unfortunately remained unwritten, show that he was already older than his years: "Visiting university students initiate me into Nihilism. Secret associations and forbidden books."

Small, dark, and intense, Berkman ever after cultivated a taste for forbidden books, forbidden ideas, forbidden ideals. His *Gymnasium* teachers considered him one of their best students but impossibly defiant. They finally expelled him for an essay entitled, "There Is No God." Then, threatened with a "wolf's passport" which would have closed every profession to him, he decided o immigrate to America. Taking steerage passage from Hamburg, he landed in New York in February 1888.

Just four months earlier the men convicted of the Haymarket Bombing had been judicially murdered in Chicago. Berkman almost immediately interested himself in the case: "My vision of America as the land of freedom and promise," he later wrote a friend, "soon became dead ashes." He became an anarchist and follower of the ideas of Peter Kropotkin. Labor strife in Homestead, Pennsylvania, in 1892, moved Berkman to fury. When the force of Pinkerton guards killed ten workers, Berkman resolved to retaliate by assassinating Henry Clay Frick, chairman of Carnegie Steel and employer of the Pinkertons. Though Berkman made a very serious effort to carry through his plan, his intended victim escaped with minor wounds.

Whatever his intentions, Berkman's act was ill-conceived. After his recovery Frick became even more adamantly antiunion. Ironically, the workers misinterpreted Berkman's motives, some assuming he and Frick had had a business misunderstanding and others suspecting him of acting as Frick's secret agent to gain sympathy for the steel baron. On the other hand, the act did prove the authfticity of his belief in his ideals. Moreover, he showed that he was willing to meet the dilemma of violence and counterviolence by sacrificing his own life for the life he attempted to take—as William Marion Reedy once remarked with insight, "Berkman sought not so much to sacrifice Frick as to sacrifice Berkman." Still, the act was in many ways disastrous and its real folly flowed from Berkman's assumption that the just life could be promoted by killing.

Berkman spent the next fourteen years in prison. Four years after his release, he published *Prison Memoirs of an Anarchist* (1912), a searching, well-written inquiry into the psychology of men behind bars. Crowded years followed as editor of Emma Goldman's monthly, *Mother Earth*—in which position he showed himself to be mercifully free of most of the revolutionary clichés which hounded other radicals—as one of the founders and first instructors in the Francisco Ferrer Modern School, as organizer of the unemployed in 1912, and as agitator-at-large for such causes as the Lawrence strike and against such outrages as the Ludlow massacre.

Late in 1915, Berkman went out to California to see if he could help with the cases of Matthew Schmidt and David Caplan, friends who had recently been jailed for their alleged part, along with the McNamara brothers, in the dynamiting, a half-decade earlier, of the Los Angeles Times Building. "Neither of the men was in favor of my idea that ONLY a country-wide campaign of agitation would save them," he wrote a friend. "They wanted to pussyfoot things, and I even had a very hot argument about it with Matt's sister. . . . [Anton] Johannsen and the whole 'radical' labor bunch was [sic] against me." Though Berkman had planned to establish a radical labor weekly in the South, he yielded to Schmidt's pleas that he carry on his work elsewhere.

Berkman was thus publishing and editing the *Blast* in San Francisco when a terrible event occurred during a preparedness parade. On July 22, 1916, a bomb explosion killed eight paraders and bystanders on the spot and wounded forty more. Berkman soon had occasion to mount his countrywide campaign of agitation.

Detective Martin Swanson, retained by local capitalists interested in public utilities, helped pin the crime on Thomas J. Mooney, regarded by his employers as a "troublesome factor" in labor disputes, and on Warren Billings, a young and rather distant associate of Mooney. District Attorney Charles Fickert, who had refused to prosecute graft charges against the president of United Railways, jumped at the chance of prosecuting Mooney, the enemy of United Railways. Mooney and Billings were arrested, without warrants, on July 26, two days after a "Law and Order Committee" raised $400,000 to rid the community of "anarchist elements." Like a boom town, the frameup was thrown together with surprising rapidity.

To make matters worse, liberals, trade unionists, and radicals in the Bay Area assumed from the beginning that Mooney and Billings were guilty. Even the libertarian Fremont Older, editor of the San Francisco *Bulletin*, stood back and expressed the feeling of the general public toward Mooney: "Let the son of a bitch hang."

Berkman and M. Eleanor Fitzgerald, his lovely, red-maned "associate worker," along with a few of their friends, were virtually alone in their conviction that Mooney and Billings were innocent. As a start, Berkman fought in the columns of the *Blast* against the unthinking and spineless acceptance of the Swanson and Fickert charges. He prevailed upon his friend Robert Minor, the gifted cartoonist and journalist, to take up the cause of the arrested men. He organized the first of the Mooney-Billings defense committees, with Emma Goldman, his great comrade, Fitzgerald, and Minor as fellow members. After some weeks of frustrating effort, the committee finally struck a spark of interest in Western radical and labor circles. Fremont Older was one of the first to admit he had been wrong—in 1931 he wrote Emma Goldman that he had been "doing amends'' for his initial response for fifteen years—and to throw his weight behind the campaign for the accused men.

Meanwhile, Emma Goldman had failed to persuade Frank P. Walsh, the nationally famous attorney, to take the case for the defense. Intent upon securing a competent lawyer, Berkman traveled across the country, interesting unions in the case on his way. In New York he sought out the highly paid and well-known figure, W. Bourke Cockran. The latter was so impressed by Berkman's eloquent description of the conspiracy against Mooney that he offered to take the case without pay. While in the East, Berkman also managed to rouse the interest and support of radicals and Jewish labor unions.

Berkman had almost singlehandedly set in motion the nationwide campaign he had talked about earlier. Years later, when Mooney's defense had been taken over by the Communists, Berkman's extraordinary achievement was deliberately ignored in historical presentations of the case. But this much was beyond dispute: thanks primarily to Berkman, Mooney had a competent attorney, some funds, and consideraE LEFT/WING SUPPORT. And this was of crucial importance ''in those early days,'' as Mooney later gratefully wrote Berkman, ''when the going was tough.''

All this, alas, was not enough. Mooney was sentenced to hang and Billings was sentenced to life imprisonment.

Berkman had known all along that he ran great personal risk in his work for the two men. Swanson and Fickert had threatened to hang him along with Mooney. Now with the latter out of the way, action could be taken against ''the real power behind the defense,'' as Fickert described Berkman. With absolutely no real evidence to go on, the district attorney secured a grand jury indictment of Berkman for murder. But by this time, fortunately, the latter was in New York's Tombs, awaiting an appeal of his and Emma Goldman's conviction for conspiring against military registration. The national government's interest, labor and radical protests against his proposed extradition, and the fundamental weakness of the case against him—all contributed to deny Fickert the pleasure of hanging him. Although the dangers Berkman braved to support Mooney were given an unmistakable demonstration, he continued the fight from his jail cell.

Russian workers in Petrograd and sailors in Kronstadt took up the campaign and gave it international dimensions. Ambassador Francis was mystified by the crowds outside the American Embassy in Petrograd chanting "Muni! Muni!" until he was informed that they were protesting the conviction of Mooney in California, half a world away. Such demonstrations, which occurred a number of times in 1917 and early 1918, were answers to messages sent to Russia by Berkman and his coworkers. Thus when Fickert tried to extradite Berkman, Emma Goldman and the committee sent off a cable to Russian sympathizers: "Uncle is sick of the same disease as Tom. Tell friends." The cable slipped by the censors and the demonstrators chanted Berkman's name as well as Mooney's.

President Wilson learned of the protests, of course, through Ambassador Francis. To make sure he felt their full weight, Berkman arranged to have a radical friend go to Washington. Soon Wilson's favorite papers were peppered with news items on the Russian agitation; government officials were personally informed of happenings on the coast. This publicity campaign was just well-started when Wilson announced the appointment of a mediation committee that was to conduct a thorough investigation.

After the investigation Wilson asked Governor Stephens of California to commute Mooney's sentence. Stephens took no action. The Kronstadt sailors again demonstrated and Ambassador Francis reportedly promised to work for the release of the imprisoned men. Then Wilson again wired Stephens that he hoped Mooney's sentence would be commuted, for it would have a "heartfelt effect upon certain international affairs." After further intercessions from the White House, and after a second federal investigation turned up further grave irregularities in Fickert's conduct of the case, Governor Stephens complied with Wilson's repeated requests. Reluctantly, protestingly, Stephens signed the commutation of Mooney's sentence, angrily charging that "the propaganda in his behalf following the plan outlined by Berkman has been so effective as to become world-wide."

Official cowardice and cruelty were to keep Mooney behind bars for more than two decades, but Berkman's campaign had helped save his life.

The pages of the *Blast* seem to smell of black powder or, better, seem to have blown out of the eye of a social hurricane. A sense of absolute emergency pervades almost every column. Unlike some other radical periodicals, this was not mere pose, propped up by a pseudodesperate barricade rhetoric. Real people were being locked up and sentenced to death. Each issue of the *Blast* threatened to be the last. After it had most improbably reached its first birthday, the editor looked back at all the crises, hurries, and harassments with some surprises himself! They had overcome "chicken-hearted printers, fearful of what their respectable customers would say; sly underhand wire-pulling by grafters, high and low; bitter opposition by Mother Grundies in silk shirts and overalls; stupid censorship and arbitrary deprivation of second-class rights; police-terrorized newsdealers, open persecution and hidden malice. . . ." Part of their compensation was in knowing the *Blast* had been "a sharp thorn in the law and order reactionists."

Here and there, apart from all this high seriousness are traces of conscious and unconscious humor. No doubt an example of the latter was an item on a 4th of July picnic, sponsored by the *Blast*, at which "we gave away the premium of Neitzsche's Complete Works, which was 'gathered in' by No. 1775A, held by E. Barabino, a young Italian comrade of Oakland. . . ."

Students of recent history will find the *Blast* useful. Published for less than a year and a half, the *Blast* still gives the careful reader insights into the causes and fights of the political far Left. It remains the best contemporary source on the early phases of the Mooney case. For those interested in Wilsonian liberalism in the prewar months, it contains interesting material on the suppression of *Regeneracion*, a Spanish-language weekly published in Los Angeles, and the imprisonment of its editors, Ricardo and Enrique Flores Magon. Their case, along with others, raised the question of the authenticity of Wilson's liberalism long before all the acts of suppression could be blamed on Attorney General Palmer. Moreover, the Magon case was of significance in its own right, for the brothers were, from all unofficial accounts, men or rare idealism and courage who undertook this early to organize the Mexican Americans—a task that remains unfinished today, as the recent strikes of Cesar Chavez and his Farm Workers Union show. Social historians will be interested in the accounts of the arrests of Emma Goldman and Margaret Sanger, when the latter was still a radical, for their birth control agitation. Students of the graphic arts will be interested in the trenchant social commentary of Robert Minor's cartoons.

Since the *Blast* was first and last a venture in personal journalism, an afterword on its editor is in order. Berkman spent the war years in the federal prison at Atlanta and, in late 1919, along with some 200 other rejects from the American dream, was deported to Russia. He was welcomed with open arms by the revolutionists and was soon enthusiastically at work helping build a new society. From the first, however, he was critical of the economic inequities perpetuated by Lenin and his followers and was increasingly disturbed by the systematic terror. After the slaughter of the Kronstadt sailors in March 1921, Berkman and Emma Goldman left Russia in dismay, convinced that the Communists were intent on "rearing generations of slaves" to the state apparatus.

In Berlin, where he lived for the next few years, Berkman served as secretary-treasurer of the Russian Political Prisoners' Relief Committee, collected most of the materials and affidavits for *Letters from Russian Prisons* (New York: Albert and Charles Boni, 1925), nominally edited by Roger Baldwin and still a valuable source on early Communist oppression, and wrote his own *Bolshevik Myth* (New York: Boni & Liveright, 1925), a discriminating attack on the emergent totalitarianism from a libertarian perspective.

Holding only a Nansen passport as a stateless person, Berkman moved to Paris in 1925, and finally settled in Nice where, save for several interruptions, he lived out the rest of his life. On three occasions in the early 1930s he was expelled from France and, while friends came to his rescue, he remained at the mercy of the authorities and the local gendarmes. Berkman eked out a poor and precarious existence with his writing and translating, and by giving his lifelong friend, Emma Goldman, assistance in writing her *Living My Life* (New York: Alfred A. Knopf, 1931). But his last years hardly supported the contention of Communists that he was living grandly on the Riviera after having "betrayed" the Revolution. Unwilling to exist in complete dependence on the generosity of friends and suffering from a serious illness, Berkman shot himself to death in June 1936.

Berkman died on the eve of the Spanish Civil War and Revolution, which in a sense really marked the beginning of our times, but a statement suitable for an epitaph was written in the 1920s by Eugene O'Neill. "As for my fame (God help us!), and your infame," O'Neill wrote Berkman, "I would be willing to exchange a good deal of mine for a bit of yours. It is not so hard to write what one feels as truth. It is damned hard to live it."

Lewisburg, Pennsylvania, 1968

Road to Freedom

STELTON, NEW JERSEY,

1924-1932

PAUL M. BUHLE

ROAD TO FREEDOM was an important reflection of American anarchist thought and activity in a most trying period when repression on the one hand, and the appeal of a new Soviet government on the other, cut deeply into the anarchists' efforts at growth or even maintenance of a small tendency. Rather than the organ of a social movement, the paper was the product of a handful of men and women who subordinated their often considerable differences to the desire to keep alive one English-language anarchist paper in the United States. And although its voice was heard by few outside anarchist circles, the *Road* did successfully preserve a little longer the hopes and dreams which found, in various ways, new life through younger generations of thinkers and political activists in the 1940s and again in the 1960s.

Road to Freedom was an exotic product even within the anarchist community, for its origins lay in experimental education, utopian anarchism, and even working-class anarchist "propaganda of the deed." Its immediate parent was the Stelton, New Jersey, settlement, which was founded shortly after World War I by the Francisco Ferrer Association (named for the martyred Spanish educator) and grew famous for its "Modern School" of pupil-oriented study, noted widely in Progressive educational circles. The Ferrer Association's first leaders were sons of activists in an Italian anarchist "New Era" movement in Paterson, New Jersey, at the turn of the century, organized by Gaetano Bresci who returned to Italy in 1900 to successfully assassinate King Humbert. By the time of the *Road*'s founding, the Stelton group served primarily as the publication body for a native American movement which had fallen upon bad times.

The anarchist movement in the United States had never been large by European standards. Despite the anarchists' affinity for the Industrial Workers of the World, no such relationship developed as on the Continent where the industrial syndicalists regarded themselves as the "practical wing" of the anarchist movement. There were brilliant figures like later Communist party leader William Z. Foster, who were attracted to French syndicalism and thus to anarchism, but most Wobblies were suspicious of all brands of intellectualism as "impractical," or were simply "Industrial Socialists" like William D. Haywood. Emma Goldman carried on her lively review, *Mother Earth*, defending strikers, freer sexual patterns and artistic experimentalism alike, but, aside from plaguing Socialist party locals around election time, had little influence on mass politics. Her companion, Alexander Berkman, spent fourteen years in prison after his 1893 attempt to assassinate Henry Clay Frick, and emerged agitator-at-large and editor of *Blast*, but was not politically potent in a lasting way. For some anarchists, a greater tragedy was the close of a nineteenth-century tradition of individualist intellectualism with the retirement of its last great figure, Benjamin Tucker. By 1920, intellectually as well as organizationally, the bulk of American anarchism existed within immigrant groups, principally Italian, Russian-Jewish, and Spanish, which, because of their language barrier, had little contact with the nation beyond.

The repression of the "Red Scare" fell very hard upon a movement with no machinery for effective defense. Moreover, the Russian Revolution seemed for a time to prove the anarchists wholly impractical dreamers—especially since the first reports from Russia convinced Socialists and syndicalists alike that the Russian workers ruled directly through soviets, in a manner similar to the IWW's vision for America. The gradual disillusionment with Lenin's belief in immediate world revolution did the anarchists scant good, for the complacency of the 1920s encouraged no dissident form of politics.

Thus the opening editorial in *Road to Freedom* was permeated with pessimism. The man who "utters a word of warning to the persecuted," it held, was forced to "lie low" unless he had the defense of a party structure. And the spectre of a "man on horseback" in America seemed to offer even dimmer prospects for human emancipation. Since the masses were "fed lies" from all the sources around them, they were (as the paper later noted) "densely ignorant, mentally lazy, and unbelievably cruel." And the more power the State possessed, the more laws it would pass, the more "criminals" it would produce, and the more excuses it would have for extending its size and power.

In their attitude toward the State lay the anarchists' primary difference from the Marxists of the Socialist and Communist varieties. Few contributors philosohhically or historically so rationalized the case as T. H. Bell, who argued that the appearance of a State and not the growth of the productive apparatus had *introduced* tyranny into human history; but all shades of anarchists shared a revulsion for the State power that the Marxists seemed unanimous in desiring to increase. During the 1928 campaign, a *Road* editorial made a typical comment:

If you want a dictatorship of cruel, ignorant men vote for the communists, k you want a reformist spell in your national life where a longshoreman may become a judge overnight and even your neighbor may be a government agent prying under your curtain, then vote for the socialists.

The Socialists seemed less culpable for their reformism and parliamentarism—they were politically impotent by the mid-1920s—than for their lack of criticism for the regime in the USSR. There, anarchist peasant leaders like Nestor Mahko had led forces against the White and Red Armies and were at last driven into exile; there, the Kronstadt Rebellion of anarchist tendencies was crushed by military forces under the direction of Leon Trotksy (whose criticisms of Stalin later drew little sympathy from the *Road*). All anarchists in general, but especially the Russian-American anarchist groups, were made profoundly aware of the political prosecution, all the harder to bear when it was delivered in the name of communism. The case of Peter Petrella, which the *Road* recorded in 1930, was exceptional in America but repeated in substance frequently across Europe. Petrella's father and brother had been executed by fascists in Italy, his remaining brother died a political prisoner in a Latin American jail, and he was himself killed in Detroit by the police following an incident at a Sacco-Vanzetti memorial meeting where he defended himself against Communist attacks by shooting two Communists. The differential treatment given political prisoners of various persuasions by the Communist-dominated International Labor Defense in the United States was only one burning reminder of the many anarchists languishing in Russian prison cells.

Nothing so deepened the hatred toward domestic Communists, or the pessimism of the anarchists in this country, as the Sacco-Vanzetti case in which the ''good shoemaker'' and the ''poor fishpeddler'' were executed in a vivid demonstration of reaction-minded attitudes toward anarchist beliefs. Veteran anarchist Harry Kelly recalled that it left him ''in a state of morale bordering on hopelessness and bitterness.'' The only excuse he could offer himself for the workers' inaction at this miscarriage of justice was that ''they do not know, and, not knowing, are indifferent.'' At last, the date of the execution became another of the times marked each year by the *Road to Freedom* for commemoration, and sometimes articles about or from the families of victims appeared, such as the notable letter from Lucy Parsons, widow of one of the Haymarket martyrs executed in 1887. By 1930, when the Marxist Left boldly predicted revolution, the *Road* commented: ''There is no single hopeful sign of an awakening spirit among the people of the West. . . . History has taught the masses nothing.''

Road to Freedom, without a movement's progress to herald, seemed to become dominated by the lives of great personalities, foreign and domestic, past and present. Reprinted writings by, and biographical sketches of, Peter Kropotkin, Voltairine deCleyre, Enrico Malatesta, and many others filled many of its columns, while ironically the only living American individualist anarchist of any note, Benjamin Tucker, wrote from his retirement in Monte Carlo only once, remarking bitterly on the critical review of a book dedicated to Emma Goldman. The paper's attempt to recruit new articles from well-known European anarchists was, in the frustrated comment of one editor, ''futile,'' and consequently its two leading European correspondents, Emma Goldman and Alexander Berkman, loomed all the larger in the paper's veneration. T. H. Bell could call the pair's disillusionment with the Soviet Union—a disillusionment which, according to another correspondent, they did not seek despite their lifelong anarchism—the ''only'' great event in the previous forty years of anarchism. Goldman and Berkman were engrossed in writing books during their European wandering, and rarely found time for special articles for the *Road*. But even intellectual crumbs were welcome, the editor commented, to an American audience that keenly felt its own "intellectual poverty."

This awareness of intellectual impoverishment manifested itself in constant dissatisfaction among anarchists as to the role and content of the paper. Its editor for five of its eight years of existence was Hippolyte Havel, who, even by the mid-1920s, was a three-decade veteran of anarchism in Europe and America, and who, after too many years of internecine strife, sought a neutral policy between the two principal currents of anarchist-communism (rather weak in the English-speaking sector) and individualism. During the easier years surrounding World War I, Havel had been active in the orbit of the Socialist magazine *Masses* and shared its Greenwich Village bohemian environment. This perhaps accounted for his amiability. But even he found it hard to keep patience with both the tendency for readers to demand an easily readable propaganda sheet and the contradictory desire by many for continual philosophical discussion.

Havel did stress the need for financial support of *Road to Freedom* by anarchist groups outside Stelton that seemed to add little constructive effort to their criticism of the paper. By 1930 he reported that the paper, which was in constant financial difficulty, suffered most of all from apathy. Some writers blamed the lackadaisical attitude of the foreign-language groups toward the creation of an American movement; a correspondent's reply, reflecting the difficulties of anarchist agitation in the United States, was that the Anglo-Saxon character was inadequate for the pursuit of an "invisible ideal," dooming the British and American movements to failure. Spanish-language editor Pedro Estreve answered analogously that English-speaking workers could earn triple the wages of their less fortunate comrades and were thus "bourgeois" and closed to anarchist propaganda. Whatever the reason, the *Road*, like the native strain it reflected, remained a collection of sometimes brilliant, often eccentric single figures rather than a united force for change.

Even the stars in the anarchists' galaxy of supporters were fading with age. T. H. Bell, a Scottish-born anarchist who had broken through London police lines to insult Czar Nicholas face-to-face, and had later chained himself to a lamppost in Paris to speak until his voice gave out, had in the latter part of the nineteenth century known "intimately" Kropotkin, Socialist heroes Edward Carpenter and William Morris,

Oscar Wilde, and other leading radical personalities. Now in his seventies, and living in Los Angeles, Bell continued to argue garrulously for a nonviolent transition to anarchism, and to debate with the ghosts, like that of Kropotkin, who continually appeared (through their republished writings) to oppose his plans. Less glamorous but perhaps more important was the veteran anarchist Jo Labadie, who revealed in *Road* his intent to found the Labadie Collection at the University of Michigan, now a repository for important radical documents. But these figures and others were not replaced or succeeded by young anarchists during the life of *Road to Freedom*. Indeed, the only active anarchist youth group published *Vanguard*, a working-class oriented, anarchist-communist publication very far from the philosophical idealism dominant in the *Road*.

Closer and more typical of the *Road* at its best was the paper's "Education Page" by Alexis Ferm who was heavily involved in the activities of the Modern School. Here, Ferm argued for the individual personality development of the child, as against even anarchist propaganda in the school. Anarchists, he candidly added, had no better ideas on child-raising than did anyone else, while the curious Progressive schoolkeepers seemed little concerned in their experimentalism with the effect on the child's individual development—indeed, conservative teachers, inadvertently, were often far better for their pupils. Thus the Modern School was a sign of great humanity, even of success, within the larger isolation and political failure of anarchism: it was the one concrete substantiation of the common anarchist belief in the reality of a new life-style before the end of capitalism.

In its style generally, rather than in its content, was the success and importance of *Road to Freedom*. As Emma Goldman and Alexander Berkman noted on the anniversary of the Sacco-Vanzetti execution, anarchists had learned from Russia that a people could not "establish new social forms on the old foundation of coercion and force." This insight offers a link to the concomitant emergence of anarchism and pacifism (notably in Dwight Macdonald's brilliant *Politics* magazine) during and after World War II. In *Road*, as elsewhere in America, anarchism was an intensely ethical movement—at worst fearful and mistrusting of ordinary people, at best able to see more clearly than the Marxists the shallowness of material reforms so widely proclaimed in Russia and America. As Goldman and Berkman concluded:

True progress is a struggle against the inhumanity of our social existence, against the barbarity of the dominant conceptions . . . a spiritual struggle . . . to free man from his brutish inheritance.

Madison, Wisconsin, 1969

Vanguard

NEW YORK, 1932-1939

ALLEN GUTTMANN

THE founders of *Vanguard*, among whom Samuel Weiner seems to have been the central figure, hoped to "Americanize" the anarchist doctrines of Mikhail Bakunin and to reform American society on the basis of industrial syndicates and decentralized communes. In the first issue (April 1932), the editorial committee indirectly criticized the anarchist organizations that worked within the confines of the immigrant subculture and published journals written in the languages of the immigrant groups: "We understand that the American people must be approached in their own language, with consideration of their local background, culture and problems if the ideas and methods of anarchism are at least to be presented and ultimately realized." In keeping with this aim, the accent was on youth, on the younger generation that had grown up in America and that was formed by American conditions. The original subtitle of the journal was "An Anarchist Youth Publication."

The desire to adjust its rhetoric to American conditions did not mean that *Vanguard* drew upon native sources. The Emersonian and Thoreauvian ideals of civil disobedience—major elements in the radical protest of the 1960s—seemed to have had little or no direct influence upon the contributors to *Vanguard*. The injustice suffered by the immigrants Sacco and Vanzetti figured in issue after issue, whereas the trials of the Abolitionists did not. Although less closely tied to European traditions and events than some anarchist journals, Samuel Weiner and his fellows nevertheless oriented themselves in relation to Bakunin and Marx. When, for instance, Max Nomad criticized Bakunin in *Apostles of Revolution* (1939), David Lawrence hurried to protest against "some of the most slanderous polemics ever written against the great figures of

Anarchist history.'' As the 1930s ran their troubled course, the pages of *Vanguard* were increasingly devoted to events abroad, to the rise of fascism, and, especially, to the Spanish tragedy of 1936-1939.

Despite their desire to find an American audience, the contributors approached political problems abstractly rather than pragmatically. They took ideological questions seriously, even solemnly. Many pages of the journal were consumed in the effort to define principles and explain the apparent paradox of libertarian communism. Although individual liberty was assumed to be a basic good, groups were defined as ''the elementary units of the anarchist movement.'' Groups, moreover, were not ''a heterogeneous collection of individuals.'' They were, on the contrary, manifestations of social solidarity, spontaneous and uncoerced collec-tivities, the primary units of the social system. The ideal was ''mutual cooperation without the State and without bureaucracy.'' The technical problems of organization and administration of an industrial society *without* bureaucratic organization were never solved. The practical dif-ficulties lurking behind the phrase ''a socialized Stateless economy'' were never examined. The slogan ''Not the Government Over Men, But the Administration of Things'' was proclaimed without considering that things are distributed to and used by men, who often differ over who gets what, when, and where.

From this position, the reforms of the 1930s seemed worse than palliatives; they obviously increased the range of centralized bureaucracy and made the state more integrally a part of the citizen's life than at any time since the colonial period. The American Federation of Labor was routinely abused and the CIO fared little better. The methods of liberal democracy were despised: ''Anarchist-Communism, being in direct con-tradiction to the institution of the state, cannot employ parliamentary tactics as a means towards its realization.'' Although the correct tactics were never spelled out in detail, the hope was apparently for the spon-taneous seizure of the entire economic system by the workers employed in it. The sit-down strikes of the mid-1930s were, therefore, one of the few instances of labor action that *Vanguard* was able to affirm.

For the American worker, not to speak of the American capitalist, libertarian communism had little appeal, even during the Great Depres-sion. For the realization of its dream, *Vanguard* had to look abroad, but not to the Soviet Union. The perversions of Stalinism represented the ultimate evil rather than the fulfillment of the promise of socialism. The place was Spain, where the anarchosyndicalists of the *Confederación Nacional del Trabajo* had participated in the bloodless revolution of 1931. The enormous influence of the Spanish anarchists made them an important factor within the Spanish Republic (which, of course, Spanish and American anarchists denounced because of its liberal and Socialist elements). When General Franco and the majority of Spanish generals revolted against their own government, in July 1936, the editors of *Vanguard* became almost obsessed with events in Madrid and Barcelona. If Franco's forces represented the nightmare of fascism, then the social revolution begun in Barcelona surely represented the realization of the dream. *The Blütezeit* of anarchism, movingly described by George Orwell in *Homage to Catalonia*, excited American libertarians. When the libertarian communism of Catalonia was sacrificed by the Madrid government, in May of 1937, in the name of discipline and respectability, *Vanguard* reacted with outrage and indignation. The Communist-sponsored government of Juan Negrín and Indelacio Prieto was condemned as "one controlled by the London bankers." Anarchist cooperation with this government, and acceptance of ministerial posts by Spanish anarchists, posed a difficult dilemma for American idealists. When the war ended in the total defeat of the Republican coalition, *Vanguard* admitted that the Spanish comrades really had had no choice; cooperation with the bad was the only alternative to destruction by the worst. The last issue of the magazine (July 1939) found some solace in the hard lessons learned in Spain.

From editorials and articles, we can derive *Vanguard*'s ideology, but we sense no enthusiasm like that embodied, for instance, in the pages of the *Masses*. The tone of *Vanguard* is almost uniformly dour. It is only in the back pages that we catch glimpses of personalities less grim than their public expressions. The issue of July 1938, which featured an attack on Trotsky by Emma Goldman and a lament over "Treachery in Spain," included also a notice under "Coming Events": "GRAND PICNIC for the VANGUARD at MOHEGAN COLONY, Crompond, N.Y. near Peekskill, on SUNDAY, JULY 10th, all day. Swell time for all. Speakers, entertainment and games. . . ." It is good to know that a world reconstructed on the basis of syndicates and communes might include picnics, even officially sponsored ones.

Amherst, Massachusetts, 1969

Man!

SAN FRANCISCO, 1933-1940

ALLEN GUTTMANN

LIKE most of the anarchist publications appearing after the demise in 1908 of Benjamin Tucker's *Liberty*, and before the rise of the New Left, *Man! A Journal of the Anarchist Ideal and Movement* was very much an intellectual import. Its editor, Marcus Graham (born Robert Parsons), was a Canadian who suffered repeated harassments from the United States' immigration service. The journal's first offices were in an Oakland, California, restaurant operated by two Italian-Americans, Vincent Ferrero and Domenick Sallitto (who were also harassed by the authorities). Many contributors were foreign-born and a large percentage of each monthly issue was devoted to eulogies of the great European anarchists and to excerpts from their work. The first issue, for instance, included a tribute to Enrico Malatesta and an excerpt from William Godwin. (Other members of the anarchist tradition appeared in subsequent issues—Pierre-Joseph Proudhon, Michael Bakunin, Max Stirner, Peter Kropotkin, Elisée Reclus.) Finally, the magazine's interpretations of American society derived from the conceptual schemes of European radicalism.

To characterize *Man!* as this kind of an import is not to denigrate it. The transcendentalism of Emerson and Thoreau was in large measure a naturalization of Carlyle and Coleridge (who borrowed freely from German sources), but Emerson's philosophy fit American conditions closely enough for him to achieve widespread acceptance. Marcus Graham, Jacob Hauser, Samuel Polinow, and other contributors to *Man!* cried out against American conditions that were truly appalling, but they never found the American audience they hoped for. Except for Hippolyte Havel, who figures in Emma Goldman's autobiography, and Ammon A.

Hennacy, who became associated with Dorothy Day and *The Catholic Worker*, the anarchists who wrote for *Man!* are almost completely unremembered.

The doctrinaire quality of the magazine is one reason for its obscurity. The initial manifesto, published in January 1933, shunned "programs, platforms or palliatives" and insisted that compromise was "the doom of so many ideals and idealists."

The Spanish Republic established in 1931 was an instance of compromise, one that rankled the editor of *Man!* because anarchism was far stronger in Spain than in any other nation. Nonetheless, in 1936, when General Franco led his *Movimiento Nacional* in rebellion against the Republic, the anarchists' union, the *Confederación Nacional del Trabajo*, supported the Republic and *Man!* followed suit. Although the editors were uneasy about the idea of anarchists serving as cabinet members, the Spanish Civil War brought forth the most ecstatic and hopeful articles of the magazine's history. In the excited words of Walter Brooks, "Amidst the sombre and abysmal night of reaction spreading its deadly pall over a submissive world of serfs and eunuchs, you have raised the glaring torch of revolt, O Spanish comrades." But the Republic, under the influence of the Soviet Union, acted to repress anarchists and their Trotskyist allies in Catalonia, and *Man!* returned to bitterness against the "marxist gangsters in the service of Spanish and International Capitalism."

Marxist "gangsters" were frequent targets for anarchist abuse. The Soviet Union itself was worse than an example of compromise. In March 1933, Graham wrote, "The Marxian Bolshevist State of Russia will . . . go down in history as the stranglers of the October Revolution of 1917." Ironically, *Man!* agreed with the Communists about the nature of World War II, at least in the period before Hitler's attack on Russia. *Man!* warned late in 1939 that American involvement in the "imperialist" war would be a terrible error.

Roosevelt was, therefore, no hero to *Man!* His "newly conceived Double Deal of Capitalism" was a fraud, an approximation of fascism. In February 1935, Graham denounced Roosevelt in language characteristic of the journal: "As long as the people will continue to look for deliverance with the aid of politicians and religious hucksters, the Roosevelts and the Longs, the Hitlers and the Mussolinis, all these will insidiously be safeguarding the perpetuation of the exploiters' Hell on Earth."

It is easy to smile at the rhetoric and to indicate important differences between Roosevelt and Hitler; it is also necessary to read a journal like *Man!* and to remember (or discover) what the depression was like and what American justice meant to a man like Graham. The execution of Sacco and Vanzetti outraged him as it outraged Maxwell Anderson, John Dos Passos, Felix Frankfurter, and Ben Shahn. The men who worked without protection and died of silicosis at Gauley Bridge, West Virginia, are memorialized in Muriel Rukeyser's poetry as well as in the rage of Samuel Polinow's article in *Man!* The arrest and conviction of the journal's editor proved the truth of at least some of the journal's accusations.

On October 6, 1937, Marcus Graham was taken into custody. He was found guilty under the same laws that had been used to expel Emma Goldman and Alexander Berkman, and sentenced by Judge Leon R. Yankwich to six months in jail. When Yankwich's decision was overruled by the Circuit Court of Appeals, Graham was jailed on a contempt charge. Crippled by litigation, the journal lingered until April 1940.

Amherst, Massachusetts, 1968

Challenge

NEW YORK, 1938-1939

MARTIN GLABERMAN AND GEORGE P. RAWICK

CHALLENGE was a libertarian-syndicalist tabloid weekly published in New York in 1938 and 1939. It should not be confused with other publications of the same name, which were Socialist youth periodicals. It was an attempt to create an English organ of the libertarian-syndicalist movement in the United States to supplement *Vanguard*, which served as a theoretical journal for various predominantly foreign-language libertarian groups, particularly Spanish and Russian.

Under the editorship of Abe Coleman, *Challenge* was sharply distinguished from most organs of the American Left. It rejected most variants of communism and socialism and called for a ''free communism.'' The perspective was both revolutionary and democratic. Coleman thus summed up his platform:

> Equal liberty for everybody—Free Communism. . . . And this liberty can only live in a Democratic Form of Society. . . . The majority of the people will have to want a change before anything can be done about it. They will have to realize that it cannot be done by the Government, nor within the Constitution. Liberty is our goal. . . . Libertarian and democratic procedure our method. . . . Labor unions and consumer co-operatives our organizations.

The paper dealt extensively with the events of the American labor movement and reported and commented on a wide range of internal union struggles. *Challenge* took a neutral attitude toward the impending permanent split between the AFL and the CIO because they regarded the

CIO leaders as procapitalist. They rejected the unions' intervention in traditional politics, which they saw as nothing more than a fight over the division of the spoils.

The paper opposed the centralization of power in the CIO. While this view allowed them to see and criticize the bureaucratization of the labor unions, it also led them to ignore completely the genuine rank-and-file upsurge of the 1930s as well as to some glaring errors of judgment. For example, in the bitter struggle in the United Automobile Workers Union between the Homer Martin wing and a united left wing that included Communists and Socialists, *Challenge* not only kept aloof from both sides but predicted the imminent destruction of the union.

In keeping with the paper's internationalist views and libertarian-syndicalist sympathies, there were frequent articles on anarchist and syndicalist movements and activities around the world, particularly from Latin America, Eastern Europe, and, above all, Spain. In the fifteen months of its existence the paper closely followed the Spanish Civil War. *Challenge* supported, and was closest to, the anarchosyndicalist parties and unions of Spain, in particular the *Confederación Nacional del Trabajo* (CNT) and the *Federación Anarquista Iberica* (FAI). They were highly critical of the Communists in Spain for their crushing of workers' independent movements and for their domination of the famed International Brigade. However, when during the last stages of the Loyalist regime the CNT and FAI joined the government of the Spanish Republic in alliance with nonrevolutionary forces, *Challenge* called their entry into the government suicidal. But they could not find it in their hearts "to condemn so long as we, and the workers of all countries outside of Spain, failed to help them as they deserved."

As the tragedy of the Spanish Civil War ground to an end and the stories of fighting were replaced by ones about the plight of the refugees, more and more prominence was given to the international crises that were leading to war. For example, an issue that reported French antiwar resolutions was followed by one that reported on Munich.

The reports of international events became a major part of the paper. But they also contributed to its death. The radical world of the 1930s was giving ground to the impending catastrophe, and the entire Left, so dedicated to opposing the war, was split as World War II opened. The August 26, 1939, issue of *Challenge* dealt with the Stalin-Hitler pact, which it attacked. This was to be the next-to-last issue of the paper, which disappeared in September 1939, reflecting the internal division in all sectors of the Left.

Although it was outside the mainstream of American radical politics, *Challenge* reflected an American radical tradition that went back to the Western Federation of Miners and the Industrial Workers of the World. It was a current that often seemed to be sustained more by immigrant groups than by native Americans, but it nevertheless reflected a revolutionary yet humanistic trend that never disappeared from the American labor movement.

The humanism that was part of this tendency stands out in an obituary written on the death of B. Charney Vladeck, a Social Democrat of the extreme right wing. Yet *Challenge* managed to say some complimentary things about him.

> It is men like Vladeck who often make us wonder what is it that turns an avid revolutionary into a petty reformer. Is it age—or a comfortable living—or perhaps the good fortune of being successful in so many undertakings? But whatever it is, there must have been something to a man who made so many friends and so many enemies. . . . Many years hence we will say that though he is dead so long, we still miss him.

That might provide a model for someone writing a friendly obituary for *Challenge*. It did not represent a major force, even within the American Left. But it did help sustain the humanity that is occasionally lost in the struggle for a better world. It went down in the face of catastrophes that even more substantial periodicals could not withstand. But it did not compromise with its humanity or its principles as it saw them.

Detroit and Rochester, Michigan, 1969

Retort

BEARSVILLE, NEW YORK,

1942-1951

DONALD CLARK HODGES

ANARCHISM is so often associated with propagandists of the deed that it comes as a surprise to learn that it also has a theoretical basis in biology as well as the social sciences. During the 1940s this theoretical basis was reviewed and elaborated in *Retort*, one of the most sophisticated journals in the literature of American anarchism. Theoretically, it was on a par with its libertarian successor, the magazine *Liberation*, which is far better known and financially more successful. *Retort* was essentially a one-man quarterly, edited by Holley Cantine, Jr., bearded prophet, artist, craftsman, and social philosopher, who was at once the journal's typesetter, printer, binder, business and circulation manager, and owner of the homemade printshop on the hillside farm in Bearsville, New York.

Although most of the luminaries of the anarchist world were being published in its pages, Cantine's own contributions in the form of articles and editorials outweigh in theoretical scope and penetration those of the better known figures. Thus it is a pity that the recent paperback anthologies of anarchism, *The Anarchists*, edited by Irving L. Horowitz (New York, 1964) and *Patterns of Anarchy*, by L. I. Krimmerman and L. Perry (New York, 1966), make no reference at all either to Cantine or to *Retort*.

My first impression of Cantine came from a chance meeting in the early fall of 1944, in the department of philosophy office at New York University. He had come to solicit an article from Professor James Burnham. Later, outside in Washington Square underneath the statue of

Cantine's illustrious forbear sharing the family name, he told me about his magazine and the community of fellow anarchists in nearby Wood-stock. The printing press had originally belonged to the Italian anarchist, Carlo Tresca, never much of a theorist, but rather a man of action, organizing strikes for the IWW in his younger days, and carrying on a large number of vituperative polemics in his paper (*Il Martello*) toward the end of his life. Tresca was murdered in the street outside his office in January 1943. The case is still officially unsolved.

The fate of *Retort*, like that of Tresca's own journal, was to be crushed by outside forces. While the splendid isolation of anarchism explains the survival of libertarian groups, their walls to the outside world have not been hermetically sealed. Moreover, in venturing outside, *Retort* took Marxism for its sparring partner rather than its ally in the class struggle. Its chief mistake, like that of anarchists generally, was to multiply enemies instead of dividing them, to attack its enemies' strongest instead of weakest link, i.e., to aim its main blows against the State instead of a parasitic and otherwise dysfunctional ruling class. In other words, it pursued a strategy so unrealistic as to be scarcely worth heeding, much less refuting.

We cannot overlook the fact that *Retort* was a quarterly of the arts as well as of social philosophy, and that these two had (and have) good reasons for linking up. In the past, anarchism had been most successful as an art form. It is the personal touch and the imaginative side of libertarian thought that has been its major selling point. The big names in *Retort* are not those of social, economic, and political philosophers, much less scientists, but poets like Kenneth Patchen and Kenneth Rexroth, and essayists, critics, and novelists like Paul Goodman, Saul Bellow, Alex Comfort, and Sir Herbert Read. Anarchists have been far more successful in creating a vision of an ideal community than in actually changing the world. Not for nothing did Cantine himself turn his main efforts to fiction once he suspended publication on *Retort*.

For the anarchism of the natural man represented by Cantine, man needs for his daily health a comparatively wide range of activities, plenty of fresh air, exercise involving the use of all his muscles and not just a few, the use of his brain in sufficiently challenging ways to maintain a high level of interest, and a change of pace and occupation to prevent apathy and dullness. One consequence of reviving productive units small enough so that authority does not have a chance to become oppressive is reduced consumption, if not a lower standard of decency. Even so, whatever bleakness is suggested by this picture may be more than compensated by greater spontaneity and opportunity for varied activities from day to day. Decentralization of industry is possible without returning to a handicraft and peasant economy, while advances in science and technology have more humane applications than to techniques of mass production, much less to the manufacture of armaments, luxury items, and gadgets geared to an artificial treadmill dominated by planned obsolescence and the tyranny of fickle and futile fashions.

This brings us to perhaps the major contribution of *Retort*, its uncompromising opposition to militarism and war, again on physiological rather than economic or political grounds. After all, one might be crippled or even killed. Although this consideration is obviously insufficient to deter the millions of cowards in the face of life willing to take the risk and play at the mere game of heroism, it is reason enough to anyone who has the courage to live. Such courage is a consequence of self-love, itself a product of an interesting and variegated life. In marked contrast, the industrial workers of the world, victimized by monotony and corresponding self-hatred, have little to lose but their brains. Fed up as they are with boredom, war offers them at least the promise of a change. Even so, they have infinitely more to gain by warring against the causes of their self-hatred than against their own kind. Hence, even nonpacific anarchism has more to recommend it than misstyled love of country. "Onward, Christian soldiers! Duty's way is plain, slay your Christian neighbors or by them be slain!"

This refusal to fight except in self-defense is not exactly pacifism. The anarchist is not a conscientious objector, unless he also happens to be religiously or at least morally motivated—and then his anarchism is partly self-defeating. Morality, like religion, is historically wed to altruism, whereas Cantine's anarchism, as reflected in *Retort*, is firmly rooted in egoism. After all, the worker's altruism only reinforces the bosses' egoism. If he allows himself to be exploited and fights his employers' battles for them, then he behaves altruistically. Neither his life nor his labors can be called his own.

For Cantine and others, anarchism is the beginning of political wisdom, but it can also become a dead end. Marx, too, was an anarchist in his commitment to a stateless and classless society; he was also an archenemy of bureaucracy, but parted company with Bakunin over questions of strategy and tactics. A frontal assault on the State or even the rights of inheritance was dismissed as so much nonsense; the State has to be captured before it can be smashed or even wither away. Hence the division of Marxists into revolutionary and reformist, Communist and Socialist, depending on the ways and means of capturing power. For anarchists of Cantine's persuasion neither alternative is convincing, for, as Bakunin intimated, capture the State and you become the State's man; in fact, power befriends as soon as it is possessed, remaining an enemy only to outsiders. Marxists, pink or even red, have a longer time perspective; anarchists want their pie neither in the sky nor at the end of history. Hence Cantine's option for building up a nucleus of the classless society within the shell of the old by dropping out of the Welfare State and Great Society altogether.

Cantine's views, as expressed in his editorials, articles, book reviews, and section on "Retorting," reflects the mainstream of anarchism from J.P. Proudhon through Albert Camus and Paul Goodman, the tradition of mutualist, associationist, or communitarian anarchism. Relying heavily on contemporary developments in the social sciences, notably in anthropology and social psychology, Cantine also impresses us with occasional incursions into the economic and political foundations of anarchism. One of the characteristics of communitarian anarchism is to stress at once mutual aid or cooperation and also the importance of the individual ego as the sole repository of dignity and authority. As a matter of fact, communitarians represent a *via media* between two extremes: the individualistic or libertarian anarchism of Max Stirner, Benjamin Tucker, down to and including the indomitable Henry Miller; and the collectivist and Communist anarchism of Michael Bakunin and Peter Kropotkin, together with anarchosyndicalism and left-wing conciliar and self-management communism. The latter have made common cause with the labor movement and the proletariat of exploited workers, instead of representing the interests of individuals as such.

Were we to follow the practice of classifying anarchists in the manner of Socialists and Communists into Right, Center, Left—corresponding to the class basis, interests, composition, perspective, and potential future of each—Cantine's brand of anarchism would belong in the Center. In this group we find religious anarchists who are for the most part pacifists, from primitive Christians to Tolstoi and members of the Catholic Worker movement, such as Dorothy Day and Ammon Hennacy, along with the more direct followers of Proudhon. This associated or communitarian form of anarchism is rooted in a class that belongs more to the past than to the future, but is nonetheless able to survive under socialism: the class of independent petty proprietors, small peasants, self-employed artisans, craftsmen, artists, and professionals, owning their own means of production, yet victimized by monopolies and indirectly exploited by the operation of the market. The middle-of-the-road position of *Retort* is evident in its anticapitalism and critique of bourgeois commercial society on the one hand, and its anti-Marxism and anticommunism on the other. Hence it was an expression not so much of the outlook and interests of the major groups then involved in the class struggle between capital and labor, as of the plight of innocent bystanders caught in the crossfire. The mainstream of anarchism, in other words, was not part of the historical mainstream, but represents rather a largely futile struggle against both socialism and capitalism. Although its self-image points to the future, its biological conservatism and abhorrence of politics have encouraged withdrawal and inaction rather than revolution.

Because of its ambiguous position, the Center of anarchist thought is definitely less influential than the individualistic and Communist wings. On its extreme Right, which merges with the left wing of nineteenth-century bourgeois liberalism, can be found the champions of sexual anarchism or free love, from D. H. Lawrence and the early Bertrand Russell through Henry Miller to Jack Kerouac, Allen Ginsberg, and more recently, the Hippies. In this camp also belong the champions of philosophical, cultural, and educational anarchism, like William Godwin and his son-in-law, Shelley, Sir Herbert Read, and A. S. Neil of Summerhill. This wing of anarchism was and remains completely dissociated from the actual struggles of the unemployed, exploited, and oppressed, having its roots mainly in the precocious and well-to-do children of the old and new middle classes.

Even more vital and considerably more influential is the left wing of anarchism, which merges with the left wing of revolutionary communism. Here we find a wide range of doctrine: first, the now largely defunct conspiratorial and criminal anarchism of Johann Most, the notorious Nechayev, and other propagandists of the deed; second, the anarchist communism or Communist anarchism of Kropotkin, Malatesta, and Alexander Berkman, committed to immediate egalitarianism and the ꞈctarian principle of distribution based on need;

third, the collectivist anarchism of Bakunin and his many followers in the First International, who directed themselves to the common ownership of the means of production and to rewarding each according to his work; fourth, the anarchosyndicalism of F. Pelloutier and W. Machajski, through the IWW, the Spanish anarchists in the *Confederación Nacional del Trabajo,* to the theoretical and historical contributions of Rudolf Rocker and George Woodcock; fifth, and still more influential, the conciliar communism of those left-wing Communists criticized by Lenin in his pamphlet of that title, notably Anton Pannekoek, who published in *Retort*, Paul Mattick, a Marxist economist, Marxist philosophers like Karl Korsch, Maximilian Rubel, Herbert Marcuse, and Raya Dunayevskaya, the psychiatrists Wilhelm Reich and Erich Fromm, the anthropologist Pierre Bessaignet, and the novelists Jean Malaquais and Norman Mailer; and sixth, the self-management or associated workers' communism of the League of Communists of Yugoslavia and of most Yugoslav philosophers associated with the international journal *Praxis*, edited by Gajo Petrovic of the University of Zagreb, which has also published articles by Fromm, Rubel, and Marcuse. The main enemy for conciliar Communists is exploitation, whereas for self-management Communists it is the remaining vestiges of the State and bureaucracy. If anarchism portends anything of international significance, the present Yugoslav experiment of whittling away the State is its most important link to the future.

Yet for the group of artists and intellectuals published in *Retort*, anarchism stood for a present way of life rather than a vision of a future society, and for the interests of the biological or natural man rather than so-called political man. *Retort*'s response to the wormwood of Western European civilization was not merely an aesthetic one. The industrialized, mechanized society of Megalopolis is not only ugly; it is unhealthy and injurious to the senses. Cantine's brand of anarchism focuses on fundamentals, the joy to be had from the simplest and least expensive pleasures, physical cultures, and handicrafts. Like the Epicureans, he would have us drop out from the world in order to maximize not just pleasures, but the balance of pleasure over pain. For him the question is not just ''How can we improve our circumstances?'' but, no less important, ''What does it cost?'' Economic development purchased through hard labor and revolution at the risk of human life are prices which the anarchist, unlike the Communist, is seldom willing to bear.

The mistake of *Retort*, as of anarchism generally, was to underestimate the mythology of the State, and to call it bunk. But there are more true believers than unbelievers, and enlightenment is not sufficient for social change. The superstitious must be maneuvered and pushed into a different pattern, the force of example notwithstanding. In effect, the anarchism of *Retort* was limited in relevance to a minority of highly enlightened and self-reliant individuals, who wanted to enjoy life while they could, and were wise and resourceful enough to know how to do so. But as a way of life it pointed to community redemption rather than to mass salvation, and it never constituted a social movement in any sense. Although Cantine appealed to the tradition of Proudhon, Bakunin, and Kropotkin, we have seen that their anarchism was not all of one piece. In its aloofness from political squabbles and plague-on-both-your-houses attitude to the Cold War, *Retort* assumed the privileged role of critic and spectator. For a few individuals it went a long way, but for the most part it was an irrelevant distraction.

Tallahassee, Florida, 1968

Part Nine

INDEPENDENT AND
AD HOC JOURNALS

HISTORIANS of radicalism in the United States, as well as labor historians, inclined for a long time to focus on *organizations*, even when those organizations were tiny and weak. This is understandable enough. "Labor history" soon became "the history of organized labor" because the unions left records whereas the great unorganized mass of workers did not. Similarly, the smallest Socialist sect could be easily identified by the historian, while independent and scattered radicals were too confusing and, hence, easily ignored. At certain times, especially during the first two decades of the twentieth century, and again during the 1930s, radical history *was* dominated by large and active organizations. But even during these periods, individuals and groups which had little in common with the comprehensive programs of the parties, or thought they could best function independently—these, too, have been a part of the radical scene.

Sometimes such groups were "front" organizations. That is, they were either covertly dominated by the better known parties, or they were genuinely open alliances—but with a single purpose. At other times, the urgency of special issues such as "peace," the status of women, the cause of the Spanish Loyalists or that of the Chinese Communists elicited committees or loose alliances to propagandize for them. In other cases such groups simply could not be classified other than as "independent." The obvious example is Dorothy Day's Catholic Worker Movement, which is certainly "radical," but is not socialist or quite anarchist or communist.

With the exception of the Catholic Worker Movement, these independent radical groups generally charted very specific ends or, in the case of the "feminist" groups and the pacifists, tackled a specific problem. Usually, such movements did not envision that they would achieve permanency as full-fledged political movements. Rather, they regarded themselves principally as propaganda agencies or as "lobbies" within the radical movement. As such, these independent groups—even more so than other radical tendencies—were little more in substance than periodicals. These independent and specialty journals were essential to propaganda, and frequently filled gaps left not only in the establishment press but in the organizational radical press as well.

The Forerunner

NEW YORK, 1909-1916

MADELEINE B. STERN

IN 1906, during a visit to the United States, H. G. Wells was interviewed about his particular American "curiosities." He replied that he wished to meet Charlotte Perkins Gilman. Mrs. Gilman, in the course of her productive life as lecturer, writer, and editor, inspired not only curiosity but impassioned admiration and virulent abhorrence. She was called the George Bernard Shaw of America. Carrie Chapman Catt exalted her as one of the "twelve greatest women." Floyd Dell, who found her an intransigent feminist, admitted that she endorsed only "that work which has in it something high and free, and that love which is the dalliance of the eagles." While Ambrose Bierce regarded her with hostility, the sociologist Lester Ward spoke of her "cosmological perspective" on society. Zona Gale characterized her best perhaps when she wrote that Charlotte Gilman "has burned her way about the world" with her message that life is growth and that man is not his brother's keeper but his brother's brother.

The slender, lithe Charlotte Gilman was indeed a woman of plunging mind and of bright incandescence, a latter-day intellectual Victoria Woodhull whose piercing eyes blazed without heat, a "militant Madonna" whose voice, thin as her body, was singularly penetrating and impassioned. It is in the pages of *The Forerunner* that her voice carries farthest, for—her greatest single achievement—that periodical was owned, edited, published, and written in its entirety by Charlotte Perkins Gilman. It was, in essence, Charlotte Perkins Gilman's magazine. A glance at Mrs. Gilman's life will, therefore, elucidate the nature of *The Forerunner*.

The woman who was destined to be called a world rouser, an

awakener, a social inventor, was born in Hartford, Connecticut, in 1860, to a heritage as distinguished as it was unhappy. Through her father, Frederick Beecher Perkins, she was descended from those strong-minded Beechers whose ministries made man's perfectibility seem imminent. Yet her father, an editor and scholar who became chief librarian of the San Francisco Public Library, had a restless nature and soon deserted his first wife, Charlotte's mother, Mary Westcott Perkins. The child grew up, therefore, in an unhappy, fatherless home burdened with poverty and debt. Between cooperative housekeeping experiments and Swedenborgian associates, she found little stability. Extensive reading took the place of formal education; yet at eleven she conceived what she called a "color concert" and she was subsequently able to earn money by teaching art and painting trinkets. At twenty-four, Charlotte Perkins married a Rhode Island artist, Charles Walter Stetson, by whom she had a daughter, Katharine Beecher Stetson. Like her parents' marriage this union also proved unhappy. Ten years later, in 1894, they were divorced, Charles Stetson marrying Charlotte's closest friend, Grace Ellery Channing. Charlotte's personal loyalty to her husband and his new wife persisted —and raised eyebrows—through the years.

A decade of intense struggle followed. During part of the time, Charlotte's "domicile was a trunk" in which she carried the necessities of her life, necessities that included two books, Whitman's poetry and Olive Schreiner's *Dreams*. For much of the time she was ill with a deepseated melancholia and loss of energy, a disease labeled as "breakdown" and mistreated by the eminent Dr. S. Weir Mitchell. She lived for a while in California, that state of many cults and theories, where she was exposed to the Nationalist movement, a "political sequel" to Edward Bellamy's *Looking Backward*. Then, in June 1900, she entered upon a second, happier marriage with her cousin, George Houghton Gilman of New York City.

Long before, however, as early indeed as 1890, she had begun her public life as lecturer on various phases of ethics, economics, and sociology. Like all the Beechers, she too was a preacher, albeit less on morality than on social philosophy, and her pay frequently came from collections. She traveled abroad, attending the International Socialist and Labor Congress in England, where she joined the Fabian Socialists led by George Bernard Shaw and the Webbs. Besides lecturing, she wrote, beginning her literary career with a remarkable short story on insanity,

"The Yellow Wall-Paper," inspired by Dr. Mitchell's mistreatment of her ailment, and continuing with poems and extended essays of children, the home, and human work. Her major book, *Women and Economics* (1898), was a "revolutionary sociological essay" on the economic relations between men and women, ranked with Mary Wollstonecraft's *Vindication of the Rights of Woman* and Olive Schreiner's *Woman and Labor*.

By 1909, when Charlotte Gilman was nearly fifty, she had developed in her mind a host of universal heresies and in her desk an accumulation of rejected manuscripts originally designed for magazine consumption. As a repository of both the heresies and the manuscripts, she established *The Forerunner*, a monthly that would run from November 1909 through December 1916. Only half its cost of production ($3,000 a year) would be met by its income; the other half Mrs. Gilman would meet by additional writing and lecturing. This literary *tour de force*, this one-man show, would begin with "no capital except a mental one." But its mental capital, especially in the fields of women's rights and socialism, would forcefully engage the attention of a small group of intellectuals for seven eventful years of American history.

They were the years when America turned from isolationism to its startling rise to world power. They were the years when "Mrs. So-and-so and maid" were drowned on the *Titanic* and the years when the search for social and economic security made its tentative beginnings. Between 1909 and 1916, America lived through Taft's dollar diplomacy and the Progressive era of La Follette. The technological revolution, a shifting population, and the social problems involved in both were major developments of the time. The Panama Canal, the auto or "private locomotive," the movies, Langley's aeroplane—all were making the machine age a reality. The Socialist party, first organized in 1900, was growing rapidly; the "liberals" were concerned with social insurance legislation and the regulation of child labor, safety and health codes, and the eight-hour day for railroad workers. They were the years of Jane Addams' Hull House and the Balkan War that would soon become the "European nightmare." Women were sufficiently "advanced" to bring down upon themselves the jeers of an "Association Opposed to the Extension of Suffrage to Women." The books of the time—books to which Mrs. Gilman would often give attention in *The Forerunner*—included Gustavus Myers' *History of the Great American*

Fortunes and William Allen White's *A Certain Rich Man*. Upton Sinclair was exposing the dangers of ignorance and silence, Emma Goldman was writing on anarchism, and Ida Tarbell was an antidote to Booth Tarkington. Most people were reading *Queed* and *Daddy-Long-Legs*, but the special few to whom Mrs. Gilman would address herself were reading the *Diary of a Shirtwaist Striker* or the frank and revolutionary *Love and Marriage* by Ellen Key. With the rise of the modern newspaper came the rise of yellow journalism and William Randolph Hearst's "frantic jingoism," which Mrs. Gilman violently abhorred.

There were magazines, too, magazines for women, like *The Woman's Journal*, the Boston suffrage paper edited by Alice Stone Blackwell that served as the official organ of the National American Women Suffrage Association. A Kansas periodical, *The Progressive Woman*, aimed at woman's political and economic freedom, as did New Orleans' *Woman's Era*. But by and large the women's magazines were either large mail-order papers, led by *The Ladies' Home Journal*, or smaller periodicals concerned with food, motherhood, and needlework. In the field of socialism, there were magazines like *International Socialist Review*, the party's official publication, and the *Masses*, which Mrs. Gilman strongly endorsed.

There was no magazine, however, that combined, as *The Forerunner* would combine, a crusade for women's rights and a plea for socialism. There was no magazine that served, as Mrs. Gilman's magazine would, as a special medium designed to appeal "much to the few," not "a little to the many." Its purposes were entirely its own: "to stimulate thought; to arouse hope, courage and impatience; to offer practical suggestions and solutions, to voice the strong assurance of better living, here, now, in our own hands to make."

Begun as a thirty-two page monthly, priced at ten cents a copy or one dollar a year, *The Forerunner* emerged from the press of Charlton Company (a variant of "Charlotte") at 67 Wall Street, New York City, in November 1909. Although it needed only 3,000 subscribers to pay its running expenses, it never attained that number and it continued to be published at the expense of the owner-editor. It had no newsstand edition; it was distributed by such organizations as the Rand School of Social Science and the Women's Political Union, the National Women Suffrage Association and the Socialist Literature Company. It was printed by a subscriber, Rudolph Rochow. Otherwise, *The Forerunner* was entirely the production of Charlotte Perkins Gilman, a monthly issue of Gilman's Works. Even its advertisements, which it carried for a short time, were written and vouched for personally by Mrs. Gilman—advertisements of Moore's Fountain Pen or Fels-Naphtha Soap, Lowney's Chocolate, or Holeproof Hosiery. Mrs. Gilman, who would advertise only such products as she could honestly endorse, soon ceased advertising anything at all and reduced her magazine to twenty-eight pages of solid text.

In that text she promoted discussions of what she considered the real problems of life, applying to them fresh standards afforded by the larger knowledge of the day. Preeminently her text was original, the product of a thinker who abhorred the deep ruts of mental habit. In the course of its seven volumes, Mrs. Gilman supplied her public with seven serial novels, all of them concerned less with literary style and inventiveness than with propaganda for the emancipation of women; seven provocative serial studies that included "Our Androcentric Culture" and "Social Ethics," "The Dress of Women," and "Growth and Combat"; and such a variety of essays and articles, short stories, and verse, comment and review, that each of her seven volumes equaled in bulk four books of 63,000 words each.

Besides being a fountainhead of words, Charlotte Perkins Gilman was an iconoclast with two major strings to her bow: the emancipation of women and socialism. To understand the nature of *The Forerunner*, it is essential to understand Mrs. Gilman's particular brand of each of these concepts. Her credo on women was, superficially at least, a simple one. She wished to point out the expanding implications of the notion that women were people. "We have the masculine and the feminine," she put it, "but above them both is the human, which has nothing to do with sex. The argument for equal freedom and equal opportunities for women rests not on . . . Blackstone but on the law of nature." *The Forerunner*, therefore, was less a suffrage paper than a woman's paper, and less a woman's paper than a paper passionately interested in humanity. It advocated woman suffrage of course, for this was essential to a true democracy; but the political equality of men and women was not in itself sufficient to emancipate women. To be fully emancipated, women must be free to develop not merely in "femaleness," but in "humanness." They must be awakened to active individual and social existence; they must especially be economically independent. Domestic industry, Mrs. Gilman believed, should be professionalized, with children in the care of experts, so that the home would be no confining "workshop," and marriage would be more than a mere livelihood. With such aims realized, the great body of voting American women could indeed become the hope of the world, legislating and working for better homes and towns, better health and education.

The idea of women as human beings naturally had a vital part to play in Mrs. Gilman's variety of socialism. This was of the early humanitarian kind, opposed to Marx, and not even strictly Fabian. She was, as Alexander Black remarked, "warmly responsive to the religion of socialistic effort but cold to the theology of Socialism." Socialism she conceived as a natural evolution of our economic system and society as the human unit in whose interests it would legislate. Every step in the direction of such a socialism would benefit humanity, reducing class privileges, enlarging opportunity, and insuring employment. Why, she demanded, should the man who produces the apple get 10 percent of its price and the man who sells it to the consumer get 40 percent? Socialism, she reiterated, "is an economic system which requires the public ownership and management of all natural monopolies (such as land, water, coal, oil, copper, etc.), and the means of production, the last meaning mills, factories, shops." Less interested in economic determinism and the class struggle, Charlotte Gilman proselytized in the pages of *The Forerunner* for the social administration of social functions, for collective production and the public ownership of natural resources. Like her brand of women's rights, her socialism was imbedded in her omnipresent belief in "humanness" and "growth."

Along with these two major crusades, Charlotte Gilman championed other causes in *The Forerunner* and exhibited other sparkling facets of Gilmania. As an iconoclast she refused to be "overawed by authority and precedent." Her unborn grandchild was, she felt, more real than her buried grandfather. In her magazine, therefore, she proceeded, month by month, to obliterate graveyards and to build in their place her particular brave new world. It was a world that would mark the apex of the ethical movement of the preceding twenty years, a world that practiced the new ethics which was social. As she explained, "a society, to endure and to grow, must guarantee to its component individuals such conditions as will enable them to live in physical health, in personal happiness, in the successful reproduction of the species, and in free progress. So far this has never been done.''

In the pages of *The Forerunner*, Mrs. Gilman cleared the ground for that society. Openly and frankly she discussed private morality and public immorality, prostitution, social diseases, and marriage, the statistics of what was euphemistically called the social evil. While her attacks upon child labor and her pleas for social sanitation and a minimum wage are dated (for the simple reason that civilization often catches up with radical thinkers), in much of her thought she was in advance not only of her own time but of ours. She championed academic freedom and a world city as the seat of a world government; she endorsed a constructive internationalism and a world federation outlined in a proclamation of interdependence. She even objected to the smoke menace and the offensive noises of 1909-1916! She opposed American imperialism in Mexico. She wrote the following, still prophetic, sentence: ''Segregation by nationality with schools of special race or church does not tend to promote American citizenship.'' Especially she believed in youth, whose duty it was to ''lift the world forward.''

She was, in a manner, an early existentialist. ''It is always NOW!'' she exclaimed. The three governing laws of life she defined as ''To Be (Existence); To Re-be (Reproduction); To Be Better.'' The basic fact of her sociology was continuous, active, ever-increasing human life. She ended her decalogue with this commandment: ''Thou shalt not worship the past nor be content with the present, for growth is the law of life.''

In December 1916 four months before the United States went to war, the last number of *The Forerunner* was issued. Although its subscription list had always been small, it had circulated Mrs. Gilman's ideas for seven years to some five to seven thousand readers, a figure obtained by the editorial arithmetic of multiplying the number of subscribers by five to estimate the number of readers. Mrs. Gilman stopped *The Forerunner* for several reasons, principally because she had said what she wished to say, because there were not sufficient people to support it financially, and because, understandably, she could no longer carry on the tremendous burden.

By and large her work was done. With America's entry into the war, Mrs. Gilman stood with the Allies, writing for a newspaper syndicate and lecturing for one of the smaller Chautauquas. She was preoccupied with the writing of her autobiography—*The Living of Charlotte Perkins Gilman*, which was published posthumously. After her husband's death in 1934, Mrs. Gilman lived with her daughter in Pasadena, California, and there, afflicted with cancer, she committed suicide on August 17, 1935. Her final act was in itself a form of service. She wrote, "Believing this choice to be of social service in promoting wiser views on this question, I have preferred chloroform to cancer."

On the day her obituary appeared in the *New York Times*, President Roosevelt was expected to nominate a woman to the Social Security Board, and bank and rail pension bills were speeding through Congress. Each of these announcements dramatized in a small way the work of Charlotte Perkins Gilman and the purposes of her *Forerunner*. The woman who had a passion for ideas, who sought at all times to shake complacency, had lived to see the partial fruition of her causes. In the enfranchisement of women and the development of the labor movement, with increased wages and reduced hours, a few aspects of the larger humanism she championed were realized. On the other hand, she who scorned compromise stormed that enfranchised woman was still "the slave of fashion"—"the world waits while she powders her nose." Socialism she found confused with bolshevism, and race consciousness on the increase rather than decrease. In the population explosion she foresaw the cause of war.

When it first appeared, *The Forerunner*—that one-man receptacle of Mrs. Gilman's ideas—took the place for which it was designed, appealing to a slightly different and slightly wider audience than did the so-called "reform publications" and suffrage papers of the day. Fifty years ago, it was "a treasury of the advanced development of the social awareness" of its era. Since in much of her thinking Mrs. Gilman was in advance of her time, *The Forerunner*, being prophetic, is still timely. The periodical still stands for the complete emancipation of women and the progress of economic socialism, for humanness in women and in men, for the New Ethics and the New World. But now that half a century has passed, *The Forerunner* takes on an added historical significance as a documentary panorama of the socioeconomic philosophy of the early twentieth century. "I hope to see a 'library edition' some day," Charlotte Perkins Gilman once wrote. In retrospect, *The Forerunner* takes a more important place than it did with its first emergence from the press. The New England conscience that preached revolutionary doctrine half a century ago today utters convictions unbound by geography. What was prophetic in *The Forerunner* has become timely; what was timely has become historical.

New York City, 1968

Socialist Woman

CHICAGO AND GIRARD, KANSAS, 1907-1909

Progressive Woman

GIRARD AND CHICAGO, 1909—

Coming Nation

CHICAGO, 1912-1913

MARI JO BUHLE

AMERICAN Socialists promised a golden future for women within the cooperative commonwealth, where the end of economic oppression would bring complete human solidarity. But this expectation could not easily obliterate the real experiences of women or change their practical, less abstractly political approaches to day-to-day problems. Socialist women themselves sought to create a theory and practice to bridge this gap and to force the Socialist movement to alter its position toward women's particular needs and strengths. The *Socialist Woman* (renamed the *Progressive Woman* in order to reach larger audiences) was a unique venture in Socialist journalism, conscientiously planned to advance these goals. Under the editorship of Josephine Conger-Kaneko, the magazine operated politically within the limitations that capitalism had imposed upon women, describing the relationship of household economics in the largest sense to their concerns of home, child, and the family purse.

The *Progressive Woman* was not a feminist journal by today's standards: it was published solely to stimulate the awakening of women to socialism and to encourage Socialist party membership. The party itself formally guaranteed equal participation of women members, which was an advanced position for the time. Within and around the party milieu, the *Progressive Woman* gained considerable influence by promoting the sense of importance that Socialist women could assume in their own distinct political activity. Yet even to the degree that women Socialists were obliged to find their special tasks, the independence of their effort was ultimately viewed within the party as, at best, a drain on needed energies and, at worst, a potential threat to party unity. Almost without intention, the magazine helped create an autonomous and self-conscious women's Socialist movement, a movement that in turn was stifled by the neglect and outright hostility of official socialism.

From the time of the party's formation at the Unity Convention of 1901, women across the country had established study clubs and auxiliary branches to the Socialist locals. Organizing separately, under their own impetus, these women began an intensive campaign to educate themselves in the principles of socialism. As a result, they gained the theoretical proficiency and self-confidence to participate in regular party affairs, and to broaden their agitation among neighboring women. The women's activities touched isolated towns in the Midwest and West as well as the familiar urban centers of Socialist agitation, and spread rapidly into Kansas, Oklahoma, and Texas. The most committed organizers hoped to build a nationwide union or league, similar in form to the federative structure of the Temperance, Suffrage, and Women's Club movements. Many of the women had in fact learned their methods of organization and procedure from these movements and simply transferred their experiences to Socialist politics. By 1907, when Josephine Conger-Kaneko began her plans for the *Socialist Woman*, the California-based Women's National Socialist Union had affiliates in scattered localities across the country and promised a small but enthusiastic audience for such a magazine.

While many of the women organized into these special clubs were dues-paying members of the party, the sense of their own unique role immediately created political frictions within the regular locals. Many party members, including some of the most prominent women organizers, voiced strong reservations about any dual network of women. Converting women to socialism, while an admirable goal, might detract from the enlistment of women directly into the party, by providing a comfortable half-way station. Moreover, left to their own devices the women might concentrate solely on such "bourgeois" reforms as suffrage. A margin of independence for the women's branches was guaranteed by the local autonomy established in the party's constitution, but from their beginnings the clubs found themselves defending their political legitimacy. For Josephine Conger-Kaneko, there was no inherent divisiveness in women's organizations. With her training in reform and Socialist magazines to write on the "Woman Question," she perceived a need only for a forum for discussing the issue and for intensified agitation among women.

In May 1908, the party convention responded to the increasing numbers organized into the burgeoning women's branches, hoping to draw all converts directly into the party. In 1907, the International Congress of Socialists (the "Second International") had formulated a special woman's rights plank in its constitution, and had urged its affiliates to actively support woman's suffrage. The American party's neglect of women now became a vital topic of internal discussion. Prominent Socialists, both female and male, urged the establishment *within* the party of a committee to provide methods of organization and propaganda among women. The convention adopted plans for a special committee, supported with sufficient funds to maintain a woman organizer in the field. While the response from the women's branches was less than enthusiastic, the practical efficiency of the Woman's National Committee eventually dispelled their hesitancy. The Socialist party, however minimally, provided financial support and organizational connections to advance the needed, special work. Conger-Kaneko gratefully accepted the decision and encouraged women to put their best efforts into building party membership. Thus the *Progressive Woman* became, in practice, an effective organ of the Woman's National Committee, carrying reports from the field organizers and local branches, plus regular contributions from "intellectual proletarians," as Conger-Kaneko called the professional Socialist propagandists.

During the peak of Socialist women's activities, from 1908 to 1912, the *Progressive Woman* achieved the kind of success that only a social movement can sustain. After a brief beginning in Chicago, the magazine moved to the more efficient printing operations of Girard, Kansas, home of the leading Socialist national newspaper, *The Appeal to Reason*. Conger-Kaneko gained the volunteer work of local Girard women to supplement the help she had from her husband, Kiichi Kaneko. The *Progressive Woman* rapidly grew from its initial list of 120 names to a peak subscription rate of 3,000, and a total circulation of 18,000 copies of single issues on special subjects. Conger-Kaneko took special pride in the magazine's economic solvency, which allowed a 50-cent subscription price to pay its bills without the political burden of paid advertising. Much of the *Progressive Woman*'s success could be attributed to her own organizational prowess. By publishing large samples of letters from individual subscribers alongside regular features, the *Progressive Woman* did much to break the sense of isolation and self-doubt experienced by small groups of women, and even lone Socialist converts in the countryside and the rural townships of the Midwest. No matter how unsophisticated or trivial these communications appeared compared to the articulation of Socialist beliefs by party leaders, they nevertheless symbolized the women's growing attraction to a vital and growing movement—as the fervent praise for the *Progressive Woman* intimated.

Organizational evangelism and self-education permeated the pages of *Progressive Woman*. Field workers from the Woman's National Committee sent in summaries of their activities in various locals, the number of women enlisted, subscriptions sold, and receptions by male comrades. Topics were suggested for discussion at meetings, and songs and entertainments were offered. In addition, model plans were submitted for leafletting campaigns, with special materials on women, and for "Socialist Sunday Schools," designed to supplement children's public education with a day of cooperative learning. The *Progressive Woman* even offered its counterpart to the prizes given by other Socialist magazines for the largest number of subscribers solicited by campaigners: an Oregon comrade awarded a pair of elk antlers to the Yonkers' leader Theresa Malkiel, symbolizing, perhaps, the growing unity of the movement. The Woman's National Committee also suggested monthly plans for internal education, including such "classic" works as Darwin's *Descent of Man*, Lester Frank Ward's *Pure Sociology*, as well as the Socialist standards, Lewis Henry Morgan's *Ancient Society*, Engels' *Origin of the Family*, and August Bebel's *Woman Under Socialism*. Many of the articles summarized and simplified this theoretical material for the purposes of making propaganda available. Regular women organizers of the party contributed generously, as did individual male Socialists, like Eugene Debs, who were special supporters of women's agitation.

Conger-Kaneko effectively combined the agitational purposes of the *Progressive Woman* with an attractive, readable magazine which could draw wide interest from non-Socialist women. Special issues on woman's suffrage, child labor, and white slavery balanced the theoretical fare and the specific Socialist insights on current questions. A regular feature lionized the individual efforts of exemplary workers for socialism. The front cover often displayed a photograph of an outstanding woman Socialist such as Kate Richards O'Hare surrounded by her children. Inside, a biographical sketch, including personal and political details, explained her conversion to socialism and her personal philosophy of activism. The most frequent contributions, however, came from Josephine Conger-Kaneko and her husband Kiichi: editorials, political analyses, and historical essays (unique for their coverage and interpretation of Japanese women's efforts), along with Conger-Kaneko's own poetry (which was published in nearly every issue). The reprinted works of the leading woman literary figure on the Left, Charlotte Perkins Gilman, along with the other features, helped make the *Progressive Woman* the most stylish Socialist magazine between the death of the *Comrade* in 1905 and the birth of the *Masses* in 1911.

During the spring of 1911, however, the *Progressive Woman* was confronted with its first great technical problems, which ultimately would prove fatal. *The Appeal to Reason*'s printers decided to drop all publications except their own. This sudden crisis forced Conger-Kaneko to take the magazine back to Chicago, where she had to rely on the volunteer work and facilities of the party's National Office. Meanwhile, her husband's health, which had partly precipitated their move to Kansas, worsened and he returned to his native Japan where he lapsed into the final stages of consumption. Now lacking the necessary funding and publication aid, Conger-Kaneko turned to an expedient which she had proudly avoided for four years: opening the pages of the magazine to paid advertising. Caroline Lowe, then national correspondent of the Woman's National Committee, helped by sending promotional materials through her office, increasing the scale of the usual appeal for new subscriptions. For the first year in Chicago, the *Progressive Woman* survived more or less intact, but the initial financial deficit seems to have been a severe blow to the editor's sinking morale.

While the *Progressive Woman* already served as the official organ of the Woman's National Committee, the continuing financial burden encouraged Conger-Kaneko to hope that the committee would absorb the magazine financially as the organ of the party's women's department. The National Office advised against this move, due at least nominally to a longstanding policy against a party-owned press. Yet because of the magazine's known value as a propaganda tool, the *Progressive Woman*'s case was taken under consideration by a party subcommittee, which resolved to fund through a joint-stock company whose shares would be sold exclusively to locals. Caroline Lowe urged the membership's cooperation in this novel undertaking. Conger-Kaneko hoped this move would be a step toward eventual party ownership, once the political objections seemed less threatening. Such illusions were dimmed by the political maneuvers within the party in 1912.

The Socialist electoral campaign of 1912 heightened political tensions throughout the party. On the one hand, the party made massive preparations for what was to be the most successful campaign in its history. On the other hand, it was confronted with antagonisms and defections to the Left and the Right. When the National Convention of 1912 proscribed sabotage and IWW leader "Big Bill" Haywood was recalled from his office in the National Executive Committee, thousands of union-oriented militants dropped out of the party. When the Progressive party campaign of 1912 drew reformers away from Socialist ranks, party officials warned against further encouraging nonwage earners to join. Women's activities, always controversial, drew fire as suffrage agitation for all women was shunted aside in favor of programs which would appeal to working-class women alone. Some of the finest women organizers turned directly to party campaigning, including Caroline Lowe, who resigned her office as national correspondent of the women's department to go into the field as a speaker.

The fate of the *Progressive Woman* was sealed when the party's national secretary chose functionary Winnie Branstetter to take up the national correspondent's position. Branstetter's hostility toward feminism brought the public resignation of several Woman's National Committee members. While the magazine was being struck from the Left as insufficiently proletarian, the *Progressive Woman* was simultaneously hit from the Right as well: Branstetter accused the new managing editor, Barnett Braverman, of being an IWW—by that time a serious charge in the National Office milieu. Stock sales fell, and the remaining elements of cooperation within the Woman's National Committee disintegrated. Official relations between the National Committee and the *Progressive Woman* were dissolved by mutual consent. Conger-Kaneko and Braverman changed the magazine's name to the *Coming Nation*, attempting to recall the popularity of that Socialist newspaper of the 1890s in a format similar to the *Progressive Woman*. For a time they attempted to continue the special appeal to women, albeit in a format of a general circulation, only semi-Socialist magazine.

In the final number of the *Coming Nation*, July 1913, Josephine Conger-Kaneko offered a lengthy, bitter epilogue to her career as editor of Socialist propaganda among women. She traced the history of the *Progressive Woman* from its early, hopeful days in Girard to the final wrangling in the National Office, publishing publicly for the first time the damaging resolutions from the Woman's National Committee printed earlier in the party's internal bulletin. To add insult to injury, the reorganized woman's department had barred financial support to the *Coming Nation* on the basis that it was no longer a woman's magazine, and recommended that the magazine be dropped from the listings of agitational literature recommended for propaganda among women. These vindictive actions were the closest approximations to personal expulsion from the party that a privately owned Socialist magazine could receive. The *Progressive Woman* and the *Coming Nation* had not been alone in receiving such attacks; but perhaps of all the dissident factions, the women supporting Conger-Kaneko were the most vulnerable precisely because they had relied so completely on party support.

As was the case with other successful Socialist periodicals of the time, the audience of *Progressive Woman* included those who were becoming political for the first time. It transformed its image as much as possible into that of the movement's organizers and subscription sellers. At the same time, the fate of the *Progressive Woman* was a monument to Socialist shortsightedness. Outstanding women like Margaret Sanger, as well as many unrecognized feminists, would continue to search for an appreciation of woman's struggle among Socialists and would ultimately become discouraged by its absence. More importantly, the *Progressive Woman* demonstrated that a mass, Socialist organization of women could be achieved, and that it had to be achieved through its own strengths, beyond the power of a mainstream radical movement which, at will, could give or withdraw life.

Providence, Rhode Island, 1973

Common Sense

NEW YORK, 1932-1946

GEORGE P. RAWICK

COMMON SENSE was the last flowering of nineteenth-century American agrarian liberalism-radicalism, with its commitment to a radical popular democracy and with its emphasis upon both extreme individualism and intense social cooperation. In the pages of *Common Sense* Populists and Progressives, technocrats and labor radicals, civil libertarians and certain Marxists, all jostled each other.

The contributing editors of *Common Sense* in 1932 included John Dewey, Upton Sinclair, Roger Baldwin, the founder of the American Civil Liberties Union, V. F. Calverton, the neo-Marxist anthropologist and editor of *Modern Quarterly* and *Modern Monthly*, Lewis Mumford, Howard Scott, the leader of the technocrats, Max Eastman, literateur and friend of Leon Trotsky, A. J. Muste, founder of the Brookwood Labor School, and such labor radical intellectuals as Mary Heaton Vorse, Benjamin Stolberg, and J. B. S. Hardman.

Among others who were associated with the magazine were the novelist John Dos Passos, John Chamberlain, the journalist and radical critic of American society whose *Forward from Liberalism* was one of the most popular books of the early 1930s, and John T. Flynn, the radical opponent of the New Deal. The two young editors who founded the magazine and kept it alive, Selden Rodman and Alfred Bingham, had cast a very wide net and gathered in the nonparty opponents of twentieth-century American capitalism.

Common Sense is an important periodical for the study of social and intellectual life in the United States in the 1930s, because in its pages those who dissented from the dominant direction of American society set forward an opposition to Franklin Roosevelt and the New Deal, which the

450

contemporary liberal consensus no longer remembers existed. That which united all those who supported *Common Sense* was a critique of the centralization of power in industry and government. It is not surprising that almost all of those who wrote for the magazine either moved to the democratic Socialist Left, as was the case with Muste, Hardman, Mary Heaton Vorse, and John Dewey, or became part of an antistatist conservative grouping—for example, John Chamberlain, John T. Flynn, and John Dos Passos.

Common Sense supported the League for Independent Political Action headed by John Dewey. The league had grown out of the People's Lobby and the United Conference for Progressive Political Action. Writing in *Common Sense* on the "Imperative Need for a New Political Party," John Dewey said:

> Power today resides in control of the means of production, exchange publicity, transportation, and communication. Whoever owns them rules the life of the country, not necessarily by intention, not necessarily by deliberate corruption of the nominal government, but by necessity.

America's leading philosopher argued that as a consequence of this, power would either be directly controlled by the people themselves, through some form of direct democracy and the creation of a strong, united, radical, new party, or else even the admitted progressive gains of the New Deal would ultimately not be preserved.

The general tendency of the *Common Sense* group was to look for a democratic socialist alternative to American capitalism, but, in the ideological vacuum of American politics and intellectual life in the 1930s, they could find nothing other than the resurrection of the old American Populist goal of a Farmer-Labor party which would include strong support from the lower middle class. Editor Alfred Bingham was most concerned with centering the rebel tradition in the United States in the middle classes. To this effect, in 1935 he published his book, *Insurgent America: the Revolt of the Middle Classes*. But the new center of power was not to be the middle classes; rather, it was to be the new industrial union working-class movement—and the *Common Sense* group could find no firm relationship to the Congress of Industrial Organizations.

Unlike that liberalism of the 1930s represented by the *Nation* and the *New Republic*, the *Common Sense* group had no interest in following the leadership of the Soviet Union. The writers for *Common Sense* not only rejected drawing their inspiration from the Russian Revolution, but they actually disavowed any fundamental interest in Marxism. And yet, even this center of American liberalism and dissent was influenced by a brand of Marxism.

There was a small but influential grouping of figures in the labor movement, and certain intellectuals, followers of Jay Lovestone, the deposed leader of the American Communist party, were important to the development of the ideas of the *Common Sense* group. Lovestone and his followers had argued in behalf of a theory of American exceptionalism, that is, a view which argued that classic Marxism was not directly applicable to the unique American experience. This view was clearly attractive to the editors of *Common Sense*.

The pages of *Common Sense* were an important repository for many strands of American social and intellectual life in the 1930s. Very often an analysis of a direction not taken helps us understand what did occur. Thus, historians searching for the roots of the power of the contemporary American state can learn much from the different direction advocated by *Common Sense*. For those who look upon the 1930s as an important watershed in American life, *Common Sense* is a significant benchmark of this transformation.

Rochester, Michigan, 1968

Alfred M. Bingham writes of *Common Sense*:

The choice of the name of the new magazine was mine. Selden Rodman's rebellion was the rebellion of an artist and a poet, and until we met in the summer of 1932, I am sure—he felt that common sense was a bourgeois concept. But I reminded him that Thomas Paine's *Common Sense* had been a revolutionary weapon. The name of Paine's other revolutionary pamphlet, *The Crisis*, had long been preempted by the National Association for the Advancement of Colored People, whose own crisis was still thirty years off; so *Common Sense* it was.

Crisis would have been better. For the magazine was a journalistic response to crisis. It was first of all a child of the Great Depression. To an extent hard for a later generation to imagine, it seemed in those days as if our whole civilization were caving in. Then, as the depression conjured up Hitler, the economic and social crisis became the crisis of World War II.

To contemporaries, no doubt, every historical period seems a period of crisis. And when, after thirteen years, the last issue of *Common Sense* appeared, it was strident with the new crisis of the Bomb and the Cold War. But its own special approach to social problems was perhaps too closely identified with a particular period to survive after the war.

It belonged to the Roosevelt era. Its first issue appeared only days after FDR's election. "In the next four years," wrote Arthur M. Schlesinger, Jr., in *The Politics of Upheaval*, the third volume of *The Age of Roosevelt*, "*Common Sense* became the most lively and interesting forum of radical discussion in the country." Its focus shifted, as did Roosevelt's, from the New Deal to a world at war. It outlived Roosevelt by less than a year.

History has no sharp edges, however. Only in our own lives and memories are there clear beginnings and endings, and perhaps also in magazines that begin with Volume I, Number I and end with a final issue. The Age of Roosevelt gave way to the Atomic Age. And now, a generation later, there is again war, and talk of revolution.

Each age produces new voices, for whom the past is only a dim echo. When Selden Rodman and I started *Common Sense* as a voice of native American radicalism, we were following closely on the liberal thought and progressive politics of the 1920s, though we tended to think of an earlier and therefore more glamorous past. Now, a generation later, a "New Left" has emerged. If there is any present validity to a reprint of a period magazine, other than as raw material for academic dissertations, it may be for the light it can shed on and for today's currents of thought.

What, then, did we accomplish in these few thousand pages? Were our ideas valid? Did they have any effect? How do they compare with radical expression today?

On the tenth anniversary of *Common Sense*, in the issue of December 1942, the editors asserted that "though ten years older and possibly wiser than it was in December 1932, *Common Sense* feels every bit as obstreperous, experimental, skeptical, and optimistic as it did then." Those four adjectives were, I think, rather apt.

We were obstreperous because we were young. I was twenty-seven and Selden Rodman four years younger. Coming from a top-drawer Eastern social background, our manners were polite, but when my father, just defeated for reelection as an Old Guard Republican senator, saw the first issue of our magazine, he flung it across the room, and never, so far as I know, subjected himself to the shock of reading another issue.

Rodman's obstreperousness, being more aesthetic than political, had first exhibited itself in *The Harkness Hoot*, a Yale undergraduate magazine thumbing its nose at Gothic college architecture and other sacred cows. My revolt emerged more slowly when, after getting a law degree and being admitted to the Connecticut bar, I could not face the drudgery of beginning a law practice, went instead on a Grand Tour of Europe and Asia, and came back believing that Russia had most of the answers to depression, even if I could not stomach its politics.

We teamed up with a couple of older hands, who left us when our money ran out. For a while an Australian writer, Hartley Grattan, gave us the help of a few years seniority. But for the first eight years *Common Sense* was the product of Rodman and myself, assisted by our wives and a shifting staff of other amateurs. Rodman remained the cultural rebel, but he had a deep commitment to the idea that the arts must deal with society and its problems. And he had a creative vitality, and an ability to wring creative expression out of others that produced issue after issue of significant social criticism. *Common Sense* writers, however well known, were never paid more than a pittance. And it was Rodman's courage and enthusiasm that kept the magazine going from one financial crisis to another.

My contribution, oddly enough, came from the same family background against which I was in revolt. It was not only the limited financial independence that enabled me to work without a salary (though not enough to help much with paying the bills after the first year). It was more the intellectual discipline of legal training, and the sense of practical political realities of a household where winning elections had been a major preoccupation. These assets, plus whatever perspective on world affairs my travels had given me, provided a balance to Rodman's flair for the written word.

Later we were joined by others, also young. My own active editorship ended in 1940, though it was not until Rodman was put into uniform in 1943 that any other name appeared on the masthead as editor. Richard

Rovere, Sidney Hertzberg, Maurice Goldbloom, and in the last year, Varian Fry, put their own different, yet in many ways consistent, stamp on these pages. But they were all young, and in their own ways obstreperous.

They were also skeptical of conventional wisdom. Any magazine of social protest, particularly if it considers itself radical rather than liberal, as we did, is necessarily going against the main current. But in one respect, I think, the later editorial policy was less distinctive than in the earlier years. For the later editors had been identified to a greater or lesser extent with the more established currents of liberal and Marxist thought, and when they joined *Common Sense*, it was because they liked its lack of identification.

From the beginning, Rodman and I had tried to find a place independent of both the older liberalism and the then newly fashionable intellectual Marxism. We felt neither was attuned to American realities. In politics our efforts to inspire and promote a third party—fusing the Progressive and Farmer-Labor parties of the Midwest into a new national party—were pitifully ineffective alongside the massive coalition that Roosevelt put together, but they made more sense than the attempt to build Socialist or Communist parties on nineteenth-century European models.

And in our economic and social proposals we were equally skeptical of liberal efforts to reform capitalism, and of the traditional socialist concern with public ownership of the "means of production." We picked up the newer slogans of "production for use," the "economy of abundance," "technocracy," "planning." We came close, but missed, the largely Keynesian devices of managing the economy by controls at strategic spots, which have, in the intervening years, saved and transformed capitalism.

Yet I believe that it was in this area of economic and social pragmatism—the third adjective we used about ourselves was "experimental"—that we may have made the most valuable contribution. Our advocacy of a third party came to nothing. Our specific proposals for a planned economy were not taken seriously by anyone but ourselves. But our basic premise that man now has the resources and the skills to control his global environment is a valid one. Man has but to apply his intelligence and goodwill, we believed, and he can end poverty and war. This assumption flies in the face of inherited beliefs in man's helplessness and depravity. But it underlies all that organized society, particularly at the national and international level, professes as its goals, however brutally it acts.

Perhaps it is this disparity between what a society says and what it does that is the major cause of social protest today. We called ourselves optimists a generation ago, but pessimism, even despair, is now the prevailing mood in the "New Left." The young radicals of today so distrust the "establishment," the "power structures," whether of traditional democracy, or military authoritarianism, or communism, that they tend to oppose all rules, all government, all law and order. One is reminded of the nihilism and anarchism of rebellious youth in nineteenth-century Russia, although hopelessness then derived from an apparently impregnable autocracy, while the frustration of youth in 1968 seems more to derive from the sheer complexity and intractability of our computerized world. Too many young people in revolt against things as they are have abandoned the Great Society to the politicians. They have turned back to nature, or inward to new states of consciousness.

Common sense is still a useful tool. It may become naive, even utopian, if it assumes that man is by nature a reasonable animal. And today it must recognize that inherited emotional responses to symbols and forms of words—particularly those associated with nationalism and communism—may foreclose all expectations based on intelligence and goodwill. But it still seems to me, some thirty-five years after picking the name for a magazine, as good a bet as any.

Salem, Connecticut, 1968

Catholic Worker

NEW YORK, 1933—

DWIGHT MACDONALD

VOL. 1, No. 1 of the *Catholic Worker* hit Union Square on May Day 1933, with an ambiguous thud. The Marxian natives couldn't classify this political chimaera: its forequarters were anarchistic but its hinder parts were attached to the Church of Rome, whose American hierarchy then stood slightly to the right of Herbert Hoover. One editor, Dorothy Day, was known as a writer for the Socialist *Call* and the old *Masses* and a friend of radicals like Hugo Gellert, Maurice Becker, and Mike Gold (to whom she was engaged for a year). But the other editor was a mystery: 14th Street cafeteria savants who could distinguish at the drop of a coffee spoon between Manuilsky and Mayakovsky, Dan and Denikin, Malenkov, Martov, Miliukov, Muralov and Muranov, were stumped by Maurin (Peter). Their conclusion, reasonable enough from their premises, was that the *Catholic Worker* was either a Trojan horse rigged up by the Vatican to betray the oft-betrayed proletariat or, more charitably, an ''adventure'' by confused idealists (the noun was as bad as the adjective that invariably accompanied it) who would be forced by the logic of Historical Materialism, the Class Struggle, and the Marxian Dialectic to choose between radicalism and Catholicism. The very name was a simple—that is, a nondialectical, or unfruitful—contradiction: Catholic *Worker*?

They were, however, as sometimes happened, wrong. Unless the Vatican's machinations are subtler, and more long-range, than I can grasp, the *Catholic Worker* has not been a Trojan horse. Nor has the contradiction between its radicalism and its Catholicism been resolved. Both still get equal space. A chimaera perhaps, in Marxist taxonomy —but also a phoenix.

Among the leftist periodicals of my time, the *Catholic Worker* is unique in combining longevity with consistency. *Partisan Review*, Methuselah of little mags, is almost as old (b. 1934) but it has gone through some drastic changes, beginning as the organ of the John Reed Clubs, the literary front of the CPUSA; revived in 1938 as an anti-Stalinist revolutionary-Socialist literary monthly, etc. My own *Politics* was always radical but the meaning of that term changed—radically—in a mere five years of existence. Dorothy Day's *Worker* has stuck to the same general line for almost forty years and a good thing too because it's still, as we say now, relevant. Had I been sophisticated enough to know what they were talking about, I would probably have agreed with the 1933 Marxian ideologues that the Maurin-Day combination of Catholic piety and anarchopacifism was a discrepant mixture that couldn't last. The difference between us is I don't mind being proved wrong by events in such prophecies. I welcome the viability, as we said then, of the Catholic Workers as one of those frequent, indeed chronic, irruptions of the unexpected that shows history is not a well-trained valet to any system of ideas but a human, and so chancey, affair. One of those surprises that makes life life.

The thirty-sixth anniversary issue of the *Catholic Worker*—May 1969, Vol. XXXVII, No. 1—looks, reads, and costs about the same as that of May 1, 1933, Vol. I, No. 1. Only the *New York Times*, another of our few stable institutions though its editorial line is jittery compared to the *Worker*'s, has a longer typographical tradition (by some thirty years). Unlike the *Times*, the *Worker* costs the same now as it did in 1933: a penny a copy, 25 cents a year—the only periodical in journalistic history that costs twice as much by the year as by the issue.

The contents of Vol. XXXVII, No. 1, are also continuous with the past. The front page is shared by articles whose common denominator is nonviolent militancy, a principled tactic that Dorothy Day, along with the late A. J. Muste and Martin Luther King, Jr., introduced into American radicalism.

"Good Friday at Fort DeRussy"—the perfect *Catholic Worker* headline—is a detailed report from a local correspondent on an episode I didn't see reported in the press. "Demonstrations to protest the American War in Vietnam were held last month in over forty American cities," it begins. "One of the most dynamic centered on Fort DeRussy in Honolulu and climaxed on Good Friday with nonviolent civil disobedience against American military power."

Two columns in the center, "God's Coward," were devoted to a long extract (*Catholic Worker* writers tend to expansiveness; it takes them a thousand words to get really warmed up) from the memoirs "continued from last month" of the late Ammon Hennacy about his prison experiences as a draft resister in the *first* world war. Not front-page stuff, except in the *Worker*, but it turns out to be good journalism—specific, lively, and shocking—which may show younger readers there is no new evil under the sun. The author died recently at seventy-six after a heart attack on a picket line, an old-style American radical, a "nut" to the cops, who called himself "a one-man revolution" and, after his conversion to Catholicism in middle-age, "a Christian anarchist." He was a regular contributor to the *Worker* for some twenty years. "Unlike many crusaders," I wrote in a 1952 *New Yorker* profile of Dorothy Day ("The Foolish Things of This World"), "Hennacy is a man of gentle good will. Some of his best friends are FBI agents, and on his most recent birthday the wife of one of them baked him a cake." There is a fine memoir of Hennacy in an obituary by Michael Harrington in the *Village Voice* of January 29, 1970. Harrington, who is Norman Thomas' successor as leader of the Socialist party, was an editor of the *Worker* in the early 1950s. He was one of "Dorothy's bright young men" (and women). There has been a long line of them now, an ever-renewing flow of young idealists who work a few years with her and then move on; a *rite de passage* that has scattered *Catholic Worker* alumni widely throughout the radical world.

The third front-page item is a long letter from Cesar Chavez, leader of the California grape-workers' strike, to the president of the growers' organization: "I am glad to hear your accusations that our union movement and table-grapes boycott have been successful because we have not used violence and terror tactics. . . . During a most critical time in our movement last February, 1968, I undertook a twenty-five day fast. I repeat to you the principle enunciated to the membership at the start of the fast: if to build our union required the deliberate taking of life, either the life of a grower or his child or the life of a worker or his child, then I choose not to see the union built." A negative moral choice—abstain, don't do it—which seems to be hard for Americans. I don't recall seeing Mr. Chavez' letter anywhere else. Nonviolence is hard to make news out of, and it is not as chic a mode of radical action as it once was. But the *Worker*, like the *Times*, is a "journal of record."

The other seven pages of the thirty-sixth anniversary issue are also the mixture as before. Two are devoted to carryovers from the front page. One is a theological essay, "The Wheat and the Vine," a title not redeemed by the first sentence: "To recapitulate then (and beginning in reverse with the sinner): The pruning knife of the Vinedresser may be used to punish the godless or the faithless (as we frequently see in the Old Testament)." I just can't keep my mind on this kind of language and I was not inspirited when I read that the tract was "continued from last month" and is "to be continued." Judicious skipping is necessary to enjoy the *Worker*. There were also three not bad "Prison Poems"; a page and a half of letters, always a lively department in the *Worker*; and a long, relaxed chronicle of doings on the Workers' communal estate up the Hudson, "Tivoli, a Farm with a View." This was often interesting except for the nature writing, which is another blind spot of mine. (Though I was intrigued by "Now and then, a traveller to more northern woods, the sweet-songed white-throated sparrow, sings yearningly: sweet, sweet, Canada, Canada, Canada." Aesopian language, maybe?) Last but not least, the current installment of "On Pilgrimage," a diary Miss Day runs in each issue that is the paper's most popular feature. Certainly it's always readable since she is as direct in print as in conversation—an actual person is talking to you and to herself. " 'On Pilgrimage' is an odd composite of Pascal's *Pensées* and Eleanor Roosevelt's 'My Day,' " I wrote in 1952; and the description still fits. "A good hostess, on the printed page as well as off, Miss Day is constantly introducing the sublime if not to the ridiculous at least to the commonplace. . . . The union of the everyday and the ultimate is the essence of the Catholic Worker movement."

For the amateur who dips into these volumes here and there—the best way to enjoy them—some historical background will be helpful. And even the pros may get some hints about the strange anatomy of the *Catholic Worker*, the better to dissect it for reassembly into a doctoral thesis in—what? Political "Science"? (Precious little science in Miss Day's paper.) History of Religion? Comparative Ethics? Abnormal

Psychology? Or maybe American Studies, that all-covering academic maxicoat.

A few excerpts from my *New Yorker* articles of October 4 and 11, 1952, may be useful.

Early in 1933, when, at the age of thirty-five, Dorothy Day, a woman in whom lightheartedness and spiritual fervor are strangely and effectually intermingled, joined hands with the late Peter Maurin to launch the Catholic Worker movement, the Roman Catholic Church in this country was still deeply uninterested in liberal social causes. Abroad, especially in France, "social Catholicism" had already become strong, but in the United States the hierarchy felt it wiser not to meddle in such matters.

Miss Day, who had long been a radical and who had joined the Church only five years previously, and Maurin, a French-born religious zealot who had spent most of his fifty-six years tramping about America, living like a hobo and expounding his doctrine to all who would listen, felt that the Church as a whole should concern itself more with the problems faced by ordinary men and women in adjusting themselves to the economic pressures of an industrial capitalist society. Inspired by Maurin's idealism and Miss Day's intensity and drive, the Catholic Workers became agitators among the people; they foreshadowed that renaissance of the "lay-apostolate" that has since arisen in the Church. The *Catholic Worker*, the organization's monthly paper, to which Miss Day and Maurin contributed voluminously and which later on in the thirties reached a peak circulation of 150,000, gave the Workers a vastly larger audience than is enjoyed by most radical organs. "There were never any committees around the *Catholic Worker* office," a veteran of the paper's early days recalls. "We just went out and *did* things. We didn't form a Committee to Promote Improved Interracial Relations. We took Negroes into our homes and lived with them. We didn't get up big-name letterheads to raise funds for strikers. We went out on the picket lines ourselves."

This direct-action approach, coupled with the fact that 1933 was the bottom year of the depression, gave the Workers a crusading appeal that struck fire in certain Catholic circles, especially among young priests, students in the theological seminaries, and some of the more enlightened members of the laity. Catholic Worker groups started up all over—often by spontaneous combustion, without any help from headquarters.

A curious social paradox was involved. Theretofore, American Catholicism had been a lower-class affair, its followers consisting mostly of post-1840 immigrants from Catholic countries like Ireland, Poland, Italy, and Austria-Hungary; the upper classes—rated as such simply by virtue of having got here earlier—were solidly Protestant. But by 1930 the immigrants had begun to rise socially and economically, their children and even their grandchildren were going to college, and Catholicism began to produce middle-class intellectuals as full of reforming zeal as their Protestant counterparts had been for a century or more. As long as the majority of Catholics were proletarians, the hierarchy could, if it liked, deal with them in an authoritarian way and dragoon them into a conservative social pattern, but as the laity became richer and better educated, there was an increasing ferment of liberalism in the old bottles of the Church. Today, the hierarchy is still largely conservative—Cardinal Spellman, of New York, probably being more typical than Bishop Sheil, of Chicago—but the lower clergy and the laity have produced such Catholic phenomena as the interracial Friendship Houses; the St. Francis Xavier Labor College, in New York; the Chicago Catholic pro-labor monthly, *Work*; and a whole crop of so-called "labor priests," like Father John M. Corridan, who played an important part in the insurgent longshoremen's strike here last fall.

Many of the individuals who are now working in such strange Catholic vineyards were given their first impulse and their training by the Catholic Worker movement. As Father Dennis Geaney, a Catholic educator, recently wrote of Miss Day in *Work*, "It was a Christian revolution she was starting. She was opening the minds of bishops, priests, seminarians, and lay people to the fact that Christianity was not a stuffy sacristy affair. She was a trumpet calling for all of us to find Christ in the bread lines, the jails, as a tenant farmer, migratory worker, or Negro. We think of Church history as being made by popes and bishops. Here is a woman who has placed her stamp on American Catholicism. The seed she sowed in the thirties is bearing fruit a hundred-fold in the fifties."

The *Catholic Worker* was started, as the name suggests, as a competitor of the Communist *Daily Worker*, and it was no accident that most of its first issue, in 1933, was distributed in Union Square on May Day. In their maiden editorial, which asked, in effect, "Why should the Devil have all the good tunes?," Maurin and Miss Day wrote: "It's time there was a Catholic paper printed for the unemployed. The fundamental aim of most radical sheets is conversion of its readers to radicalism and atheism. Is it not possible to be radical and not atheist?" The Church's social program is contained largely in two papal encyclical letters—the *Rerum novarum*, of Leo XIII (1891), and the *Quadragesimo anno*, of Pius XI (1931). These rebuke the greed of unrestrained capitalism, encourage labor unions, and in general put the interests of the worker above the interests of private property. "Our job is to make the encyclicals click," Maurin once said.

A graph of the *Catholic Worker*'s influence would show a long trough between 1940 and 1960. My *New Yorker* profile, quoted above, was written at its dead center, in 1952, twelve years after the social ferment of the 1930s had been smothered by wartime patriotism and prosperity, eight years before Kennedy's election broke up the Eisenhower stasis. World War II made the *Worker* part of their title obsolete by removing the working class from our radical scene, so far permanently. The postwar depression predicted by all Left-thinking prophets from Trotsky to Henry Wallace—and by many Right-thinking ones too—never materialized. The poor were there but didn't become visible until the mid-1960s. The blacks were also there, more visible—the 1954 Supreme Court decision integrating the schools; the 1956 Montgomery bus boycott that made Martin Luther King, Jr., a national figure—but their problems were not a crucial issue. There were no crucial issues then, by presidential order. There were no military adventures overseas either, to be fair—no Bay of Pigs, no Dominican occupation, no Vietnam horror. Ike was at least consistent: his foreign policy was as undynamic as his domestic.

The graph has turned upward in the last decade. The *Worker*'s circulation has risen from 58,000 in 1952 to 85,000 today. Vietnam has made pacifism no longer the "embarrassment" it was in the martial forties or the moot issue it became during the Ike Pax. Draft resistance comes naturally to the Workers—they had plenty of (rather lonely) practice during World War II, many have gone to jail since 1965 and many are still there, including David Miller, the first draftee to burn his card after Congress made it illegal. Their anarchism, an eccentricity, almost a solipsism, in the Marxian thirties, has become the norm of radical behavior in the sixties: direct action (''We just went out and *did* things''); their antibourgeois, infrarational, free-form style (when Abbie Hoffman told Miss Day: ''You were the first hippie,'' she was flattered). And the communal trust their houses of hospitality—there are still fifteen—have as their disorganizing principle: everybody welcome, everything free, the Marxist utopia, ''To Each According to his Needs, From Each According to his Abilities.''

As for their Catholicism, the conflict between it and their radicalism of which Miss Day was as conscious as her Union Square critics—Cardinal Spellman's Chancery impressed it on her frequently—has been relaxed of late, and it is the Church that has given ground. Slowly, grudgingly, with last-ditch defensive sorties from the Holy Office; but that a freer spirit is breezing through the rectories and seminaries hardly needs documenting.

The long, dogged insistence of the Workers on practicing what other Christians preach has been a major factor in radicalizing many American Catholics. Their example may have been in the minds of those Catholic priests, like the Berrigan brothers, who have participated in midnight raids on draft boards or Dow Chemical offices to destroy records —violence that is restricted to inanimate objects, a sabotage technique borrowed from earlier American anarchists, the IWW or ''Wobblies.'' The ''Milwaukee Fourteen'' who in the fall of 1968 incinerated some ten thousand draft cards with homemade napalm before the cops arrived were mostly Catholic priests, scholars, and laymen, including two staff members of the local Catholic Worker house of hospitality. And Emmaus House, founded in 1967 in New York City by some extremely emancipated—in both political and the ''swinging'' sense—young Catholic clerics, was directly inspired by the Workers. ''I am a spiritual stepchild of Dorothy Day,'' says one of its leaders, Father Kirk. ''Since the thirties, the *Catholic Worker* has used the word 'revolution' in its non-violent sense. . . . Emmaus is trying to bring the same kind of activism into the problems of religious freedom, race relations, draft resistance.''

cardinals and policemen; and finally—specially useful for guiding a free-form collective enterprise—a direct, easy way with people. Long before Peter Maurin died in 1949, the Catholic Worker style had been established by his grateful proselyte and admiring co-founder.

At seventy plus, Dorothy Day is still what she was in her thirties—the active, personal center of the movement and its paper. Not the least of her qualifications for the job is that she never really wanted it. "Low in mind all day, full of tears," is a typical entry in "On Pilgrimage," her public-private journal. "What with Easton, New York, Boston, Ottawa, Toronto and Missouri groups all discouraged, all looking for organization instead of self-organization, all weary of the idea of freedom and personal responsibility—I feel bitterly oppressed. I am in the position of a dictator trying to legislate himself out of existence. They all complain there is no boss. Today I happened to read Dostoevsky's 'Grand Inquisitor,' most apropos. Freedom—how men hate it and chafe under it, how unhappy they are with it!"

This was written in 1936, three years after she and Maurin had founded the Catholic Workers. Things are still about the same.

New York City, 1970

Dorothy Day writes of the *Catholic Worker*:

Peter Maurin, French peasant, former Christian brother, member of the lumpenproletariat in Canada and the states (he never entered the United States legally, but came over the Canadian border with a lumber camp) was the founder of the *Catholic Worker*. He arrived on the scene in December 1932, via the Bowery and Union Square and suggested the following program of action:

Clarification of thought through round-table discussions, workers' schools, and the publication of a paper to reach the man of the street. Houses of hospitality to feed the hungry, clothe the naked, shelter the harborless, where worker and scholar, young and old, people of all races and creeds could live together in community and which would branch out into the countryside and become farming communes.

This was the program he felt would be the best way to live a life of love of God and love of brother. It will be seen from even a cursory paging-through of these volumes of the *Catholic Worker* how we have continued in these pursuits.

My own part in the work was that of journalist and housekeeper. I had worked with the old *Masses*, written for the *New Masses* and worked on the *Liberator* with Bob Minor, who was secretary of the Communist party. On my conversion to the Catholic faith, I had continued for a time to work for the Anti-Imperialist League, which was in 1928 upholding the cause of the Nicaraguan guerrilla Sandino. Having always been more inclined to the IWW and the anarchist position, I was not interested in socialism or the dictatorship of the proletariat, or any other dictatorship, and I did not have much faith in the idea that the State would wither away. I was a firm believer in direct action, and that we learn by doing.

There has been what Cardinal Newman would term a development of doctrine in the pages of the *Catholic Worker*, and we are still learning. But there has been a consistent theme throughout the thirty-six years, and it is that we must work for the common good, that men are responsible for each other, that God has a special love for the poor and the destitute, the insulted and the injured, and that where they are, we must be, too. We have been consistent in our pacifism and our endeavor to portray nonviolent means of bringing about a new social order. We have opposed the Japanese-Chinese War, the Ethiopian War, the Spanish Civil War, World War II, the Korean War, the Vietnam War, and can point with pride to the many editors of the *Catholic Worker* who have spent time in prison for their refusal to serve in the Vietnam War. We advocate the nonpayment of income tax and a life of voluntary poverty in order to have more to share with others. We try to do without as much of the bounty of the State as we can. "The less we have of Caesar's, the less we will have to render to Caesar." But all these ideas will be found illustrated and developed over and over again in the pages of the *Catholic Worker*.

"Freely ye have received, freely give." We try to live by scripture and that means we never receive salaries and never charge people for the hospitality they receive. We charge a penny a copy for the *Catholic Worker*, or twenty-five cents a year for mailing it out, and we do that only because we could not get a second-class mailing permit without having a valid circulation and that, of course, entails people sending in money for subscriptions. Fortunately, people who take the paper to their bosoms and read it faithfully each month send much more, and since the wolf is at the door often, we send out appeals once in a while for help. Somehow the bills get paid. After all, we live as most poor families do—from hand to mouth.

Meals are important and that is why I speak of meals served. The word *"compañero"* means those who break bread together. The word *"comrade"* means those who sit in a Chamber of Deputies together. There is a story in the Gospel of two travelers who sat down in an inn by the road, and suddenly knew the Stranger, who joined them *"in the breaking of bread."* Mary Magdalene encountered Jesus in one whom she thought was the gardener. In other words, our brother, anyone we encounter, is another Christ, to be loved, not to be feared.

The Catholic Worker family is so large now, with 85,000 papers going out each month, that there is a continuity in the work. There is always a hard core of oldtimers so that a visitor can drop in from Australia or Tanganyika after being away for twenty years or so, and find someone he knows around the farm or house of hospitality. Students come and go, as to a university, as though they were taking postgraduate courses in history, sociology, or theology, and go out again to the vocation for which they have been trained, to the vocation which they perhaps have newly discovered through their months or few years at the Catholic Worker houses. There are even of recent years serious high school students who come before and after school to help.

Property in the New York area is held as trust in the form of a corporation which is like a safe-deposit box to hold property, and is controlled by the unincorporated association of the Catholic Workers, wherever those who are carrying on the work happen to be at the time. The trustee, who may be changed from year to year, has filed a letter with our lawyer, John Coster. The letter states that she or he will do whatever the unincorporated association of Catholic Workers orders him or her to do if we wish to sell the land or give it away, in whole or in part.

The State, by the right of eminent domain, can take away house and land at any time, though it does offer compensation. When the city paid us a year's interest, a few thousand dollars, for the house and land at 223 Chrystie Street some years ago, we sent the interest—which we termed usury—back to the city, much to its consternation and that of our friends, many of whom announced that they would no longer give donations to workers who indulged in such folly. When the city also wondered what to do with such funds, we urged it to use the money in the operation of the fine city radio station, WNYC, which had long served us with the best of music and lectures. After this brief exchange we have not had any other communications with the city. We pay taxes on our real estate, which we communally own, because we enjoy such city services as these radio programs, fire protection, the help of the department of sanitation, the city hospitals, and so on. We do not believe that church property should be exempt for such taxation, except for schools and charitable hospitals. Every time an estate is deeded to a religious group, it is removed from the tax rolls, and the village, county, and state taxes on the property of the surrounding owners is raised.

In the *Catholic Worker*, we try to write of people, money, food, education, work, and so on, in the light of the pacifist and anarchist principles we profess, and if we confuse people rather than enlighten them, we pray God to send writers who live these principles more consistently and so write better about them.

What is the future of the *Catholic Worker*? The postscript of my book, *The Long Loneliness*, published by Harpers in 1952, reads:

We were just sitting there talking when Peter Maurin came in.

We were just sitting there talking, when lines of people began to form, saying "We need bread." We could not say, "Go, be thou filled." If there were six small loaves and a few fishes, we had to divide them. There was always bread.

We were just sitting there talking and people moved in on us. Those who can take it, take it. Some moved out and that made room for more. And somehow the walls expanded.

We were just sitting there talking and someone said, "Let's all go live on a farm."

It was as casual as all that, I often think. It just came about. It just happened.

I found myself, a barren woman, the joyful mother of children.

It is not easy always to be joyful, to keep in mind the duty of delight.

The most significant thing about the *Catholic Worker* is voluntary poverty, some say.

The most significant thing is community, others say. We are not alone any more.

But the final word is love. At times it has been, in the words of Father Zossima, "a harsh and dreadful thing compared to love in dreams" and our very faith in love has been tried as though by fire.

We cannot love God unless we love each other, and to love we must know each other. We know Him in the breaking of bread, and we know each other in the breaking of bread, and we are not alone any more.

Heaven is a banquet and life is a banquet, too, even with a crust, where there is companionship.

We have all known the long loneliness and we have learned that the only solution is love and that love comes with community.

It all happened while we sat there talking, and it is still going on.

New York City, 1969

Monthly Review

PLAINFIELD, NEW JERSEY,
1934-1935

OAKLEY C. JOHNSON

THE 1930s have been described in a variety of terms, but for me one essential fact has not been stressed: *it was a time of danger*. There was the threat of world war, which came in 1939, and the threat of American fascism, indicated by such developments as the America First Committee (which rapidly moved to the political Right), the goose-stepping organizations, and the eventual rise of McCarthyism.

The *Monthly Review* came to life in 1934 with a sharp awareness of the perils. It had a double aim and a single appeal, which I may summarize as follows:

Stop the United States from going fascist;

Stop the war that was surely coming;

Appeal directly to the middle class, including professionals and white collar workers, to reject and to strive against the twin danger.

There was in the 1930s a tendency to blame the middle class for the rise of fascism, both abroad and at home. *Monthly Review* denied this, and urged professionals of all kinds to refute the slander and fight the menace.

The *Monthly Review* was conceived and launched by Joseph Koven. It was patterned in superficial appearance after the *Saturday Evening Post*, a slick paper publication. The inside front cover would carry an essay in definition of a current political term: fascism, capitalism, democracy, imperialism, the aim, of course, being to educate the mass of nonpolitical white collar citizens. There was to be in each issue a main political article on a pressing current problem, or a descriptive social study in depth. There were to be short commentaries by Koven himself in a light, satirical vein. And there were to be editorials, cartoons, short news articles, book reviews, occasional verse, even short stories—all in line with the magazine's objectives.

Koven was a dark, smallish man, intense, nervous, already—when I knew him—beginning to go grey. He described himself as a businessman who had made some previous literary experiments of which he spoke deprecatingly. In 1915 he had collaborated with Gustave Davidson on *Melmoth the Wanderer*, a play in five acts. In 1924, under his own name, he had published a slender volume, *The Miracle of Saint Masha, and other plays*. In 1934, his main interest was the *Monthly Review*.

Koven believed the *Monthly Review* would appeal to the white collar people he wanted to reach, and that writers and artists could be found to supply content. No one was to be paid for either articles or services.

Politically, the magazine regarded itself as independent and nonaligned. It was designed to be a "sympathizer" publication. It would support the Communist party on the narrow platform against fascism and war, paying no attention to minor issues. I was, so far as I know, the only Communist on the editorial staff. These included Koven himself as editor, Ann Laine as our technical (printing) expert, and Theodore Kheel for art. Koven invited me to serve as managing editor. I wrote most of the longer political articles, or helped select the special features that, on alternate months, would be used in place of the polemical pieces.

We had considerable success all around. I remember particularly that V. J. Jerome, editor of *The Communist*, complimented me on my Madison Square article in the first issue. I was involved in getting James Shields, a brother of the *Daily Worker*'s Art Shields, to write about how he was forced out of his teaching job, and in having Irving Adler, long before he achieved recognition as a pedagogical expert in mathematics, write about the "loyalty oath" danger. I found Clara Severn (this was her *nom de plume*), a social worker, and asked her to describe the campaigns of the Unemployed Councils. The story of M. J. Olgin's battle with the chief of the New School for Social Research was, like the others named, a scoop for us.

As for the definitive essays on page two of each number, the first,

"Who Are the Professionals?" was by Koven himself, but the others were largely my work.

We were fortunate in getting able writers, even without payment. We were all proud of Isidor Schneider's series, "Who's Who in Jail," and of Harvey O'Connor's "Thumb-Nail Biographies" of people in the news. The names of James T. Farrell, novelist; Kenneth Fearing, poet; Margaret Monahan, Hungarian journalist; Mary Van Kleeck, social critic; and Haakon M. Chevalier, author, were well-known, and gave lustre to our pages.

I vividly recall working in the late fall of 1934 on my third major study, which was to deal with Jay Lovestone. He was at that time still heading what he called the "Communist Majority." I went a couple of times to hear him lecture. I read his pamphlets. Afterward, on the telephone, I asked him if I could have lunch with him (Dutch treat), and he consented.

It was a stiff, nonenjoyable meeting. I found his personality unpleasant, as I sought to learn his real views and plans. Finally I asked him point-blank if he would like to see the Soviet Government overthrown. He hesitated a bare instant, then said "Yes." We paid our separate checks, and I went home to work further on "The Jay Lovestone Instance."

As December drew to an end, I looked forward to seeing this article in the *Monthly Review* for either February or March, as the January number was already made up. Then Koven told me he couldn't go on. The expense, he said, was greater than he had bargained for, and the subscriptions had not come in fast enough to pay the bills. This was the end. Even the January material, edited and prepared, was scrapped.

In view of Lovestone's later career, I have often regretted the death of the *Monthly Review* at that particular moment. I feel that a sharp, analytical study of Lovestone's personality and ideas at that time would have helped labor and the Left today to understand what I consider his reactionary role.

Times have changed, and whether I would now write precisely the same thoughts in precisely the same way as I did thirty-odd years ago is hardly the point. The *Monthly Review* was a power for progress, despite its brief life. It was a brave response to a historic need.

New York City, 1968

China Today

NEW YORK, 1934-1942

PHILLIP J. JAFFE

ONE evening in May 1933, a few men and women met in a small Bronx apartment in New York City to organize what became known as the American Friends of the Chinese People. I was present at this meeting at the invitation of Chi Ch'ao-ting, a leading American Communist party member, who happened also to be the husband of a third cousin of mine. There is probably no question that, except for me, everyone in the apartment that evening was a member of the American Communist party.

Very quickly we rented a very small office on West 23rd Street where our only activity for the balance of 1933 was to issue about three multigraphed bulletins announcing our birth, and within those bulletins to reproduce two or three political releases sent to us from Shanghai by the Chinese Communist party underground.

It wasn't until January 1934, that we moved into larger quarters at 168 West 23rd Street, where we began to publish a magazine that we named *China Today*, as well as to give frequent lectures on Far Eastern problems. From January through August 1934, *China Today* was issued in mimeographed format of 8-1/2 x 11 inches in size, with a simple printed two-color cover. For prestige purposes we arbitrarily designed our magazine as Volume 2. There was no "Volume 1" except for the bulletins mentioned above.

Most of the writing, if that's what one would call it, was done by me and one or two others. All of it was in the main a rewrite of material received by the Chinese Bureau of the American Communist party from Shanghai in the form of carbon copies on rice paper.

During this brief period, Chi Ch'ao-ting, whose Communist party name was Doon-ping, used the name C. T. Chan, while I used the name

John Phillips. Chi used an assumed name primarily to protect his student immigration status while I used mine for no particular reason that I now remember. However, both of us lectured frequently in and outside of New York City under our assumed names so that our identity was certainly no secret.

Beginning with October 1934, *China Today* underwent a radical change both physically and politically. The new format was a large (10 x 13 inches) conventional one, well-printed with many photographs and with a two-color illustrated cover. Its articles were now no longer re-writes but mainly original pieces written by the editors as well as by invited writers not connected with either the magazine or the organization.

One can easily see what we thought of our previous mimeographed *China Today*, by noting that the new printed one became Volume 1. The editors of this new *China Today* were Hansu Chan (Chi Ch'ao-ting), Philip J. Jaffe (J. W. Phillips), and T. A. Bisson (Frederick Spencer). Chi Ch'ao-ting, in fear of his immigration status, used on a very few occasions also the names of Huang Lowe and Futien Wang. It was not until July 1934, that Frederick Vanderbilt Field (Lawrence Hearn) was added as the fourth member of the editorial board. Both Bisson's and Field's identity were ultimately revealed by Bisson in congressional testimony.

E. P. Greene (his real name) as managing editor was not of great importance. His title was gratuitous, since his chief function consisted of finding photographs and giving titles to them, writing an occasional piece, and editing the section, "Eyes on the Far East." The three and then the four editors worked very hard at making *China Today* a well written and influential magazine. Most of the technical work such as dummying, proofreading, seeing each issue through the press, etc., fell on my shoulders. My only regular column was "Comment by Sinicus." Ideologically, Chi Ch'ao-ting was our political guide—no one ever questioned his directives or his political editing.

The circulation of *China Today* between subscriptions and book store sales reached a peak of about seven thousand. The income from the sale of the magazine, from lectures, from two banquets, and from a few fundraising meetings was almost sufficient to support both the magazine and the surprisingly small Friends of the Chinese People organization. Despite testimony to the contrary, both *China Today* and the Friends, except for a very few donations, none larger than fifty dollars, were self-supporting.

The last issue of *China Today* to be edited by the four editors previously noted was that of October 1936, listed as Volume 3, Number 1. This cutoff date coincided significantly with the Yosemite Conference of the Institute of Pacific Relations (IPR) in which Chi Ch'ao-ting, T. A. Bisson, and Frederick V. Field were participants. Field was then not only secretary of the American Council of the IPR, but also a widely recognized expert on the Far East.

Before the three left for Yosemite, the four editors decided that it was high time to publish a magazine of greater academic stature than *China Today*. Thus, with important spade work done by Field at Yosemite, there came into existence *Amerasia*, a magazine that continued uninterrupted publication from March 1937 through July 1947.

The older *China Today*, however, did not miss even one month of publication. Beginning with November 1936, with a less imposing format than before, it continued uninterrupted publication through March 1942, under several different editorships. It published a great many documents and original reports from the Communists of China that students of the Far East would be well advised to compare with later texts of the same.

New York City, 1968

Amerasia

NEW YORK, 1937-1947

PHILLIP J. JAFFE

THE four editors of *China Today*—Chi Ch'ao-ting, Phillip J. Jaffe, T. A. Bisson, and Frederick V. Field—ended their connection with that magazine after the issue of October 1936, in order to publish a new magazine of greater academic stature.

The timing of this projected change coincided with the Yosemite Conference of the Institute of Pacific Relations in which Chi, Bisson, and Field were participants. Since Frederick V. Field was secretary of the American Council of the IPR, his spade work in Yosemite was instrumental in obtaining an impressive board of editors for the new magazine. Thus, *Amerasia* was born with the issue of March 1937, and it continued uninterrupted publication through July 1947, as Volume 11, Number 7.

The question has frequently arisen as to what connection there was between *Amerasia* and the American Communist party. Of the original board of editors only Ch'ao-ting Chi and possibly Frederick V. Field were party members. Although Field was listed as chairman of the board of editors, he took almost no part in the actual editing of the magazine. As managing editor, I was in complete charge and control of every phase of each issue, including the editing of all articles. Although for at least the first two or three years, Field's name was signed to all letters of request for articles, they were all written by me and his name was signed by me. Even Ch'ao-ting Chi (for *Amerasia* he put his family name last), in contrast to his role on *China Today*, played a very small part in the affairs of *Amerasia*.

There is no question that I was a very close fellow traveler of the American Communist party. However, I believe I was scrupulous in protecting and preserving the mixed character of our board of editors.

The board met regularly, at least once a month, to discuss articles submitted for publication and to recommend subjects to be covered in later issues. There were occasions when I refused to publish articles submitted by Fred Field and by Ch'ao-ting Chi. Moreover, there were several occasions when *Amerasia* published articles that were diametrically opposite in political conclusions to those on similar subjects covered by the Communist press.

It may be of passing interest here to note that Ch'ao-ting Chi severed his connection with *Amerasia* with the February 1941 issue, in order to work officially for the Chinese government. From that date on his rise in Kuomintang circles was meteoric. He ultimately became a close associate of H. H. K'ung, the powerful vice-premier and minister of finance in Chungking. However, during Chi's entire association with K'ung he also worked secretly for Chou En-lai. All of this was revealed at his funeral in Peking on August 9, 1963, which was attended by many dignitaries including Chou En-lai. He was eulogized as a "fine member of the Chinese Communist Party" and he was praised for having been "engaged in underground work for a considerable period." (For an exciting full biography of Chi, see *Biographical Dictionary of Republican China*, Vol. 1, Howard L. Boorman, editor; New York, Columbia University Press, 1967.)

Despite a very small circulation, *Amerasia* became a very influential magazine. Dr. Stanley K. Hornbeck, then chief of the Far Eastern Division of the State Department, wrote an important statement of official American policy for the first issue. The *New York Times* greeted the very first issue with an editorial welcome. A number of well-known figures in the Far Eastern field were openly disappointed at not being invited to join *Amerasia*'s editorial board. Frequently, unsolicited articles arrived from nationally recognized scholars and teachers.

The largest circulation *Amerasia* reached was 1,700 by subscription and another three to four hundred through book shop sales. However, of the 1,700 subscribers, about a third were from government agencies all over the world, particularly from the United States, Great Britain, and the USSR. At one time the total of American government subscriptions came to sixty-four. Approximately another third of the subscribers were editors, newscasters, teachers, and major libraries.

For the first four years, the political direction of *Amerasia* was in the main anti-Japanese. With the publication, in March 1941, of Anna

Louise Strong's article, "The Kuomintang-Communist Crisis in China," *Amerasia* became critical as well of the Kuomintang in general and Chiang Kai-shek in particular.

With the entrance of the United States into the war after Pearl Harbor, more and more of our editors were drafted for official positions in Washington, until so few were left that I decided to discontinue the board of editors entirely. Thus from the January 7, 1944 issue (Volume 8, Number 1), to the last issue of July 1947, first as a fortnightly and then as a monthly, Kate L. Mitchell and I were the sole editors, and except for a small number of signed articles by others, the two of us wrote every word of all the issues.

Perhaps the most sensational and historically important article *Amerasia* ever published was Anna Louise Strong's "The Thought of Mao Tse-tung," in the June 1947 issue. This article caused a worldwide stir and ultimately led to Miss Strong's arrest in Moscow in February 1949, as well as to the purging of Borodin, who died in jail under suspicious circumstances. This article has come to be recognized by scholars as being important to an understanding of the current Sino-Soviet dispute. *Amerasia* ceased publication with the next issue (July 1947) because the task of producing it became too demanding for two people. There is some evidence that the journal was missed. After I sent Stanley K. Hornbeck a bound set of the 1946-1947 volumes of *Amerasia*, I received a letter from him, dated April 21, 1948, that included the following remarks:

> Over the years, although it [*Amerasia*] has often presented opinions and interpretations with which I could not agree, I have enjoyed and profited by reading it and I have found it useful for purposes of reference. I regret its discontinuance.

It is entirely probable that other specialists on the Far East and on American foreign policy had much the same reaction as Dr. Hornbeck.

New York City, 1968

Spanish Revolution
(United Libertarian Organizations)
NEW YORK, 1936-1938
Spanish Revolution
(Workers' Party of
Marxist Unification)
BARCELONA, SPAIN, 1936-1937

RUSSELL BLACKWELL

FOLLOWING the outbreak of the Spanish Civil War and revolution in July 1936, the need was felt for an English-language publication in the United States to present the positions and reflect the ideals of those fighting in Spain for a new revolutionary society. Fascism in its various forms was dominant in Germany and Italy and was threatening in several other European countries, including France. Its most active opponent at that time appeared to be Stalin's Russia, which posed as the champion of freedom and democracy and the only alternative to fascism. Many people of goodwill throughout the world, suffering through the Great Depression, bewildered by the rightist propaganda and the demagogy of Stalinism, were turning with hope towards Russia.

Anarchists had long realized that between the two totalitarian solutions there was little or no real choice. For them the revolution in Spain was a new opening in the direction of freedom. Russian policy at that time was based on the formation of People's Fronts in all countries. This meant alliances with such diverse elements as Chiang Kai-shek, Franklin D.

Roosevelt, Fulgencio Batista, Leon Blum, and Francisco Llargo Caballero, and a denial of revolution everywhere including Spain. The Communists claimed that in Spain there was purely and simply a civil war between democracy and fascism, and that to work for a social revolution was "counterrevolutionary."

Libertarians felt that the message of Spanish anarchism should be made known to the world. Its relative isolation had to be broken down in order to offset the vicious propaganda of the Communists, the half-truths and distortions of the press agencies, and the clouds of confusion emanating from the chancellories of the Western democracies.

Maximiliano Olay, the representative in the United States of the National Confederation of Labor (CNT) of Spain, left his job as a professional translator in Chicago, moved to New York, and opened an office on lower Fifth Avenue. An additional delegation of three representatives of the CNT then arrived from Spain to stimulate interest in the libertarian point of view and to seek support in the American labor movement.

At that time, the anarchist movement in the United States consisted of a number of groups largely organized around foreign-language newspapers and having but minimal coordination of activities. On the initiative of Olay, it was decided to establish an ad hoc organization, the United Libertarian Organizations, to publish *Spanish Revolution*.

The United Libertarian Organizations embraced the Jewish Anarchist Federation (publishers of *Freie Arbeiter Stimme*), the Russian Federation (*Dielo Trouda*), the *Vanguard* group, several branches of the Industrial Workers of the World, a federation of Spanish-language groups publishing *Cultura Proletaria*, Carlo Tresca's group publishing the Italian newspaper *Il Martello*, several Canadian anarchist groups, some Italian groups in New England, and a scattering of others. Although not actually affiliated, the Gillespie, Illinois, branch of the Progressive Miners of America contributed substantially through a regular monthly assessment on its membership. Mass meetings were held in many cities and thousands of dollars were collected, all of which was sent to the Spanish movement with no deductions for overhead expenses.

The central activity of the United Libertarian Organizations was the publication and circulation of *Spanish Revolution*. Its editorial policies were the collective responsibility of all. Most articles were unsigned since they expressed the ideas of many people and their line had been worked out in general editorial meetings. The paper was not especially concerned with the military aspects of the civil war, which were adequately covered in the capitalist press. It emphasized the much more fundamental revolutionary developments that gave meaning to the military struggle. Special attention was paid to the constructive work of the revolution, with the collectivizations in agriculture and industry being reported in considerable detail. More important policy statements of the CNT were printed in translation.

The editorial in the issue of September 5, 1936, expressed the hope among many radicals throughout the world that a new revolutionary center was in the making in Spain, where the presence of a mass anarchist movement would be able to prevent any party from monopolizing the course of developments as had happened in Russia, where the revolution degenerated as a result of the Bolshevik dictatorship.

Spanish Revolution consistently reflected the activity and thinking of the Spanish libertarians. Its editorial line reflected the hopes and policies of the Spanish movement. However, at times these policies were contradictory, reflecting disagreements within the CNT itself.

To everyone who at the time followed the Spanish events, and especially for those of us who personally lived the exciting, hectic, thrilling, and frustrating days in Spain, a reading of these pages brings alive once more the great aspirations, hopes, and heartbreaks of an earlier decade.

The Spanish workers, with more than a half-century of revolutionary indoctrination and struggle behind them, saw themselves on the threshold of victorious social revolution. The liberal republican politicians had failed to prevent or stop Franco's revolt, and those places where the latter had failed were mainly the result of the action of the working class in defiance of the established authorities. The governments of Madrid and Barcelona had virtually ceased to exist. They were replaced at every level by revolutionary committees in a confusion of colors and shades.

Out of the apparent chaos, the libertarian forces of the National Confederation of Labor and the Iberian Anarchist Federation (FAI) took gigantic steps towards the organization of a society based on freedom, justice, and mutual aid. To the extent of their influence over large areas (and in some they were the majority force), both industry and agriculture were collectivized and/or socialized. The Socialist workers in many sectors participated actively and loyally in this revolutionary work.

In those early days, within the antifascist half of Spain the middle-class liberals had resigned themselves to accepting (in effect if not in so many words) the revolutionary transformation of Spanish society. Only one political sector—Stalinism—actively opposed the revolutionary road. The Communists standing at the extreme right in the anti-Franco coalition denied that there was a social revolution and did everything possible to block it. They entrenched themselves by appealing to the capitalist and petty-bourgeois elements, recruiting thousands of the latter into their party, and into "unions" and auxiliary front groups to serve their purposes. From a small minority party they became a powerful movement.

Eventually they were able to crush the revolution, largely through political and military blackmail. Stalin's Russia sent in a limited amount of supplies, always paid for in gold in advance, and on condition that Stalinist policies be followed. Their personnel flooded Spain. Starting with technicians and advisors, they shortly introduced the GPU and its methods of terror against the revolutionary movement.

The libertarians were no match for the Bolsheviks in political intrigue. For the sake of a false unity against fascism, the libertarians yielded one revolutionary position after the other until the revolution was lost. And with the revolutionary fervor gone, the military fight against Franco (an unequal one at best) was also lost.

In its earlier issues, *Spanish Revolution* followed quite closely the line of the CNT. It published the official documents and policy papers of the Spanish organizations and it emphasized the positive economic and social achievements of the libertarians in the revolution—and these were many and impressive. In a sense, however, its hands were tied, and it glossed over the lack of revolutionary intransigence in such matters as the reluctant acceptance of the "militarization" of the Workers' Militias and the anarchist entry into the governments of Spain and Catalonia.

Soon, however, the editors of the paper found it impossible not to criticize their Spanish comrades. In the issue of January 8, 1937, Emma Goldman attacked the softness of the anarchists in yielding to the Stalinist pressure and political blackmail. Other material in the same vein is to be found in succeeding issues, and there is a rising tone of criticism. The Stalinists were attacked head-on for their policies of strengthening the revivified capitalist state, for their opposition to the revolution and their attempts to liquidate its achievements. They were attacked for their reorganization of the repressive police forces and for their campaign against the "semi-Trotskyist" POUM (Workers' Party of Marxist Unification).

POUM sent its own journal, also called *Spanish Revolution*, to the United States. It was edited by Charles Orr, of the Revolutionary Policy Committee of the Socialist party of the United States, with the very able assistance of his wife, Lois. They had been touring in Europe in the summer of 1936 and went to Barcelona shortly after the outbreak of the revolution to do their part for a cause to which they felt deeply committed. Mary Brea of Australia and other English-speaking comrades contributed on occasion. Publication continued until it was interrupted by the suppression of the POUM. The Orrs were arrested by the Russian GPU at the same time as the POUM leadership. This was featured in a Matthews dispatch to the *New York Times* as a "Fascist Nest Uncovered in Barcelona." Relatives learned of the Orrs' arrest, and they were released, thanks mainly to the intervention of Senator Alben Barkley of Kentucky and to the U.S. State Department. The Orrs were permitted to leave Spain, after spending ten days in a private prison operated by the Russians in Barcelona.

This other and distinctive *Spanish Revolution* faithfully reported events during its period of publication from the point of view of the POUM. Its first issue appeared on October 21, 1936, at a time when the revolutionary process was already beginning to decline. Its final issues dealt with the historic May Days of 1937 and the events immediately following, which led to the Stalinist takeover. These events were also dealt with in the pages of the *Spanish Revolution* of the United Libertarian Organizations. Those times marked the last point at which the Stalinists would have been crushed and the revolution possibly saved.

After the May Days, the Llargo Caballero government was overthrown by the Stalinists and replaced by the government of Juan Negrin. This regime, heralded as the "Government of Victory" by the Communists and by itself, proceeded to lose the war piecemeal, due largely to the demoralizing effect of its antirevolutionary policies on the morale of a revolutionary people. Upon taking power, Negrin crushed the POUM and brought its leaders to trial as fascist agents, just as many of the Old Bolsheviks in the Soviet Union had been framed and liquidated by Stalin, accused of being Hitler's agents. The Russian GPU operated actively and almost openly in Spain. Andres Nin of the POUM, and many anarchists as well as a number of foreigners of anti-Stalinist Marxist groups, were murdered by its agents.

The CNT now went into open opposition where it was joined by the Left Socialists around Llargo Caballero. The repression reached mammoth proportions. The press censorship was crippling and the anarchists and Socialists issued illegal papers in order not to lose their identities altogether. The Stalinist International Brigades were taken into Aragon to smash the peasant collectives by force of arms.

Spanish Revolution had been founded to bring the message of the revolution to the Anglo-American people. As the revolution declined and news became increasingly unfavorable, the enthusiastic support that had made its publication possible petered out. *Spain and the World*, published in London, filled the need for further information in the English language.

Spanish Revolution ceased publication in the spring of 1938. The Negrin government was firmly in power and the revolution was over. The counterrevolution was triumphant. The war dragged on as a purely military affair for another year. Hitler and Mussolini had made their point. So had Stalin. Less than six months later, the Stalin-Hitler Pact was signed and World War II was launched.

New York City, 1968

The Conscientious Objector
NEW YORK, 1939-1946

STEPHEN SITEMAN

USUALLY the author of even the merest of polemical documents feels required to describe the "need" for his particular production. The group of pacifists, who met in the home of Abe Kaufman, then executive secretary of the War Resisters League (WRL) in the summer of 1939, and decided to publish *The Conscientious Objector*, felt no such need. They took for granted a common knowledge of it and, indeed, required their potential subscribers to affirm their belief in it. Putting first things first, the coupon asked each contributor to agree that "*The Conscientious Objector* serves the purpose of enlightenment on the war and peace question and acts as a bond between men and women of good will." The coupon on page two of Vol. I, No. 1, quite modestly did not ask for subscriptions but only for an unspecified sum of money for "the next issue." There was not to be another issue until the February-March one of 1940. This was followed by five more issues in that year, seven in 1941, and then the paper settled down to once-a-month publication for the duration of the war.

This frequency of issue does not indicate an irresistible demand for another publication on war or peace, but *The Conscientious Objector* was to perform a useful and sometimes pioneering role in the years of strain and suffering that were to come. It will be useful to try to describe the pacifists or, as the draft came into existence and swept the young men of America into its embrace, the conscientious objectors for whom the paper spoke.

They were not the young men of the historic peace churches—the Quakers, Brethren, and Mennonites. (They comprised the great majority of objectors in the Civilian Public Service camps. Out of 9,835 assignees, the Mennonites accounted for 4,610, the Brethren for 1,468, and the Friends or Quakers for 902.) Nor were they the Jehovah's Witnesses. (Out of 6,086 convictions for violation of the Selective Service Act for religious reasons or conscientious objection in one form or another, the JW's supplied 4,411 and all other groups the rest.) These groups, especially the rather standoffish Jehovah's Witnesses, felt adequately represented by the apparatus of their well-organized institutions.

Nor were they, in large part, the members of the older peace groups, the Fellowship of Reconciliation (FOR), the Women's International League for Peace and Freedom, or the National Council for the Prevention of War.

There remained the mildly religious or purely political, philosophical, or moral objectors. Many of these had already found an organizational home in the relatively young War Resisters League. This group had begun as a committee of the Fellowship of Reconciliation, an organization of Christian pacifists, to service those pacifists who were either not Christian or not religious. This committee had grown into a separate entity, but by the outbreak of war in 1939, it had not brought forth a publication of its own. From the beginning of publication on *The Conscientious Objector* was given desk space in the crowded offices of the League, at 2 Stone Street, New York City.

The evolution of organizational support for *The Conscientious Objector* can be followed by a look at the masthead of each issue. The first issue had no editor and was described as the "organ of the American section of the War Resisters International, including the Fellowship of Reconciliation, the War Registers League and Women's Peace Union." Pax, described as a group of Catholic conscientious objectors, and the New History Society (undescribed) were listed as "cooperating" groups.

The second issue, a few months later, was "published . . . by the Fellowship of Reconciliation, the Peace Committee of the New York Yearly Meetings of Friends, and the New York Section of The War Resisters League." Pax and the New History Society had disappeared, never to be heard from again.

For the third issue, support had shifted from the New York section of the WRL to its national organization, but in the FOR had shifted from the national to its New York section. Support of the Friends had been handed from their yearly to their monthly meeting, perhaps reflecting the increased frequency of the paper's appearance.

This lineup was to continue for nearly two years, or until the United States entered the war in December 1941. With the March 1942 issue (Vol. IV, No. 3), *The Conscientious Objector* became an independent organization with its own board of directors, headed by A. J. Muste of the Fellowship of Reconciliation and Dr. Evan Thomas (brother of Norman) of the War Resisters League. (In the pacifist movement, Evan Thomas has filled much the same role as his brother has done in the Socialist party.) Although the change took place in a peaceful and friendly fashion as befitted such organizations, it nevertheless reflected a feeling of caution that, in a time of war, with its increasing regulations and suspicions, they did not want to be responsible for a publication which they could not wholly control.

The publication of *The Conscientious Objector*, at all, much less with any regularity, was a feat of lively gymnastics, devotion, and ability. Compare it with events in the United States of the 1960s, when publications with hundreds of thousands of subscribers and millions of dollars of advertising cannot sustain themselves. The subscribers of *The Conscientious Objector* were usually vanishing into prison or Civilian Public Service camps and in either case had no money to pay even a minimal subscription price. The advertising was bravely pathetic and an example of sympathetic organizations and publications taking in each other's laundry or, to switch metaphors, whistling to keep up each other's courage.

In the summer of 1940, the paper hired its first paid employee, a business manager, who was expected to work 10 hours a week for $5.00. The rest of the staff, of course, was not paid and, worse, was continually being drafted or arrested. A young newspaperman, Jay Nelson Tuck, performed the yeoman and highly competent job of editing *The Conscientious Objector* from its second issue until he himself was drafted in February 1945. In October 1942, the board of the paper, in a flush of optimism, voted to raise $1,500 and hire their first full-time employee, still the business manager. The paper was always very cagey about its circulation, but on its first anniversary in 1940, it announced that it hoped to raise its circulation from 2,000 to 4,000. In November 1943, the paper increased its budget to $3,300 a year and two years later announced that it "hoped to become a weekly with a circulation of 20,000" and a budget of $15,000. But such affluence was beyond its reach.

Quite properly, *The Conscientious Objector* concentrated on the treatment conscientious objectors were receiving and was probably the first to attack the organization and philosophy of the Civilian Public Service camps. Although the objectors had been promised work of "national importance under civilian direction," they were given work that was often of no importance whatsoever and, although the camps were operated by the peace churches, their conditions were dictated by Selective Service. The men assigned to CPS were not only not paid but were at first required themselves to pay $35.00 a month maintenance costs. This cost was, however, absorbed by the religious organizations. Matters improved somewhat as the war went on but church sponsorship and lack of pay remained the chief source of dissatisfaction and frustration. To this day, the money earned by CPS men on detached service to farmers, who were required to pay the prevailing wage, which was seized by the federal government, remains in the United States Treasury. At the end of the war it amounted to more than a million dollars.

There were two side effects of the wartime pacifist movement. One was the pacifist's attitude toward racial discrimination. The pacifist groups had always advocated an end to racial discrimination as part of their philosophy of fraternity of peoples but it wasn't until many of their young men were thrown into prison, with its rigid segregation of the races, that the issue exploded in their ranks. Probably the reforms in the Federal Bureau of Prisons' handling of racial discrimination owe more to the change in social attitudes and the pressure of Negroes' demands, but the work and hunger strikes by imprisoned conscientious objectors achieved the first success in calling public attention to this social evil and in breaching the bureau's policy of segregation. Upon release from prison, conscientious objectors of the Fellowship of Reconciliation organized a Committee on Racial Equality which spun off from the Fellowship and became the Congress on Racial Equality. A. Philip Randolph's March on Washington movement in the middle of the war adopted nonviolence as a principle of action.

The second issue had to do with India. Attracted by Gandhi's satyagraha, pacifists took up the cause of India's independence at a time when it had few friends. It was good for India and it was good for the pacifists because it educated many of them on the nature of colonialism and the exploitation of what they had not yet learned to call underdeveloped countries. This led to some ambivalence in the pacifists' attitude toward Britain, which was the chief colonial power and oppressor of India, but also the home of the strongest antiwar movement and the greatest number of conscientious objectors.

The Conscientious Objector came to an end in June 1946, with Vol. VIII, No. 6. Sixty-eight issues had been published, and the journal never achieved a circulation of more than 4,000 copies. The management optimistically spoke of a return to publication in the fall of 1946, but it never did. The paper attributed its end to ''an acute shortage of personnel and a creeping financial paralysis,'' but war had been the health of *The Conscientious Objector* and with its end, the closing of the CPS camps, the release, finally, of the conscientious objectors still in prison, the interest and devotion necessary to a publication like this one faded away. By the time of the Korean War, brief though the interval was, a new generation was appearing on the scene which had already begun to look away from the old institutions. Another fifteen years, when the United States had plunged into Vietnam, the pacifist situation and the attitudes of the young men who were refusing to fight had changed even more drastically. For these developments, close the pages of *The Conscientious Objector* and consult your daily newspaper.

New York City, 1968

Pacifica Views

GLENDORA, CALIFORNIA,
1943-1947

WILLIAM APPLEMAN WILLIAMS

PACIFICA VIEWS, a Weekly Journal of Pacifist Thought is one of the more stimulating and prescient radical journals of the 1940s. "Pacifism is the revolutionary movement of the twentieth century," the editors announced on June 11, 1943, arguing that "successful opposition to war depends upon a far-reaching social program that will offer other means than war for the adjustment of international differences." Thus "War Resistance is Revolution." And it followed that the central problems were those involved in making the transition from conscientious objection to general radicalism, and from individualistic, neoanarchist action to a social movement.

One approach called for attacking the wartime Civilian Public Service system for COs as a "forced labor program" as part of an effort to create a more general "resistance movement" among those who refused to serve in the armed forces. "The prevention of war was never a valid aim," the editors asserted, "let alone an argument, for pacifism." The objective was to end the war system, and they described their "major avocation" as "propagandizing and working for the non-violent revolution." Describing American society as too far gone to save through piecemeal reform, and the world as "insane," *Pacifica Views* mounted an attack on "the very bases of our economic and political order."

The editors insisted, from an early date, that imaginative and effective intellectual leadership was essential. As they defined the problem, the head, rather than the heart or the guts, was the crucial part of the human anatomy in evolving a "radical social philosophy" and building a social movement. The environment, whether in terms of the Cold War, poverty, frustration with one's work, or racism, generated all the necessary emotion and determination. As the editors pointed out, in an insight very similar to the one used much later by Norman Mailer, the experience of the CO could give him an understanding of what it meant to be a black man in the United States. The fundamental need was to define the broad objective in concrete terms and to articulate strategy and tactics capable of generating movement toward that goal.

The early optimism (1944-1946) that the "sure leaven" of pacifist thought would create a "technology of social change," and that the pacifist could "put the non-pacifist on the defensive and keep him there," did not withstand the impact of five contrary developments. First, there was no tradition of agreement among pacifists on general objectives. That was because, second, there was no established movement, and because the existing individualistic and anarchist ethos blocked the creation of a social outlook.

Third, the editors concluded that the emphasis on resistance likewise imposed serious limitations on achieving long-range goals. "Opposition by itself, even as an assertion of moral responsibility, does not create alternate institutions." Fourth, there was no sustained effort to formulate alternatives that, by promising a better life, would unify the pacifists as revolutionaries and attract wide support from leftists and liberals. Finally, those weaknesses served indirectly to strengthen the existing and impressive power of the established system.

Other leftists made a similar analysis of the situation in the United States at the end of World War II, but *Pacifica Views* was notable for its rigor and toughness about the Left itself, and for refusing to slide off into routine rhetorical criticism. "We face a world worse today than in 1939," the editors judged on July 12, 1946, and warned that "its capacities for growing worse are even greater." And their evaluation of the Truman Doctrine, and what it represented and portended, was perceptive and courageous. "American imperialism is growing with sickening rapidity. It is meeting with almost no opposition."

In response, the editors concentrated on encouraging and supporting three kinds of activity. The first, which began on June 1, 1945, was an assault on peacetime conscription. That campaign might serve to give the radicals of the 1960s and 1970s a sense of the time required to generate the kind of action that provokes serious national attention. For one of the first significant episodes of draft-card burning occurred early in February 1947, when sixty-six men defied the system at the University of Chicago. Two full decades passed before that particular tactic became at all effective.

Second, *Pacifica Views* publicized and praised the noble action of Ammon Hennacy, particularly his refusal (beginning in 1944) to pay income tax as a way of striking at the system. For a time, in 1946, the editors neglected such tactics in favor of a convoluted discussion of the sexual theories of Wilhelm Reich. Leftists, along with men of other ideological persuasions, were certainly correct in viewing American sexual repression (and resultant sexual obsessions) as both a cause and a symptom of its more generally oppressive nature.

But the discussion of the issue in *Pacifica Views*, like those in related journals, served more to illustrate how deeply the Left was permeated with an individualistic ethos than it did to present a convincing case that personal liberation in sexual matters played a primary causal role in creating a revolutionary movement. A reader sometimes gains the feeling that the Left was engaged in a curious reversal of the classic Freudian doctrine: that instead of sublimating the libido in politics, it was sublimating politics in bed.

The editors of *Pacifica Views* may have reached a similar conclusion, for they shortly dropped Reich in favor of a sustained discussion of how to reach the worker with an alternate conception of the economic order. The existing labor movement, the CIO as well as the AFL, was dismissed as a bureaucratic institution of the establishment. More significantly, they perceptively discounted the value of traditional producer cooperatives on the grounds that the members remained locked in a marketplace system. Such a worker, "as a consumer," they noted, "is so remote that his interests are never democratically expressed and he suffers the same frustrations as does any industrial worker."

Starting from the premise that "it is the need of the worker to feel he is an integral, essential part of an important activity," the editors tried to use Veblen's theory about the instinct of workmanship as a dynamic axiom for devising an alternate political economy. Their strategy was to construct worker-controlled industries directly tied to consumer outlets that would provide "the nucleus of a revolutionary dual power." They realized that a revolutionary central credit agency would be required to fund such a system, but they hoped to use it to encourage and sustain

—rather than to control—multiplicity of decentralized economic units. As with the political tactic of burning draft cards, the concept of a dual (or counter) society emerged twenty years later as a primary theme in the discussions of the Students for a Democratic Society and other groups of the New Left.

Very little had been done during that long interval, however, to carry the dialogue (or thinking) beyond the point reached by *Pacifica Views*. Nor did it move very rapidly after 1966-1967. The individual and group protests and demonstrations did politicalize and even radicalize increasing numbers of American citizens. But the lack of a concrete, attractive, and workable alternate conception of a new American community left the new radicals—just like the old—suspended in the limbo between rhetorical revolution and repetitive, isolated acts of opposition and resistance. As *Pacifica Views* sensed as early as 1945, the result could well strengthen the established order through a process of piecemeal adaptation. On many grounds, therefore, the files of *Pacifica Views* provide sobering—and perhaps illuminating—reading for contemporary radicals.

Madison, Wisconsin, 1968

Part Ten

THEORETICAL JOURNALS, LITTLE MAGAZINES, AND THE ARTS

NINETEENTH-CENTURY American anarchists made important contributions to the development of libertarian thought. But since the turn of the century, and especially among Socialists, American radicals have not been strong on theory. They have contributed little to the growth and the study of ideology.

The most frequently cited exception is Daniel De Leon, who was admired for his fine mind even by his enemies who found no other redeeming quality in the man. As has been mentioned earlier, Lenin was quoted as saying that De Leon was the only individual anywhere who added anything to the Marxist *corpus*. De Leon certainly does stand alone as a theorist in the United States, but, curiously, neither he nor his successors produced a creditable theoretical journal. De Leon's own abstractions were publicized in pamphlet form or in his contributions to the Socialist Labor party's newspaper, *The People*. After his death in 1914, the SLP not only failed to build on his insights, but did nothing more than reprint the master's sayings into the 1970s.

None of the other radical groups has been notably successful in producing a first-rate magazine of theory either. What Martin Glaberman and George P. Rawick have written of Louis Fraina and *The Revolu-*

tionary Age of Boston applies generally to the American experience with theoretical inquiry. Although Fraina was "the leading theoretical figure" of his time, they write, he

> was not a profound theoretician on the level of many in the European Socialist and Communist movements. Lenin, Plekhanov, Luxemburg, Bernstein, Kautsky, and some others towered above him. It is not at all a matter of comparing lists of attainments; it is simply the theoretical poverty of American socialism and communism. Although there was some excellent political journalism in *Revolutionary Age*, nowhere did it (or its antecedents or successors) reach the levels of seriousness or originality of some of the European Marxist journals.

In fact, the most successful radicals in America were those who drew on the national attribute of practicality. When the Socialist party poised briefly on the brink of political significance early in the twentieth century, it was characterized by its pragmatism and its indifference to ideological niceties. Similarly, the Communist party achieved its greatest strength in its easy-going "Popular Front" period when theoretical laxity was party policy. Indeed, in those periods when American radicals have immersed themselves in theory, necessarily of European origin, it was then that they promptly sank into the tragicomic bickering and splintering that mars so much of the history of the Old Left. Or, at best, they have been unsuccessful. It is worth noting in passing that *The Marxian*, called by its analyst "undoubtedly one of the most learned and scholarly of the radical periodicals to be published in this country," is also singular in managing to put out the absolute minimum of issues (two) necessary to qualify it as a "periodical."

The story of the New Left added another dimension to this generality. After 1960, disgusted by the hairsplitting of some of the old radicals, New Leftists abjured ideology so extremely—so "ideologically"—that the movement degenerated into an empty thrashing-about and a self-righteousness quite as fruitless as the dogmatism of the older movements. But a paucity of theoretical underpinning was also characteristic of the American Left before the 1960s.

In contrast, in the arts American radicals have been more active and even more productive than their European counterparts. Part of the reason for the theoretical poverty may, in fact, derive from their emphasis on the arts. That is, when hardnosed "realists" like the Wobblies decried the influence of "intellectuals" in the radical movements, they were speaking not only of ideologues like Daniel De Leon but of—intellectuals to them—the aesthetes who have periodically attached themselves to social radical movements in America. From the salons of Mabel Dodge to the "radical chic" of the 1960s, middle-class cultural *emigrés* have rallied to symbolic red flags and political associations where, in Europe, they might more likely have been content with more familiar bohemianisms. One result of this has been the confusion of "life style" with revolution that blossomed in the 1960s. But, in addition, revolutionary-artists also created some fine literature and dramatic propaganda such as the "Paterson Pageant," a massive tableau presented at Madison Square Garden in 1913 by John Reed and some associates in support of striking broadsilk weavers in Paterson, New Jersey. And, finally, in dozens of "little magazines" of a notably political bent, culminating in the *Partisan Review*, and in near unanimously lauded publications like the *Masses*, radical intellectuals of artistic inclination bequeathed a periodical heritage far exceeding anything done in the realm of theory.

The Marxian

NEW YORK, 1921

DALE RIEPE

THE MARXIAN was published in 1921 by the Marx Institute of New York City. Its guiding spirit was Harry Waton, the author of *Philosophy of Marx, Pain & Pleasure*, and *Fetishism of Liberty*. Among the writers, only Max Lerner, who wrote one of the editorials, is widely remembered. He was only nineteen when he pointed out the mistakes of members of the Socialist party, including the fact that they did not bother to read Marx although they were quick to quote him to suit their purposes. Other writers for the short-lived *Marxian* included Nathan Moser, Rose Wortis, Charles Brower, and Leonard Day. Foreign writers represented in translation (often supplied by M. Heller) included Marx, Engels, Karl Kreibach, the Czechoslovakian Marxist, and Katayama San [Sen], the Japanese Marxist. Sen, who wrote *My Socialism* in 1903, was an early leader of Asian Marxism, and with Ho Chi-minh, M. N. Roy, and others formed the third world congress of the Comintern in 1922. To my knowledge, his article on ''Rice Riots of Japan (1918)'' was the first of its kind to be printed in the United States and it was not until the late 1940s that an occasional Japanese Marxist was again published in American Socialist periodicals.

The Marxian was undoubtedly one of the most learned and scholarly of the radical periodicals to be published in this country. It made no bones about appealing to intellectuals who were eager to master the principles of Marxism. The editors, Waton and Lerner, expected nothing short of complete dedication to an understanding of such classics of Marxism as *Capital, The Eighteenth Brumaire of Louis Bonaparte, The Poverty of Philosophy, Wage Labour and Capital*, all by Marx and Ludwig Feuerbach, *The Dialectics of Nature*, and *The Peasant War in Germany* of

Engels, as well as Lenin's *State and Revolution* and the *Empirio-Criticism*. To this end they published translations which were not generally available to English readers until the 1940s: Marx's *Critique of the Gotha Programme*, his "Class Struggles in France" from the *Neue Rheinische Zeitung* of June 29, 1948, Rosa Luxemburg's "Mass Action and Revolution" with a foreword to the Swedish abridgment, and "Address of the Central Committee of the League of Communists to its Members in Germany (March 1850)" by Marx and Engels.

The editors were concerned to give help to dedicated Marxists who might be studying the central classics of Marxism such as *The Communist Manifesto* and *Das Kapital*. Charles Brower wrote two installments of "Historic Background of the Communist Manifesto" which probably could be used today to great advantage in preventing the usual reaction to the *The Communist Manifesto* by readers who do not know what went before it. Harry Waton supplied two installments of "An Aid to the Study of 'Capital' " which were one of the very few such studies in English.

The first editorial of *The Marxian* briefly analyzed the state of Marxian studies in the United States and stated that one "can boast of little worthwhile in this field." America is so concerned, the editorial said, with immediate gains and practicality that shallowness and superficiality are the order of the day. The Socialist movement "has been a child of its environment, confused, empty, shallow—mainly concerned with 'practical' and immediate objectives. The essential opportunism of the Socialist movement was a natural development in this country where the sharper class antagonisms had not had a chance to develop." Above all, in the practical struggle, Marxian studies must be pursued in order to unmask the opportunism of the leaders of the Socialist party. Let us remember, nevertheless, that "Marxism is a science of action, not a closet philosophy." Marxian action must be contrasted with opportunistic Democratic Socialist treason noted throughout the world in World War I.

The general tone of the journal's two issues was optimistic but wary. If Americans were ever to master Socialist history and goals they must know Marxism. Bolshevism had held out in Russia for four years against drought, revisionism, counterrevolution, blockade, and foreign intervention. Now was the time to accelerate the wave that made it possible, and basic to it must be the study of Marxist classics.

Although heavily emphasizing foreign affairs and the international nature of Marxism, *The Marxian* was not completely aloof to local issues. Its treatment was of a uniformly high caliber largely because of the historical framework given to local or American issues. "The Lusk Bill" which went into effect in New York State in September 1921 "requires the licensing of all schools and classes by the State except those conducted by religious organizations and fraternal orders." This concern with loyalty has persisted of course down to the similarly worded Feinberg Law in New York. *The Marxian*'s comment on such licensing of loyalty was that "New York State curtly tells us, 'I am to be the censor of what is to be taught.' This is the open dictatorship of the capitalists." Every effort must be made to nullify this educational weapon of the ruling class, said *The Marxian*.

Max Lerner in "The *New York Call* and the Critique of the Gotha Program" warns against the opportunism of the Socialist party press, particularly the *New York Call*. The argument of the *Call* was that Marx had nothing to say about distribution. Lerner responded by quoting Marx from the Gotha Program: " 'From everyone according to his ability, to everyone according to his needs.' " The difficulty with the *Call*, he said, is that its staff doesn't know, read, or study Marx, but merely perverts and adulterates Marxian socialism.

Much of Rose Wortis' article on "Problems of American Trade Unionism" reads like it had been written last month. "The officials . . . at one time the pioneers of the labor movements, are no longer responsive to its needs," she claimed. But despite them, World War I provided a fine opportunity for more intelligent and broader leadership because "the most backward masses had been drawn into political life." Instances of leadership treachery may be seen in the New York harbor strike of January 1919 when 17,000 maritime workers went out and where the labor leaders broke the strike. They also perverted the aims of the Musicians' Union, and the Teamster's Union. The laziness of the rank and file needs correcting, Wortis claimed, as does the divisiveness of such brilliantly conceived unions as the IWW. Five percent of the workers are as brave and unselfish as any in the world. What we need to do is to get inspiration from the encouraging labor situation in England.

Finally, to turn to a more intellectually demanding article, and one practically unknown in English literature, is Karl Kreibich's "Preface to the Czecho-Slovakian Edition of the Critique of the Gotha Program." The main value of this is to sharply trace the growth of "bourgeois parliamentary sham democracy" from the political reaction of 1848 to 1920. From La Salle to Bebel, to the Eisenacher Program in 1869, to the Gotha Unity Program of 1875, to the Congress of Erfurt in 1891, and finally to the Social Democratic acceptance of nationalism in World War I, Kreibich traces the mistakes of liberalism, Ricardianism, the Hegelian view of the State, the "full product of labor" and the "co-operatives financed by government credit." To know the history of this welfare statism is to understand its weaknesses. Such articles turned some readers away from the "fluff" being printed in the *Call* but were not sufficiently in demand to require issues of *The Marxian* beyond November 1921, when it stopped publication.

Buffalo, New York, 1969

The Marxist

NEW YORK, 1925-1927

DALE RIEPE

THE MARXIST was published in New York City from 1925 to 1927. Its editor, Harry Waton, was also editor of *The Marxian* (1921) and author of *Philosophy of Marx, Pain and Pleasure*, and *Fetishism of Liberty*. *Marxist* was published by the Workers' Educational Institute, successor to the Marx-Engels Institute and the earlier Marx Institute.

According to the anonymous introduction to the first number of *The Marxist*, because of the distractions created from 1914 onward by World War I "it was almost impossible for the working class to concentrate their mind upon serious study and deep thought." By 1925, however, it was believed that the class-conscious workers had "regained their revolutionary self-consciousness and their mental composure" and were again ready for light and knowledge. With this auspicious beginning, it was hoped that a central school for advanced students (workers) could be instituted where they could study Marxism, universal history, and philosophy under the guidance of Harry Waton.

The first issue of *The Marxist* was largely Waton's "An Aid to the Study of Capital." It began with an analysis of Marx's *Capital*, Volume I, which is concerned with a discussion of "Commodities" and continued to Section 4, "The Fetishism of Commodities and the Secret Thereof." (Chapter I or the first one hundred pages of the American [Kerr] edition of 1912.) An introductory chapter set the scene for entrance into the adventure of reading *Capital*. In it Waton emphasized the tremendous development of mankind under primitive communism which "brought light into darkness, order into chaos, knowledge into ignorance, and laid the foundation for a wonderful world." This world perfected human speech, cleared the earth's surface, tamed and harnessed animals, discovered fire, invented tools, acquired horticulture and agriculture, learned to spin, weave, sew, build houses and make pottery and thus laid the foundations of aesthetics, religion, philosophy, and science.

With civilization in the cities came property-owning, individualism, hatred, struggle, war, and misery. "Mankind's achievements during primitive communism were infinitely greater and more fundamental than their achievements during civilization. If one raises the question as to why civilization replaced primitive communism," Waton answers, "social existence . . . most proper for mankind is in the state in which mankind can rise above the state of nature. This implies a state of existence in which mankind are the masters over nature; which, in turn, implies that mankind are the masters over the tools of production and the processes of production." As a communism of consumption instead of production, primitive communism had to pass to higher communism through civilization (slave empires, feudalism, and capitalism).

Waton next advanced his own theory of progress which "is from the periphery to the centre, and when the centre is reached, all further progress is from the centre back to the periphery. . . . Self-consciousness first dawned at the periphery of society, manifesting itself among the thinkers, prophets and philosophers . . . And when self-consciousness reached the centre of society, all further progress proceeded from the proletariat back to the periphery of society. It is the historic function of the proletariat to revolutionize and reconstruct society from the centre to the periphery." At this point the proletariat becomes the ruling class which forms a new society based on communism of production.

The periphery-center hypothesis of Waton may be seen to operate in the realm of science. "Man was the last concern of man himself [periphery]. Mankind plunged into metaphysical contemplation, before they betook themselves to study the real world. . . ; they studied the heavens before the[y] began the study of the earth; they built up systems of astrology before they crystallized astronomy, metaphysics before physics, alchemy before chemistry." As we shall soon see, this novel hypothesis was used in a way that did not endear Waton to "orthodox" Marxists.

The essence of Marxism, according to Waton, is repeated many times by Marx. It is in Marx's own words: "A definite form of production thus determines the forms of consumption, distribution, exchange, and also the mutual relations between these various elements." This is the central idea of the materialist interpretation of history. The dialectic is the movement of the mutual relationships within the process.

To turn now to the study of Marx's *Capital*, the first point wort'hy of our attention is that without an "understanding of it [one] cannot be heard to express any opinion about economic phenomena, for his opinion is worthless." *Capital* was written "to guide and enlighten the international proletariat," to convince them to consciously and actively endeavor "to overthrow the capitalist order, and inaugurate a communist order, . . ." by means of the laws of economics. The major elements in understanding *Capital* are as follows:

1. Capital is the part of wealth, either in the form of money or in the form of commodities, or in the forms of both, which is used for the purposes of making more money, for the purposes of profit.

2. The capitalist mode of production is that mode of production in which capital begins the process, and in which the material means of life are produced primarily for profit, and not for the use of the producers themselves or others.

3. A commodity is a human product made primarily for exchange, and is the means for the creation of profit for the owner of the means of production.

4. Value is a social relation between the quantity of labor-power socially necessary for the reproduction of one commodity to the quantity of such labor-power necessary for the reproduction of another commodity.

Of special felicity is Waton's discussion on the determination of price. He showed the ineffectuality of the supply and demand hypothesis as well as that of marginal utility, favorites of bourgeois economics. One instance that destroys supply and demand as a determinant is shown in the example of mine owners, who despite being overstocked with coal already dug out, push the price skyward if there is a threat of a strike. It is not the supply and demand of the commodities, but the labor-power that determines market prices. Marginal utility is largely irrelevant to understanding prices because: first, it concerns the private economy of the individual who values his goods according to their marginal utilities (the more they get, the less they want) instead of realities in the marketplace where other than individualistic measures are required; second, many buyers have limited means and would not purchase if the price goes above a certain figure; and third, many sellers would hold their property (commodities) rather than take a lower price. "It is these buyers that are least eager to buy and these sellers that are least eager to sell, who hold the power of determining the ratios of exchange, all other purchases and sales, in the open market, conforming to the values set by these."

The marginal utility hypothesis is wrong for the following reasons: (1) it seems to operate only at the time commodities are already on the market, ready for exchange and does not enter as a factor at or before the time or production of the commodities; (2) it assumes that commodities are produced for use—but not so—"the manufacturer thinks of the utility of the money rather than of the utility of his suits . . ." (3) marginal utility is simply supply and demand in disguise, and finally (4) marginal utility reverses the role of factors. "Instead of interpreting psychological phenomena in terms of material factors, this theory interprets material factors in terms of psychologic phenomena. It seeks to explain the cause by the effect." What this says, in brief, is that bourgeois economics is idealistic rather than materialistic. Bourgeois economics also begins with an analysis of exchange or consumption when it ought to start with production. "The real science of modern economy does not begin until theoretical analysis passes from the process of circulation to the process of production." (*Capital*, Vol. II, Chap. XX.)

In the second number, *The Marxist* published another section of "An Aid to the Study of Capital," Waton's "Introduction to Universal History," and a commentary on "The Scopes Case." The indefatigable work of Waton is again shown in the third number in which appears his translation from the Russian of the *German Ideology* ("The Materialist Conception of History"), followed by "An Analysis and Criticism of the Materialist Conception of History," and "The Revolutionary Movement Must Go a Step Beyond the Materialist Conception of History." Just as all realities of existence change in form and interrelations, so the materialist conception of history must change. The writings of Marx took us to that point, but now we must take the next step beyond, which to our surprise takes us back to Hegel. Waton's reasoning is this: "The laws imposed upon man are those of reason. . . . Reason is transcendental in nature and universal in scope and function. . . . History . . . is the process of the realization of the destiny of man [which is] a free, rational and happy existence [given to them by] the ultimate reality of existence (God,

Spirit, the Unknowable or whatever)." One proof that even Marx foresaw something like this is, Waton says, that he never attacked Hegel directly but instead attacked the Young-Hegelians. The reason is that Marx knew that he could not attack this essentially correct philosophy. Space does not permit the elucidation of Waton's philosophy of history, but it is not without originality and ingenuity. I would characterize it as having strains of Marx, Hegel, Spencer, Spengler, and Berdyaev, although he is personally indebted only to the first three. His closing thought, which is in keeping with the present trend in humanistic Marxism is that "We deceive ourselves when we imagine that we can interpret the phenomena of existence empirically, without any metaphysical [philosophical] assumptions."

Buffalo, New York, 1969

Road to Communism

NEW YORK, 1934-1935

DALE RIEPE

ROAD TO COMMUNISM was the theoretical journal of the American Communist party (Opposition). It appeared in 1934-1935 under the editorship of Jay Lovestone, who also was the leader of the CPO. Student revolutionaries, black resisters, bourgeois democrats, and historians of the social movements of the Great Depression will find this essential reading.

In 1934, two questions crucial to an assessment of the political climate of the day were being discussed by the Communist party. The first question was, "How stabilized is capitalism?" For if capitalism is stabilized, the time is not ripe for revolution. But even though there were many leaking seams in the capitalist ships of state, it seemed likely that they would remain afloat for quite some time. The second question was whether bourgeois democracy is really any different from fascism. Fascism had come to power recently in Italy, Germany, and Austria, and it looked as if other fascist governments would soon peak in Central Europe. It was the contention of *Road to Communism* that left-wing infantilists had overlooked the notable differences between the two, and by doing so, had encouraged fascism with a shrug. "There can be no doubt about it, but that Fascist dictatorship is the elimination and smashing of bourgeois democracy." But the Communist party of Germany and the Communist Internationale both looked upon the Bruening, Papen, and Schleicher governments as carrying through the fascist dictatorship. Such blindness proved "flagrant imbecility"—a step lower, according to *RTC*, than any achieved heretofore by Socialists.

One of the main theses of *RTC* was that Social Democracy was a treacherous movement to try to win over the workingman to capitalism through parliamentary and democratic illusions. Furthermore, it "objectively furthers fascism'' by pretending that there is no difference between fascism and bourgeois democracy. The contradictory nature of these two views was often missed by the uneducated worker. Social Democracy, however, posing as anticapitalist yet unable to explain its inactivity in fighting capitalism, brought up the following red-herring (which it employs even today) that ''the growing revolutionary danger, the threat to the rule of capital by the working class has brought fascism into existence as a counter movement.'' On the contrary, replied *RTC*, ''The inability of the proletariat to struggle, the splits within the working class movement, were the conditions not only for the growth of fascism but also for bourgeoisie to risk a fascist coup d'etat because it no longer feared the working class.''

The *RTC* also dealt with the Negro question. According to *RTC*, to understand the Negro question one must first understand the South. One must also understand the North because the two sections were becoming interpenetrated. White supremacy, even among Socialists, according to an anonymous author (perhaps Jay Lovestone), impoverished any theory concerning the Negro question and reduced it to the economic question of workers against bosses. This could no longer be tolerated, especially among Communists. The economic crisis of the 1930s, unemployment, and chaos in the cotton industry had made it imperative to ''explain'' the Negro question. The major points made were as follows: (1) The Negro people represent a caste or a noncaste like the outcastes or nonscheduled castes in India; they are not a national minority. (2) Since the North prevented the final emancipation of the Negro, racial oppression has become an integral part of the bourgeois-imperialist system of the United States. (3) American farmers and workers have been brainwashed by the bourgeoisie to be anti-Negro, and this feeling is reinforced by the psychic compensation it affords them (as in Sartre's *Portrait of the Anti-Semite*). (4) Because of the migration of the Negro to the North, a Negro bourgeoisie and petit bourgeoisie has developed, and Negro society has begun to develop into a colony or subject nation. The fundamental statement of this trend is to be found in Booker T. Washington's ''Atlanta Compromise.'' Washington (1856-1915) was the prototype of the ''race leader'' to be found in church, business, labor, and entertainment thereafter. It is notable that ''Only in the proportion of clergy to the population do the Negroes show precedence.'' They were important as serving the capitalists as ''race leaders.''

RTC predicted that the Negro petit bourgeoisie would play a progressive and significant social role in the struggle of the Negro people. But they must first rid themselves of the "strange faith" that the Negro question can be solved within the framework of capitalism. Today, said *RTC*, "the Negro intellectuals and professionals are lost in the absurd utopia of creating a self-contained Negro economy, through utilizing here the 'organized buying power of the race'. . . ." Instead of political and economic reality, a fuzzy and capricious know-nothingism results. Yet this will be countered by the growth of the Negro proletariat who will separate themselves and the farmers from the Negro bourgeoisie. Ultimately the Negro proletariat must join with the white proletariat to overthrow the capitalist system. What must the Communists do to speed up this process? First, they must defend the Negro workers, peasants, and petit bourgeoisie. Second, they must weld these same Negroes against the white ruling class. Third, they must break down the barriers between Negro and white workers. Fourth, they must fight against the peonage and serfdom of the Negro farmers in the South. Fifth, they must stand for the complete equality of the Negro socially and politically. Sixth and last, they must struggle against lynching, jim crowism, and discrimination.

Another issue faced yearly by radicals in the United States is the desirability of a third party. *RTC* faced this issue in 1935. At that time it was possible to envisage a noncapitalist third party composed of workers and farmers. It seemed propitious for the workers to start such a party for the following reasons: (1) there was a noticeable breakdown of craft unionism (just before the institution of the CIO); (2) the gap between skilled and unskilled labor was being narrowed; (3) the aristocracy of labor had a diminishing base; (4) virtual cessation of immigration had helped repair the split between American-born and foreign-born workers; and (5) outbreaks of third-party spirit could be seen in Upton Sinclair's "Epic" movements and "Ham-n-Eggs" in California, La Follette's Progressive party in Wisconsin, and Olson's Farmer-Labor party in Minnesota. Furthermore, it was clear that the New Deal was helping only the big capitalists, was enlarging the bureaucracy (government-big business alliance) and was acting as a strikebreaker for business. Its real role was encapsulated in the phrase "the Roosevelt myth."

But a mere third party made up of the irritated petit bourgeoisie was not the answer. What was needed was a Labor party composed of blacks and whites, American-born and foreign-born alike. A party like the States'

Rights or Wallace's American Independent (1967) would be valueless for it would merely perpetuate the same old capitalist system. *RTC* believed the CPO must "stimulate and hasten the historical process of a Labor Party development . . . through propaganda, agitation and through its influence in the trade unions." Such a party would at the outset "have a confused program, lacking clarity in its politics, inadequate from the proletarian revolution viewpoint." Nevertheless, much good could come out of such a party; without it a firm base for change would be impossible. What is needed is a "Marxist-Leninist educational program to prepare labor for such a Third Party directed toward a socialist society."

There were no humorous columns or light touches in the grave message of the *RTC*. Yet, if one wanted to find a change of pace from political analysis it could be found in the article "The Application of Dialectical Materialism to the History of Art and Literature," by August Thalheimer, theoretician of German Marxism. Much of this article is a commentary on the critical writing of Franz Mehring (1846-1919), literary critic and one of the founders of Marxist aesthetics. Always a stepdaughter of bourgeois philosophy, aesthetics from a Marxist point of view has scarcely received any more attention. The tendency to deal in shibboleths instead of concrete analysis is particularly noticeable here, even though Thalheimer speaks against "empty generalizations."

In dealing with the history and canons of aesthetics, Thalheimer claims, we must examine "the inner structure of economic conditions, economic development, and of class relations." The stages of bourgeois consciousness must be deduced from the economic stages. Unsuspected treasures of interpretation will thus appear.

Aesthetic theory is needed, and although Mehring did not provide it, he did make a start in his examination of German classical literature, using Schiller and Kant as starting points. According to Kant, "the highest ideal of art is man. Art should be law observant without law, teleological without purpose." This was the first theoretical blow to classical art and literature, just as Marx later shattered classical economics. Kant's and Schiller's flaw was in seeing aesthetic laws as separate from the art of the "rising, revolutionary bourgeoisie." They saw aesthetic laws as eternal and absolute. This Marxism can never allow, anymore than it can take seriously the claim that capitalist laws of production and circulation are natural and eternal.

"Can a scientific history of aesthetic feelings, as they have progressed in human society, be written?'' To this question, the Marxist answer must be yes. According to Mehring, ''Every creative work of art creates its own aesthetics.'' Instead of art conforming to aesthetics, aesthetics must conform to art. This does not mean interruption in aesthetic analysis, since classical aesthetics contains laws that extend beyond a single epoch of art. Naturalism, for example, is able to describe the transitory *as it is*. Idealization, as in the characterization by Schiller of Wallenstein, gives a truer picture than is possible to draw in historical writing. Great art never blindly ignores the pressing problems of its time. But ''bourgeois aesthetics permitted bourgeois propaganda to be sowed thickly in art'' while condemning Socialist propaganda as ''true propaganda.'' Schiller and Kant separated form and content without recognizing their reciprocity. In this they were bourgeois aestheticians.

Hegel's aesthetics is not treated by Mehring. This is an oversight, Thalheimer maintains, because Hegel reveals the completion of scientific aesthetics in a bourgeois framework. Despite Hegel's penchant for explaining art in terms of religion, he did show the connections between social relations (class relations), the forms of production, and the form and content of art. For this reason he cannot be ignored. Indeed, Thalheimer says, ''[Hegel's] class characterizations of Cervantes, Don Quixote, of the chivalric epos, of Ariosto, of Dutch painting, could easily be taken over by a history of art of aesthetics base[d] on dialectical materialism.''

Marxist aesthetics has the practical task, first, of understanding the artistic expression of the bourgeoisie and, second, of rejecting reactionary bourgeois thought in its artistic form since there it is most cryptic and sly.

RTC also discussed problems facing the Communist Internationale, the Czechoslovakian question, the cause of German and Austrian fascism, the fight of the Barcelona workers against the fascism of Madrid, the United Front in France, and the definition and meaning of ''communism'' as seen by the CPO. They are treated with dignity, knowledge, and concern, adding a great deal to our knowledge of the radical movement in the mid-1930s.

Buffalo, New York, 1969

Marxist Quarterly

NEW YORK, 1937

MICHAEL HARRINGTON

THE editors of the *Marxist Quarterly* sought to create a journal of serious Socialist thought which would be both scholarly and independent of any factional alignment on the non-Communist Left. They attracted some first-rate writers and intellectuals and published material of great merit (many of the articles are well worth being read for their intrinsic value and not just as historical data). And yet the *Quarterly* only lasted for three issues. 1937 was the year of the Moscow Trials, the Spanish Revolution, and the opening political skirmishes of World War II. The passions which these events evoked simply would not permit sustained collaboration on the Left on a nonparty basis.

The board of editors was quite distinguished and, given the spectrum of the non-Communist Left in America, quite heterodox. Lewis Corey was the managing editor and did most of the actual editorial work. As Louis Fraina, he had played an important role in the early Communist movement. He had been charged with being a government agent and then with absconding with funds (in his brilliant history of American communism, Theodore Draper essentially vindicates Fraina's reputation). Under the name of Lewis Corey he had, by 1937, achieved considerable recognition for his writings on the American economy and social structure. Louis Hacker was already well known as a historian in 1937, Sidney Hook and Meyer Schapiro were both scholars and Marxist activists, Sterling Spero had written on the black worker, and Bertram Wolfe was one of the intellectual leaders of the Lovestone faction (and later was to write *Three Who Made a Revolution*).

Two other intellectuals who were involved in the planning stages of the *Marxist Quarterly*, but who did not join the board of editors, are of particular note. As both Meyer Schapiro and Sidney Hook remember the *Quarterly*'s genesis, Corliss Lamont was among the early supporters (and a contribution from him was published in the second issue). But, typical of the polarizations of the times, Lamont moved away from the *Marxist Quarterly* and toward *Science and Society*, a periodical which, though it then published articles by independent scholars of various views (and has done so much more in recent years) was within the broad Communist cultural orbit. And, Schapiro recounts, James Burnham also attended some of the first discussions of the project but withdrew on the grounds that the publication would be too politically diffuse (Burnham was a Trotskyist at the time).

As George Novack, one of the Trotskyists involved in the project, recounted his own experience in a 1968 article, Burnham and he quit the *Quarterly* because of the second of the Moscow Trials in 1937. The Lovestonites, who identified with Bukharin in Russia, supported the purge until their own idol was finally caught up in it. The Trotskyists were, of course, deeply involved in the Dewey Commission of Inquiry on the verdict against Trotsky and, Novack wrote, the *Marxist Quarterly* was simply unable to contain these different points of view. So the first issue was the occasion of the first split.

So political problems bedeviled this nonparty journal from the very first. These at least partially account for the character of the magazine. Most of the articles are far removed from immediate politics or factional issues of the day. There are discussions of philosophy by Edel, Hook, Eliseo Vivas, and others; historical narratives by Hacker, Phillip Slaner, and Stuart Brown; and translations from Europeans like Franz Mehring and Karl Korsch.

Now it is certainly true that even in such seemingly "theoretical" realms there were passionate political divisions. Hook's discussion of Dialectic and Nature in the second issue is still cited in Soviet texts as an example of a fallacious American pragmatic approach to Marxism. And Meyer Schapiro's discussion with Bertram Wolfe in Number 3 is as concerned with the fate of the Mexican Revolution as with aesthetics. Yet, the *Marxist Quarterly* did not engage in the kind of immediate, topical content which would have inevitably caused a split on the editorial board.

But there was another, more idealistic reason for the intellectual style of the *Quarterly*. The men who gathered around this publication were serious, and original thinkers. By 1937, for instance, Sidney Hook had already made significant contributions to the scholarly study of the origins and meaning of Marxism and Karl Korsch had a worldwide reputation among those concerned with Marxist philosophy. So there was a desire to found a magazine which would rise far above the level of factional journalism which then prevailed in the radical movement. In conception, then, the *Marxist Quarterly* was to be a sort of American *Neue Zeit*.

Yet, and this was the dominant factor in the magazine's demise, its environment was almost totally unlike that of the pre-World War I *Neue Zeit*. The German periodical was part of an ascendant, unified Socialist movement which was confronting major issues in every advanced nation in the world. This, and the remarkable genius of its editors and contributors, made it one of the most vital publications in the history of socialism. The *Marxist Quarterly*, on the other hand, brought together brilliant spokesmen of various Marxist tendencies which, however well-wrought their resolutions and serious their analyses, had no mass following. And it did so in 1937 at the precise moment when events in Russia and Spain were turning debates over political differences on the Left into a literal matter of life and death. Thus, even though the intellectual resources available to the *Quarterly* were quite impressive, the project could not transcend the times.

In the end, there were nonpolitical factors which influenced suspension of publication. The *Quarterly*'s format was too bulky and expensive for its finances; it could not compete with the radical parties and committees for money; and there were technical problems in distribution. As Sidney Hook remembers it, the *Quarterly* "petered out" and there was no climactic faction fight on the editorial board. At the same time, both Hook and Schapiro recognize the underlying problem of the political differences among the editors. The Lovestoneites, Schapiro notes, were not simply hostile to the members of other organized tendencies but suspicious as well of the independents.

And so, in three short but distinguished issues the *Marxist Quarterly* came to an end. Its death was part of the tragedy of American radicalism in the 1930s. The depression at home and the upheavals abroad had moved American intellectual life to the Left. The main beneficiaries of this shift were the Communists who, with their Stalinist view of the necessary subservience of thought to the party line, mainly promoted apologetics, frauds, and mechanistic popularizations of Marx. The significant number of American writers who escaped from, or avoided, the Communist trap made some remarkable cultural contributions in magazines like the *Marxist Quarterly* and *Partisan Review*. But they were never really able to relate their brilliance to the political struggle of the millions and their energies were often dissipated in internal debates; theory and practice, which Marx had insisted must be one, were sundered. Still in all, it is an achievement that, thirty years after its brief life, the *Marxist Quarterly* is still very much worth reading.

New York City, 1968

New International

NEW YORK, 1934-1936,
1938-1940

Fourth International

NEW YORK, 1940-1956

International Socialist Review

NEW YORK, 1956—

GEORGE NOVACK

SINCE its foundation in July 1934, the theoretical organ of American Trotskyism has appeared under three names: *New International* (1934-1936; 1938-1940: Volumes 1-6, two issues); *Fourth International* (1940-1956: Volumes 1-17, two issues); and the *International Socialist Review* (1956, two issues, to the present). It is today one of the oldest consecutively published magazines in the radical movement in the United States. This fact alone makes it distinctive in the field since radical periodicals, not only in this country but elsewhere, usually have a life span of brief duration.

The magazine has presented the views of the Socialist Workers party. This political organization started out as the Communist League of America (1928-1934), became the Workers party (1934-1936) after fusion with the American Workers party of A. J. Muste, and took its present name on New Year's Day 1938, following the ousting of its supporters from the Socialist party headed by Norman Thomas.

For the first six years of existence as a distinct tendency in American radicalism, the Trotskyists expressed their positions primarily through *The Militant* (1928 to the present). They felt a more insistent need for a separate monthly theoretical publication to supplement their weekly paper in 1933 after the catastrophe suffered by the German and world working class through Hitler's triumph. In reaction to this terrible defeat, the Trotskyist movement, which had functioned as a Left Opposition force outside the Communist ranks, discarded its previous policy of seeking to reform Stalinized communism and set out to build an independent revolutionary Marxist party in the United States.

Although this reorientation was decided upon by the middle of 1933, the new publication could not be launched until a year later, in July 1934. The lead editorial introducing its first issue explained the political reasons for the appearance of the magazine. These were, as its title indicated, predominantly international in character. "Our periodical appears at a most critical juncture in the life of the international labor movement," the editorial statement began. It took note of the economic collapse of world capitalism, the spread of fascist barbarism, the revolutionary stirrings among the proletariat, and the rebellions of the colonial slaves against their metropolitan oppressors. While capitalism was revealing itself to be an outlived social order, it asserted, the proletariat and its allies had developed to the point where, as the victory of October 1917 had demonstrated, they could take power and open up a new era to humanity.

However, the proletariat lacked the indispensable political instrument for that purpose, proper revolutionary leadership. "The two parties of the proletariat, into whose hands history successively gave the imposing task of overthrowing the bourgeoise and opening the road to socialism, have failed abysmally. Social democracy and Stalinism both collapsed at the first blow, like eggshells sucked dry, in Germany, then in Austria, then in Latvia, then in Bulgaria."

The default of the leading parties of the existing Internationals demanded the formation of a new International and new parties to carry through the unachieved tasks of the world revolution. "The lesson of the collapse of the *two* Internationals is not the renunciation of internationalism but its revival. And not on paper, but in deeds. Revolutionary internationalism must be active and concrete. At the present time that can mean only one thing: unfurl the banner of the Fourth International and work unremittingly to rally the vanguard elements throughout the world around it.''

The program of the projected International ''means a fight to the death against Fascism, imperialism, war. It means an intransigent struggle against treacherous social reformism, bureaucratic Stalinism, cowardly compromising centrism of all species. It means the unconditional struggle to defend the Soviet Union which social democrats and Stalinists left in the lurch when they permitted the arch-anti-Sovietist Hitler to come to power without a battle. It means the militant struggle for revolutionary Marxism, for the final victory of the working class.''

The magazine has adhered to these foundation principles throughout the subsequent decades. It has consistently sought to defend Socialist internationalism and to apply the theories of revolutionary Marxism in the tradition of Marx, Engels, Lenin, and Trotsky, even though some of its early editors and writers, including the author of the programmatic editorial, later departed from them and even abjured them.

The birth of the periodical was hailed by Leon Trotsky, then living incognito in France during his third and last exile from Russia. ''The fact that you have established a theoretical organ, I consider as a festival occasion,'' he wrote the editors in a greeting which was inserted alongside the opening editorial. ''It's name, *The New International*, is a program of an entire epoch. I am convinced that your magazine will serve as an invaluable weapon in the establishment of the new International on the foundations laid by the great masons of the future: Marx, Engels, Lenin.''

The first issue contained two articles by Trotsky. One on ''The Testament of Lenin'' was subsequently published in pamphlet form. Under Stalin's regime the very existence of this crucial communication of Lenin to the Bolshevik leadership at the close of his life was denied and the document suppressed. Its text was not made known to the Soviet public until after Khrushchev's sensational revelations of Stalin's crimes at the twentieth congress of the Soviet Communist party in 1956.

The other article, on ''The Clemenceau Thesis,'' was a previously unpublished document which had been written by Trotsky in 1927 at the height of the factional conflict within the Russian Communist party. It aimed to refute the calumnies against the Left Opposition and to clarify its attitude toward the bureaucratic regime in face of the danger of invasion constantly haunting the Soviet Union.

These contributions by Trotsky were followed by a stream of others which appeared in the magazine throughout the rest of the 1930s as he moved from France to Norway to Mexico. The flow was cut short by Trotsky's assassination on Stalin's orders in August 1940. One of the magazine's most memorable issues came out in October 1940. It contained Trotsky's last letters and articles as well as a graphic eyewitness account of the murder by Joseph Hansen, his secretary and a member of the magazine's editorial board.

Trotsky's contributions during that final period of his life include some of his most perspicacious commentaries on key issues of world politics such as fascism, Stalinism and developments within the Soviet Union, imperialist policy, the colonial revolution, the role of the United States, and the approaching world war. He also dealt with questions of morality, literary criticism, philosophy, and Marxist theory. Along with *The Militant*, the *New International* is the richest single source of Trotsky's writings in English during that tempestuous period of modern history which was among the most productive in his literary output.

After his death the magazine kept on printing literary materials by Trotsky which were otherwise unavailable or had hitherto been inaccessible to the English-reading public. It continues to fill these gaps to the present day. Its volumes from July 1934 through the fall of 1960 contain no less than 190 pieces by Trotsky. Knowledge of these writings is indispensable to any student of his maturest political thought.

The magazine's contents are especially valuable for their Marxist interpretation of the decisive world events from the rise of Stalinism and fascism in the 1930s, through World War II, to the volcanic eruption of U.S. imperialism on a global scale during the Cold War. They present a running critical commentary on all the momentous developments which have determined the history of our times and shape its future.

The concentration on world affairs is one side of the magazine's outlook. Of equal importance is its focus on American politics and economics, the major developments in the labor and radical movements, and the intellectual life of the United States over the past third of a century. When the periodical was launched, Roosevelt's reformism was still in the honeymoon stage and the initial number carried an analysis of "New Trends Under the New Deal."

At that same juncture a revivified labor movement was about to take the giant step that resulted in the creation of the CIO and the strong industrial unions of today. The founder of American Trotskyism, James P. Cannon, contributed an article to the first issue on the significance of the magnificent strikes of the Minneapolis truck drivers under Trotskyist leadership which heralded that upsurge of labor organization. The vicissitudes of American unionism from the militant struggles of the 1930s through World War II, and the passivity and conservatism associated with the Cold War, are recorded and amply documented in the successive volumes of the magazine.

These also contain a wealth of information on three decades of developments inside the radical movement in the United States which illuminate the differences and conflicts among the various tendencies and groupings contending for influence and leadership within the movement. Thus the very first issue dealt with the ferment in the Socialist party that led to the Old Guard split in 1935 and paved the way for the entry of the Trotskyists and their brief sojourn in that party. (Publication of the magazine was temporarily suspended during part of 1936 and all of 1937.) There are scores of articles giving a Trotskyist criticism of the nature of Stalinism and the policies of the Communist parties in the United States and elsewhere.

A piece by John G. Wright in an early issue took up "Shifts in the Negro Question," and an entire special number (December 1939) was devoted to that problem. Not until after the war, however, did the black liberation struggle receive sustained attention. For the past twenty years more and more space has been given to discussions of the many facets of this subject, notably from the pen of George Breitman. Several of his contributions, such as "How a Minority Can Change Society" (Spring 1964), have had a wide influence upon both white and black radicals. The same is true of Robert Vernon's "White Radicals and Black Nationalism" (Winter 1964). The *International Socialist Review* was the first radical magazine to uphold and print the speeches of Malcolm X, and it is a prime source of materials on the evolution and evaluation of the thought of the martyred black leader.

Max Shachtman, one of the three original leaders of American Trotskyism, and James Burnham, the most prominent theoretician of the Muste group, acted as principal editors of the magazine from its establishment to 1940. The radicalization of American intellectuals during the 1930s, and their revulsion against Stalinism, attracted to the ideas of

Trotskyism a number of talented young writers and skilled journalists who could be counted upon as contributors and reviewers. Among them were Herbert Solow, Felix Morrow, Elliot Cohen, Harold Isaacs, Earle Birney, Sidney Hook, Bernard Wolfe, and Dwight Macdonald. By 1946, all of these had turned away from the Trotskyist movement. As of 1967 I was the sole survivor of the group active in revolutionary politics.

The great turning point in their political evolution, or more precisely, devolution, occurred in connection with the convulsive events at the beginning of World War II. Along with the desertion of the Communist party by its more numerous fellow-travelers, many of the intellectuals and students in and around the Trotskyist movement succumbed to the environing patriotic pressures and political reaction and began to jettison revolutionary Marxist positions and principles.

After the Stalin-Hitler Pact in August 1939, and the Soviet invasions of Poland and Finland, a bitter struggle broke out within the Socialist Workers party. The minority faction was headed by Max Shachtman and James Burnham, the executive editors of the *New International*. Because of the crimes of Stalin's regime, their tendency questioned the necessity of defending the first workers' state, the Soviet Union, against imperialist attack—an obligation which was one of the cornerstones of the program of the Fourth International. Their leaders also tried to disqualify other cardinal tenets of the Trotskyist program and Marxist theory all the way from the field of philosophy (dialectical materialism) to party organization (the Leninist concept of democratic centralism).

The majority defense of the Marxist positions was directed by Trotsky himself. It was his last great ideological battle waged on behalf of Marxism. Evidences of this sharp and irreconcilable controversy will be found in the issues of the magazine from October 1939 through the split of the minority which came in April 1940.

The opposition leaders, Burnham and Shachtman, took advantage of their technical posts as trustees and editors of the *New International* to take over its name and mailing rights. However, they changed its political basis and editorial policy to accord with their new views, which were at odds with the original aims and principles of the publication. Rather than engage in a legal contest and futile squabble over this breach of trust, the Socialist Workers pary majority decided instead to choose a new name for the magazine. They selected the title of *Fourth International* because it corresponded to the progress made by world Trotskyism which, from proclaiming the need for a new International in 1934, had actually founded the Fourth International in 1938.

Even though some of the contributors were the same, the political line and contents of the *New International*, published by the Workers party from 1940 to 1958, are essentially different from those in the first period of its publication under that name. The two opposing phases of its existence should be kept in mind.

This distinction was explained by Trotsky in a stinging castigation of Burnham and Shachtman's action entitled "Petty-Bourgeois Moralists and the Proletarian Party," written on April 23, 1940, and reprinted in his book, *In Defense of Marxism*. "The discussion in the Socialist Workers Party of the United States was thorough and democratic," he wrote.

The preparations for the convention were carried out with absolute loyalty. The minority participated in the convention, recognizing thereby its legality and authoritativeness. The majority offered the minority all the necesary guarantees permitting it to conduct a struggle for its own views after the convention. The minority demanded a license to appeal to the masses over the head of the party. The majority naturally rejected this monstrous pretension.

Meanwhile, behind the back of the party the minority indulged in shady machinations and appropriated the *New International* which had been published through the efforts of the entire party and of the Fourth International. I should add that the majority had agreed to assign the minority two posts out of the five on the editorial board of this theoretical organ. But how can an intellectual 'aristocracy' remain the minority in a workers' party? To place a professor on equal plane with a worker—after all, that's "bureaucratic conservatism"!

Trotsky went on: "Long political experience has taught me that whenever a petty bourgeois professor or journalist begins talking about high moral standards it is necessary to keep a firm hand on one's pocketbook. It happened this time, too. In the name of a 'moral ideal' a petty bourgeois intellectual picked the proletarian party's pocket of its theoretical organ. Here you have a tiny living example of the organizational methods of these innovators, moralists and champions of democracy.''

The *Fourth International* experienced hard times during the early years of the war because of its Socialist opposition to the imperialist conflict. Three members of its editorial board, James P. Cannon, Albert Goldman, and Felix Morrow, were convicted as the first victims of the Smith ''Gag'' Act for their refusal to support what they regarded as the war of the capitalist ruling class, and served 16-month terms in federal prison. Nevertheless, although it had to skip an occasional issue, the magazine never ceased publication. During those difficult years it continued to present the views of revolutionary Marxism on the issues raised by the war.

From the start, the magazine enjoyed a broad circulation in other lands where it was regarded as among the most authoritative expressions of Trotskyist opinion on all major questions confronting the revolutionary vanguard. It was one of the very few Trotskyist publications in the world that managed to keep afloat at a time when every force of reaction, from fascism and democratic imperialism to Stalinism and Social Democracy, combined to hound its adherents and suppress its voices. The magazine played a key role in facilitating the resurgence and regroupment of the international Trotskyist movement toward the close of the war as it emerged from the underground where it had been driven by the dictatorial war-machines. In the immediate postwar years the publication was an invaluable auxiliary in consolidating the new forces which rallied to the program of the Fourth International in many countries.

The magazine expanded its circulation at home, from 1945 to 1947, on the crest of the brief upsurge of labor militancy. Then it ran into the adverse effects of the witch-hunt and McCarthyism, which were most malignant during the Korean war years. At times the periodical could barely hold its head above water and was forced to retrench in various ways to keep alive. With the Winter 1954 issue it had to be converted from a monthly to a quarterly printed on cheaper paper.

A brighter chapter opened up in 1956 when the American Left was shaken up by the destalinization processes in the Soviet bloc, climaxed by the Polish and Hungarian revolts and by the rebirth of student radicalism and the beginnings of civil rights agitation at home. These developments stimulated a greater interest in the ideas of Trotskyism and created a larger audience for the magazine.

As part of a project to enhance its attractiveness to the new generation of rebels, it was felt desirable to change the magazine's name to the *International Socialist Review*. This title was taken over from the celebrated theoretical organ of the left wing of American socialism before World War I. The journal lasted from July 1900 to February 1918. Its name was appropriately revived to signalize the continuity of revolutionary Socialist traditions in the United States and to carry forward the avowed aim of the original *International Socialist Review* to "produce the most clear cut and developed socialism" in the heartland of world capitalism.

After the Shachtman-Burnham period, the responsibilities of editorship were assumed by a number of people. Among them were John G. Wright, the translator of Trotsky's works, Bert Cochran, Joseph Hansen, George Clark, Murry Weiss, and Tom Kerry. The Socialist scholar, George Novack, served on the editorial board for twenty-five years and was the most constant and copious contributor. The editor in 1972 was Les Evans.

Except for one year, from the summer of 1957 to the summer of 1958, when the editorial office and place of publication were shifted to Los Angeles, the magazine has been published in New York City.

With the January-February 1967 issue, the *International Socialist Review* changed from a quarterly to a bimonthly, in a pocketbook format. It resumed regular monthly publication in May 1970.

The announcement of these changes brought forth the following comment from the editors. "In the 32 years since beginning publication, first as the *New International*, then as *Fourth International*, later as *International Socialist Review*, we have weathered many storms. But we can be proud to record that never once have we been driven off our course of serving as authentic spokesmen of orthodox Marxism."

New York City, 1967 and 1972

The Comrade

NEW YORK, 1901-1905

JOSEPH R. CONLIN

JACK LONDON pledged a short story to the editors of *The Comrade* when the first number was issued in October 1901. Maxim Gorky or his agent promised a whole series, and Richard LeGallienne and Edward Carpenter would each contribute a poem. The editors claimed that they even had a Thomas Nast cartoon in the hopper. But George Bernard Shaw, solicited for a similar donation at his cottage in Surrey, had other things to do and piqued the editors by his reply:

> Delighted to hear that deathless Socialist paper is going to fill that empty niche again. When I was young I contributed to all its first numbers—they appeared regularly every two years or so. Now I am growing old and have to limit my help to good wishes. After all it must succeed some time; and why not this?

The editors were willing to print Shaw's joshing because they believed: why not this time indeed? In that first year of the Socialist party of America, the radical movement in the United States was small, but its mood was buoyant and its prospects good. "We are in the early days of a great renaissance," the editors chortled sincerely, and as for GBS, he would soon enough be "begging" to be a contributor to the movement's literary herald.

The prospects looked good, first of all, because of the growth of the Socialist parties of Europe. At home, the new Socialist party had apparently transcended the fusty sectarianism that had retarded the growth of Daniel De Leon's older Socialist Labor party. In Eugene V. Debs, not yet canonized but famous and widely admired, the party had a formidable, attractive titular leader. In Victor Berger of Milwaukee, Wisconsin, the Socialists had a more practical tactician who was already assembling the organization that would dominate the city's politics for fifty years. Some labor unions were explicitly Socialist, and large minorities of others promised to grow and provide the party with its working-class base. And, increasingly at the turn of the century, troubled middle-class and professional people were examining Socialist ideas as well as more conventional progressive reforms.

This was where *The Comrade* came in. Despite its vague designation as "an illustrated socialist monthly," *The Comrade* was not an ordinary propaganda journal; the Socialists already had plenty of those. *The Comrade* was a literary magazine. The editors claimed that their purpose was to bring Socialist *belles lettres* to "the great mass of the world's disinherited," but, in fact, the magazine was geared to the interests of the new middle-class Socialists, the sort of people who already read and honored William Morris. This intention to reach the country's literate middle class was apparent in the magazine's promotion of its "distinguished" list of contributors. Even those luminaries who reacted equivocally to the venture, such as Shaw and William Dean Howells, were registered as sending "best wishes." This was to be no common enterprise.

As an unabashedly radical literary magazine, *The Comrade* must be reckoned a pale forerunner of the *Masses* and its own plethoric successors of the 1930s. *The Comrade* also resembled the *Masses* in the excellence of its graphics and the initial ebullience of its editors. Where it differed from the *Masses*, aside from overall quality, was in the cut of its contributions. The *Masses* blazed new trails in American letters. *The Comrade*, not excepting its socialism, was part and parcel of the genteel tradition, hardly avant-garde in 1901. Indeed, some items were hopelessly archaic for the turn of the century, such as an embarrassingly inept and unhumorous commentary after the Bigelow Papers ("the ecshun of the nashunal convenshun at Indianapolis in jining together the people workin' fer the same ends . . ."). But few "Little Magazines" ever manage to rise above the banal, and even fewer of those that are explicitly political. The *Masses* and the *Partisan Review* are the exceptions. That *The Comrade* was exceptional on occasion distinguishes it.

The Comrade was also something of a forerunner of that most famous of early Socialist magazines, the *International Socialist Review*. Actually, Charles H. Kerr's Chicago-based *Review* predated *The Comrade*, and Jack London wrote in November 1901 that with the two of them he felt like "a respectable member of society, able to say to the most finicky: 'Behold the literature of my party.' " But the early *Review*, during the years when it was contemporary with *The Comrade*, was a difficult, often abstruse, and sometimes pedantic journal of theory. In 1908, however, Kerr fired the scholarly editor, Algie M. Simons, and transformed the *Review* into a flashy, copiously illustrated popular magazine with articles on current strikes instead of disquisitions. The *Review*'s new type of article was the same sort of thing *The Comrade* had interspersed among its poems, short stories, and hopefully pithy epigrams ("It's a wise slave that knows his own master—and votes against him"). *The Comrade* was defunct by 1908, but Kerr had apparently learned a few lessons from it.

Perhaps the most interesting of *The Comrade*'s features is the magazine's series on "How I Became a Socialist." Numerous party leaders and regulars recorded their testimony, the most famous being the first essay by Eugene V. Debs in April 1902. Debs' contribution has been frequently reprinted, but those by less-famous characters have not. The articles are not literary gems; there are no Pauline conversions. With the exceptions of Jack London's, William Thurston Brown's, and one or two others, they are rather dull. But the series taken as a whole is a valuable historical document, insufficiently examined by social historians. "How I Became a Socialist" provides, in a sample almost large enough to satisfy a computer sociologist, the accounts of how some quite ordinary people were turned into political activists at a politically important time in American history. Beyond these essays there is a great deal of good reportage, especially in the later issues when the Socialist poetasters apparently ran dry and the belles-lettres section of *The Comrade* consisted of little more than a survey of current books.

What about *The Comrade*'s role in the larger history of the American Socialist movement? It was essentially passive. The magazine's duration approximated a clear, first phase of the Socialist party of America, between 1901 and 1905. Although Debs ran for president as a Socialist in 1900, the party took shape only a year later. Despite a few internal squabbles, members of the party got along fairly well in those first years. The party was decentralized for lack of homogeneity, without any real power anywhere in the country, probing for its foundations rather than disputing them. The party was, as a result, quite tolerant within. There is little disputation within the pages of *The Comrade*; disputation with other Socialists, that is. Like the party's, the basis of *The Comrade*'s socialism was ethical and moral; it was the socialism of Debs more than a programmatic ideology, and there was little reason to quarrel about the sad, obvious brutalities of American industrial capitalism. It was a wholesome, almost congenial, sort of movement. Editor John Spargo might regularly inveigh against the clergy and Christianity, but the tenor of *The Comrade* was religious in a sense that neither Spargo, nor many others, would in 1901 have comprehended. William Thurston Brown worded it in discussing his path from minister to Socialist: "I began as a moral idealist. I am as much one as ever."

But the Socialist party passed beyond merely moral protest and left *The Comrade* behind. The party did grow between 1901 and 1905, and the larger family proved opinionated and quarrelsome. On the one side emerged labor-unionist militants like William D. Haywood and ideologues like William English Walling. They scorned the style of the "parlor socialists," the parliamentary politics of the moderate "reformists," and spoke in red-hot revolutionary terms quite dissonant with the genteel tradition. On the other side were the "slowshulists" or moderates, political in their methods, restrained in style, committed to continuing missionary efforts among the middle class. *Comrade* editors Spargo and George D. Herron eventually ended up in this wing of the party. The difference was that the SPA became a party of factions preoccupied with the prosody of tactics and power and *The Comrade* never made the leap. By 1905, it was quite out of touch. In that year, for example, the party was agitated and divided over the question of unions. Should Socialists continue their efforts to capture the conservative American Federation of Labor? Or should they support rival revolutionary unions like the newly founded Industrial Workers of the World Socialists on both sides of the dispute agreed on the importance of the unions. But *The Comrade* was editorializing: "We are of the opinion that too much importance has been attached to the trade union movement" and "We shall find out later, perhaps, how little the trade unions really mean." What turned out to mean very little to a party that was going after the working classes was a magazine that reprinted Oscar Wilde. There would be room on the Left again for a literary magazine with the arrival of John Reed, Mabel Dodge's "evenings," the *Masses*, and Max Eastman. But these were not of the cultural world of the genteel tradition, with which *The Comrade* died.

Eynsham, Oxford, 1969

Masses

NEW YORK, 1911-1917

Liberator

NEW YORK, 1918-1924

RICHARD FITZGERALD

THE *Masses* (1911-1917), a monthly magazine focusing on cooperatives, socialism, art, and literature, was about to fold after a precarious year and a half existence when its graphic artists, including Maurice Becker, John Sloan, and Art Young, decided to try to keep it going. They persuaded Max Eastman to take over the unremunerative editorship and, in their December 1912 policy statement, proclaimed that "Our appeal will be to the masses, both Socialist and non-Socialist, with entertainment, education, and the livelier kinds of propaganda." They frankly hoped that the magazine, as a "meeting ground for revolutionary labor and the radical intelligentsia," would bring together art and politics.

Although Eastman later founded the *Liberator* (1918-1924) with the same intention of providing a radical but humorous journal of politics and art, the *Liberator* was in many ways a different magazine. Just as the European war and the Russian Revolution had changed the American radical movement, the *Liberator* markedly altered the nature and setting of the bohemian-Socialist rebellion which had fed the earlier *Masses*.

In the decade of the 1910s there existed a large, mass-based American Socialist movement, the Socialist party of America, which reached a peak membership of 118,000 in 1912. The SPA had been traditionally supported by native workers (a majority in 1910), but by 1919 had a foreign-born majority. Through its large membership and its ethnic

be Socialist but undogmatic, for revolution but not necessarily by violence, yet never for reform. In its simplicity the *Masses'* policy was consistent. This was not *merely* because of the little time available to develop ideology but also because the *Masses* did not choose to develop a narrow ideology. Thus, the *Masses'* "easy flexibility" allowed it to criticize Socialist politics and life with an ease and "a humor that the artists of the thirties denied themselves."

The prewar world was more vigorous than that of the postwar era. Before 1914 the social and economic life of America was apparently less fixed and determined than that of the later period. The industrial working class was growing rapidly; from 1890 to World War I the labor force in manufacturing more than doubled. The large corporations did not seem to dominate the political and economic life of the country as thoroughly as they did after the war. Various alliances of farmers, workers, and small proprietary interests still had a strong influence over some of the nation's legislative organs. The depression, of course, wiped out many of these small interests, to the great advantage of the rising corporate system, and the relative size of the industrial working class began stabilizing after the war. During the depression it even declined in some areas. Where the prewar world was enthusiastic about the prospects for social change and betterment, an optimism expressed in the pages of the *Masses*, the world of the depression seemed to be a world in decline.

But as Daniel Aaron writes, if *"The Masses* expressed the distinctive mood or attitude of the prewar insurgency . . . it also expressed its contradictions and uncertainty, and, to some extent, its vagueness." Max Eastman recalled, "I don't know how many of us really believed, or how firmly, in the Marxian paradise where the 'wage system' would disappear, liberty and organization lie down together like the lion and the lamb. . . . But that was the general idea."

The *Liberator* started with the *Masses* staff and looked back nostalgically at its predecessor, but like all Socialist publications after 1917, it faced much harder choices. The Russian Revolution soon implied a commitment to a concrete government, nation, and party line, thereby forcing an end to the ideological flexibility of the *Masses* period. Although the *Liberator* advocated no new role for the radical artist, it envisioned only one solution to the crisis in world capitalism: Soviet communism.

The protest of the *Masses* and *Liberator*—if in some ways more personal and cultural than social and political—was at least indigenous to American life. The *Masses'* and to an extent the *Liberator*'s rebellion occurred in an anarchic, native, Protestant fashion which suited the IWW's mood for participatory immediatism. For example, in the SPA's conflicts over union organization, the *Masses* sided with the IWW and its doctrine of industrial unionism, rather than with the right-wing doctrine of craft unionism. In supporting the Industrial Workers of the World, the *Masses* identified the "Wobbly" with "The proletarian hero depicted as a tramp and hobo," a tramp who elicited the natural sympathies of the Greenwich Village bohemian-Socialists staffing the *Masses*.

While the *Masses* mirrored the IWW's left wing of American socialism, the *Liberator* reflected the early American Communist movement emerging in 1919. The early Communist factions openly advocated direct action, ridiculed political electioneering, and "boring from within" the American Federation of Labor's craft unions. Lenin's *"Left Wing" Communism*, which marked the Soviet Union's recognition that world revolution was not imminent, was not available in the United States until 1921. Even after it was available, however, the American Communist parties were so accustomed to the immediatist IWW style of radicalism that only under orders from the Comintern, which had shifted to the "United Front" theory, did the Americans surrender the dual-union, antipolitical tradition. Communists were to stay in the AFL, to refrain from organizing independent unions, and to establish a legal party.

The (legal) Workers party was established at the end of 1921. The *Liberator* was friendly to the new party, but did not devote more space to politics until it was turned over to the Workers party in October 1922. Therefore, the *Liberator* concentrated on specific Communist programs, such as the "amalgamation" of all unions into industrial unions. Until that time the *Liberator* had argued that American workers should not collaborate with Samuel Gompers' AFL leadership.

Until the *Liberator* affiliated with the Workers Party, the artists of the *Masses* and the *Liberator* had always considered revolt to be a kind of personal self-expression, an affirmation of their individual integrity as artists. Though they considered themselves Socialists, socialism was only a backdrop for their thinking. Accordingly, a *Masses* editorial declared "Socialism has more to gain from a free, artistic literature reflecting life as it actually is, than from an attempt to stretch points in order to make facts fit socialist theory.''

At monthly *Masses* meetings, though articles and illustrations were voted on by all present, cartoon captions were often suggested by Eastman or Dell, who sometimes suggested the cartoon idea to the artist in advance. The question tacitly posed to the artists was: can revolutionary propaganda be art? The *Masses*, however (and, until the end of 1922, the *Liberator*), did not pose the question in theoretical terms: they simply assumed art and socialism complemented one another. The two journals attempted, if not a synthesis of art and politics, at least an equilibrium between Socialist theory and reportage, and free artistic expression. For the reasons mentioned, the *Masses* was the more successful of the two in this attempt and probably more successful than any other American radical periodical of art and politics before or since.

In practice, politics and aesthetics were not complementary and different factions waged a running battle over the *Masses'* philosophy. Dell recalls that the fights were ''usually over the question of intelligibility and propaganda versus artistic freedom.'' On the *Masses* Art Young carried the battle for greater artistic politicization, whereas John Sloan led those cartoonists who resented Eastman or Dell putting ''such a socialistic twist to the lines under our drawings that we didn't like our drawings any more.'' Such a situation doomed cooperation, and the final break came in April 1916, at the so-called ''Greenwich Village Revolt'' where the issue of personal versus social art was fought to the bitter end. Then Sloan and several other artists formally resigned from the *Masses* staff. More than any other event, World War I crystalized these conflicts within the *Masses* over the means of promoting socialism in a magazine of art and politics. The October Revolution in Russia provided the context within which the same question was debated on the *Liberator* board.

Despite the problems of politics, the *Masses* and then the *Liberator* continued to promote stylistic revolt. Through their openness, they were able to incorporate new forms and techniques. The magazines justifiably are better known for their graphics than for their fiction and verse; they did not merge with the literary avant-gardes. Even so, their reportage was notable. It provided an important point of view for the reading public on major strikes (such as Max Eastman on the Ludlow miners, John Reed on the Paterson textile workers) and on the Russian Revolution (John Reed and various Soviet leaders). These authors captured some of the drama and historical meaning of great events; thus, their excitement and optimism.

Graphically, the *Masses* was the first American publication to deal consistently with genre art, and, thanks largely to the efforts of John Sloan, featured full-page cartoons with one-line captions. Its illustrations were often independent of the text and its pages were uncluttered by decorative headings. Illustrations were reproduced by linecut which produced sharper, more graphic, reproductions than halftone. Other magazines such as *Harper's Weekly* imitated the *Masses'* style. This style was generally free and easy, purposefully sloppy, intended to create an aura, a mood, a kind of expressive crudeness which was partly the result of newer printing techniques allowing more freedom of style.

Masses cartooning was perhaps oversimplified in some respects, but the work of the best artists, such as Art Young, symbolized sharply and effectively the changing nature of power in America and its impact on various aspects of social life. Insofar as they knew how to comment on events intelligible only in the context of a general social theory or a set of general political attitudes, their work remains important.

The *Masses* was a cultural product indigenous to the spirit of socialism and bohemian revolt prior to World War I; the *Liberator* was the inheritor of the tradition and the final gasp of that ethos. Through a happy circumstance of time, artistic conventions, and social and political developments, the *Masses* made the most intensive effort to merge art and politics.

San Francisco, 1973

New Masses

NEW YORK, 1926-1948

RICHARD FITZGERALD

THE *Masses'* attempt to synthesize artistic and political rebelliousness made the magazine graphically very exciting. As its title suggested, the *New Masses* was to be modeled after the "old" *Masses*. In fact, however, the *New Masses* was a more self-consciously "political" magazine than its distant predecessor, and came to reflect the hard-line communism which emerged from the factionalism of the 1920s. An examination of the two magazines reflects many of the changes that occurred in American radicalism in the 1920s and 1930s. Unlike its predecessor, which supported all radical elements in the labor movement, the *New Masses* was bound to the Communist party's labor programs. For example, when in the mid-1930s the party switched from a policy of organizing independent unions to working within (or "boring from within") established unions, the *New Masses* focused almost exclusively on the organizing drive in heavy industries and ignored other radical labor developments.

The *New Masses* reflected the sectarian, Stalinist direction and tactics of the Communist party during the depression. Its pages were replete with interminable ideological quarrels, accusations, and literary purges. In 1935 the party decided, in response to Comintern policy, to set up a Popular Front and engage in "mass action." Mass action was a euphemism for a prolonged organizing effort, for alliances with "progressive" antifascist elements, and for seeking reformist labor gains. Under this slogan, revolutionary tactics and strategy would be set aside until the day of the supposedly inevitable revolutionary consensus. *New Masses* cartoonists quickly stopped portraying exploited workers and fat capitalists and began attacking fascists and racists at home and abroad. The AFL and Franklin Roosevelt—though not Roosevelt's opposition—were suddenly left alone. Such an abrupt, externally dictated shift would have been inconceivable in the old *Masses*.

And yet the distance between the *Masses* and *New Masses* was only nine years—obviously a more historical than chronological "distance." In considering the changing social background of American radicalism between 1917 and 1926, we should remember the following major points. In the LaFollette campaign of 1924, the AFL, the railroad brotherhoods, and the Socialists supported the Progressives; the Socialists had given their places on the ballot to LaFollette. LaFollette had excluded Communists as foreign conspirators, although they wanted to support him. The 1919 steel strike, the coal strike of 1924-1925, the Passaic wool workers' strike of early 1926, and other major strikes often split Communists and Socialists. The Communist party itself was confused over the tactic of "dual unionism" or "boring from within." This confusion was based largely on a deeper uncertainty over the weakness of American left-wing politics in the 1920s, as expressed in the long discussion over whether the United States was an exception to the general worldwide capitalist decline. In fact, American socialism also declined after 1919; even the Ku Klux Klan co-opted some members because of the Klan's populistic aspects. At the same time, the 1920s were actually a period of reform and continued Progressive agitation, an agitation which often co-opted radicalism locally.

Relativism (or the belief that moral codes, religious ethics, and artistic and legal forms are mutable within given historical contexts) was growing in intellectual life. Of particular importance was the influence of John Dewey and others who laid the basis for the behavioral sciences. Freud's theories made their entry into the United States' intellectual scene, changing forever the ways in which intellectuals thought about themselves. But Freud's impact could be felt far beyond sophisticated urban circles as, for instance, it was in Clarence Darrow's famous defense of Leopold and Loeb. However, psychoanalysis rarely appeared as anything more than "bourgeois escapism" or "Greenwich Village bohemianism" to the *New Masses*' editors.

While the influence of some immigrant communities, particularly groups of New York Jews, grew in the Communist party, the mass of immigrants was being Americanized through the spread of public education. The gap between left-wing intellectuals and militants and the rest of the country was not diminishing. The new mass production industries, such as autos, electronics, glass, and rubber, were full of recent migrants from the rural South. And the deep cultural division between urban and rural America became wider with the onset of Prohibition. The Scopes trial and the debate over Darwin highlighted this gap. Steady organizing was beginning to give way to "causes," of which the most passionate was that of Sacco and Vanzetti. The emphasis on causes can be seen as a tactic to build a popular consensus and to play down the differences between radical sects. In this latter aspect, as well as in day-to-day organizing, the flourishing of mass-circulation magazines and the rise of radio and professional sports competed for the attention of workingmen.

Another aspect of the growing isolation of the left-wing politicos was that social experimentation was no longer fused with the politics of dissent or even those of reform: Dewey became institutionalized in better public school systems; the woman's movement became increasingly middle class; family experimentation was no longer favored by Russian or American radicals; and many radicals attacked the new art forms, which a decade or two earlier would have been hailed as "revolutionary." Left politics was greatly influenced by its love affair with technology and by the increasing administrative sophistication of corporate leaders. Even Lenin admired Henry Ford. Together with an increasingly advanced technology, corporations were adopting new strategies for financing and internal management: the spread of stock sharing, options, company unions, as well as the new manipulative uses of the social sciences in industry date from this period.

In sum, the 1920s represent the triumph of Progressivism—in industry, education, religion, in most areas of politics, and in ethnic and class relations. What this means is that Socialists and radicals were presented with a cultural transformation for which they were not prepared. Neither they, nor the *New Masses*, nor union leaders were asking the right questions about anomie, alienation, new forms of exploitation, language, and propaganda. No new political organization could hope to face the future without some answers to these questions. Those who did ask the right questions (the so-called "Lost Generation") never translated their critique into a political program. It cannot be ascertained whether this failure represents an effect or a cause of the bifurcation of radical political culture into the aestheticism of the little magazines on the one hand and dogmatic sectarianism on the other. What is certain is that the effect of this bifurcation on American radicalism shows up in a comparison of the

Masses and *New Masses*. The latter, much to its detriment, emphasized the Soviet line on art and in so doing doomed its cultural prospects. The magazine, and, in general, the Left of the 1930s, combined the worst of the old (cultural conservatism) and the worst of the new (humdrum technology and politics).

The explanation for this cultural sterility lies in part with the artists themselves. Many radical artists, particularly in the 1930s, believed that artistic work was not as important as political work and should be subordinate to the latter. In the late nineteenth and early twentieth centuries, not only did artistic *products* become commodities that could be bought and sold in the marketplace of newspapers, magazines, and other media, but the *ability* to create art increasingly became a market commodity as well. The artist became less and less the proprietor of his own talents and skills. His productive activity as an artist began taking on the classic patterns of exploited and alienated labor that had already characterized the productive activities of the industrial worker. The earlier conception of the artistic role was that of the free lance illustrator or writer of the early nineteenth century, who was closer to the artisan than to the wage worker. Nevertheless, there was an enormous gap between the actual social role that the twentieth-century artist had begun to assume and the social role that he *believed* himself to have assumed. The ideological pull of the earlier conception of the artistic role was very strong, and it may have become even stronger as this conception became increasingly romanticized. Even the most radical artist did not consider himself a proletarian, despite the fact that his productive life had taken on a semiproletarian bohemian character. Thus, when *New Masses* artists undertook to wage class war on behalf of the proletariat, they did not consider that their own interests as artists were at stake. In their eyes, if artists had any interests in the struggle at all, it was more as Communist party members than as intellectuals and authentic revolutionary artists.

This confusion of the *New Masses* artists was compounded by their belief that in the transition from capitalism to socialism a pure, indigenous, proletarian culture would simply spring forth, and that the revolutionary artist's problem was to portray or reflect this process rather than to help generate and shape it. Editor Mike Gold devoted numerous articles to this hope for a "spontaneous" birth of proletarian culture. In January 1929 he announced that the magazine, working its way "toward the goal of a proletarian literature in America," was calling for contributions from a new type of writer, typically an itinerant proletarian whose writing "is all instinct with him. His writing is no conscious straining after proletarian art, but the natural flower of his environment. . . . His 'spiritual' attitudes are all mixed up with tenements, factories, lumber camps and steel mills, because that is his life."

Because the *New Masses* artists did not have a clear sense of their own worth and role as artists, they believed that their basic artistic mission was one of mere reflection. But to fulfill this duty the artist would have to reflect something—proletarian culture—that in fact never existed! For clearly, aside from the meager attempts of the radical artists themselves, there was no distinct proletarian culture arising from the industrial working class of the 1930s. What, then, was the *New Masses* artist "reflecting" if not a mirror image of his own vain attempt to reflect an idealized and idealistic image of proletarian life? Because of the very vagueness of this notion of reflecting, he apparently had no clear understanding of the dilemma he confronted.

In fact, the radical artist of the 1930s was not so much reflecting as *becoming part of* a process. Eventually this process might have contributed to the constitution of a proletarian culture of some sort. And of course the realization of such a culture would have required the fullest flowering of the artist's critical and creative faculties as he struggled to interpret the meaning of proletarian life at its different phases of development. But the complex dynamics of Stalinist bureaucratic organization and repression discouraged intellectual experiment and artistic interpretation. Indeed, since the requirement of uncritically supporting a political line was made the lynchpin of an aesthetic theory, Stalinism sought to enlist artistic energies in the cause of art as propaganda, trivializing in this way the artist's personal struggle for integrity. That is, the forms and meanings perceived by artists often could not be poured into preconceived political molds. The revitalization of capitalism through the New Deal, on the other hand, was another major factor which annihilated the embryonic development of revolutionary activism and, therefore, the potential matrix of an authentically proletarian culture. In artistic terms, the *New Masses* suffered from both the dogmatic and bureaucratic version of communism that was becoming prevalent and from the weakness of a proletarian tradition in America. As a result, *New*

Masses art acquired a highly "ideographic" style which for years relied on the same small assortment of stock symbols—for example, the brawny young proletarian giant and the fat, coat-tailed capitalist.

In theory, American communism of the 1930s, following the cultural line of the Soviet Union, espoused the doctrine of "socialist realism." It was never clear how this doctrine could be applied in an artistically innovative and useful way. Instead, its normative and classificatory impact was quite apparent. The doctrine not only identified arbitrarily a certain kind of art as genuinely proletarian, but it also attempted to stipulate what "real" art had to be. In general, socialist realism required that art, in some sense, conform to the principles of "dialectical materialism." Dialectical materialism is a philosophical theory of great generality; but in the oversimplification that became current in the Communist parties, it came to mean that historical change is ultimately intelligible only in terms of certain kinds of social conflict. In capitalist societies, this meant, essentially, the class conflict between proletariat and bourgeoisie. The radical *New Masses* artist, such as William Gropper, presumably had to depict this conflict. Not only was he to portray this conflict, but he also had to assess it and present it in terms favorable to the proletariat, i.e., in terms favorable to immediate Soviet interests.

With these intellectual strictures, not only the romantic, "decadent" doctrine of "art for art's sake," but also vanguard art and the various artistic 'isms that sprang up in bourgeois society after World War I, appeared simply as instances of bourgeois and self-delusionary masking of reality. Thus, the artistic innovations of, say, surrealism, from which these American Communist artists might have learned useful lessons, were condemned or ignored. According to socialist realism, the function of surrealistic "distortion" was to mask reality by making it unrecognizable. This narrow and sterile artistic dogma could not entertain the notion that all plastic art is, in some sense, a distortion of reality insofar as it is a reconstruction and an interpretation of it. How readily visible the "distortion" is depends purely upon how conventional or eccentric are the aesthetic means employed in the mode. Socialist realism appeared to be a less distorted view of reality simply because it was, stylistically, a more conventional and academic view. Indeed, it employed some of the stylistic devices of the worst bourgeois calendar art.

Thus, most *New Masses* artists, unlike their predecessors on the *Masses*, were caught in the aesthetic trap of their own debilitating and inadequate theories about art. Many of these artists, particularly the illustrators William Gropper and Adolph Dehn, were not without talent. Yet even the most talented artist cannot be expected to produce great art when he must work within the constraints of such dogmas, and when both art and theory are themselves subordinated to the gain of relatively short-term political advantages.

San Francisco, 1973

International Review

NEW YORK, 1936-1939

JAMES B. GILBERT

THE *International Review of Contemporary Thought and Action*, unlike so many of its companions in the 1930s, represented no political party or movement; it was a privately owned and edited magazine, devoted to left-wing causes, but broadly based in its interests. Published in New York by Herman Jersom and his wife, the *Review* contained articles and translations of articles written by a wide range of European radicals. Most of the articles and translations were composed by Jersom, who was a language teacher in the New York City public school system.

The political position of the magazine was radical but anti-Bolshevik. Jersom reprinted works written by a diverse group, including Rosa Luxemburg, André Malraux, Karl Radek, Simone Weil, Leon Trotsky, Mao Tse-tung, and many others. Much of the writing was theoretical, although after late 1936 articles began to appear on the war in Spain and the organization of industrial labor unions in the United States. The names of many of the authors of articles and translations are presumably pseudonyms for Jersom, although one American Marxist, Paul Mattick, contributed to the magazine.

Jersom took a strong stand against the Communists in Spain, but he did not turn to Trotskyism. On the contrary, the *International Review* blamed the tragedy of Spain on bolshevism, and the deformation of the Russian Revolution on Lenin as well as Stalin. Bolshevism, it contended, had little to do with communism or Marxism. Thus Jersom found his political moorings in the older writings of J. Martov, Rosa Luxemburg, and Friedrich Engels. Also under the auspices of the *International Review*, Jersom published three pamphlets: Rosa Luxemburg's *Reform or*

Revolution, J. Martov's *The State and the Socialist Revolution*, and M. Yvon's *What has Become of the Russian Revolution?*

The *International Review* suffered from the same types of financial problems as other little magazines. It announced somewhat mysteriously in 1937, for example, that available funds to continue publication were being denied to the editors and the magazine was in danger of suppression. Again, in early 1939, the magazine discussed financial affairs, this time assuring its readers that enough funds had been found to continue the journal for a year. Shortly after that, however, the *International Review* ceased publication. Jersom's attitude toward radical politics had changed after the outbreak of war in Europe. For some time after the demise of his periodical, he published a mimeographed newsletter supporting American participation in the war, and then, apparently, he disappeared from radical political life altogether.

The *International Review* is thus a strange, but interesting, radical magazine of the 1930s, for it was not devoted to any political movement, nor did it stand strongly behind a single cause. Its private view of the period led it to reprint some of the lesser known writings of older, but important, Socialists and Marxists. In addition to commentary by Jersom, it reprinted significant articles on Spain and on the Soviet Union. When the war intruded—when present politics became of great importance—the *International Review* proved perhaps too remote to support Jersom's new interest in supporting the war, and his publishing venture folded.

College Park, Maryland, 1968

Partisan Review

NEW YORK, 1934—

JAMES B. GILBERT

THE *Partisan Review* is one of the most fascinating of America's little magazines. The designation, little magazine, is generally reserved for literary journals with low circulation, but in the case of *PR* it refers to a magazine whose only nearest competitor in importance is probably the old *Masses*, which also combined literature with articles of current political interest. But the *Partisan* is undoubtedly unique in its longevity; it was founded in 1934 and continues today. More important, it developed a type of cultural criticism in the European tradition, which has, as its subject, the relationships of art, culture, literature, and politics. Since its inception, the *Partisan* has been published with an eye toward the political context of culture as well as toward literary developments.

This combination of cultural, literary, and political criticism has made the *Partisan* a fascinating archive of important intellectual developments. Reading the magazine, of course, gives one a distorted view of American culture, with a heavy bias toward the politics and sometimes the in-fighting of New York intellectuals. Moreover, some of the concerns of the magazine were never as central as they might have appeared at the time. Nevertheless, since its beginning as a minor publication of the New York John Reed Club in the early 1930s, through its discussion of Trotskyism in the late 1930s, to the debate among the editors over America's participation in World War II, the magazine shed much of its parochialism. And even the debate in the early days over proletarian literature and then the struggle to achieve an independent radical politics in the difficult atmosphere of the late 1930s are, in retrospect, important points in the history of American intellectualism.

The issues that occupied the *Partisan* editors in the beginning and that continued to interest the editorial board even as it changed centered around one key issue: the role of the intellectual in society. The 1930s with its apparently clearcut issues made this problem no clearer or more reasonable than did the 1950s. At almost any point in the 39 years of its publication one can find articles in the magazine in which writers puzzle over the changing and explosive nature of the intellectual in society. When the *Partisan* first appeared, it expressed great faith in the force of proletarian literature, a term variously defined, but which generally meant a literature that would serve a working-class revolution. From social revolution and the working-class cause, the *Partisan* gradually shifted its commitment to a different formulation of the same problem. By the end of the 1930s, the editors were deeply disillusioned with existing forces of revolution (principally the Soviet Union), and so sought a new position and justification for the intellectual, in which his self-proclaimed independence and his ostentatious freedom could promote the cause of radical culture. In the early 1930s commitment seemed radical; by the end of the decade alienation—an act of self-preservation—seemed the only proper stance for the intellectual. In part resulting from this new position, there followed after 1940 several fascinating years in which the magazine devoted itself to a reconsideration of Western avant-garde literature, existentialism, psychoanalysis and literature, and, of course, politics.

The chronological history of the magazine reveals many of its changing commitments. From the beginning it was published and edited primarily by Phillip Rahv and William Phillips, two young critics and members of the Communist-affiliated New York John Reed clubs. Through its New York location, the magazine also was aided in its first issues by the editors of the *New Masses*, which by the mid-1930s had become the chief literary organ for intellectuals sympathetic to the Communist party. In the early issues, Rahv and Phillips published a good deal of proletarian literature, and began what remained a constant feature of *PR*—their joint essays on the contemporary state of culture. Taking the notion of proletarian literature perhaps more seriously than did the more orthodox Communist journals, Rahv and Phillips were critical of much of the work called proletarian literature. Yet they were completely committed to what they thought was its essential purpose: finding a way to combine radical politics and radical art forms.

This deep commitment to literature was inevitably fated to bring them into conflict with the editors of the *New Masses*, Mike Gold and Granville Hicks in particular, as well as political stalwarts. But as late as the end of 1935, *PR* was still considered a loyal Communist journal. At that time, the magazine was joined to Jack Conroy's little magazine venture, the *Anvil*, published in Chicago. In effect, the *Partisan* absorbed the *Anvil*, for Conroy had almost nothing to do with the combined magazine when it appeared in 1936.

Despite the approval which the *New Masses* gave to this joint venture, there was growing competition and hostility between *PR* and the rest of the Communist intellectual movement. This tension first emerged in the debate over proletarian literature, largely because the *Partisan* was dissatisfied with much of what had been produced. When the Communist movement adopted the Popular Front politically, its sympathetic intellectual allies did so culturally. By 1936 the full effects of this shift were apparent. It became more important for Communist purposes to organize a League of American Writers; the meetings of the league were star-studded affairs which roused support for the general cultural and foreign policy positions of the Soviet Union. The Reed Clubs were dropped. This development left the editors of *PR* in a hopeless position. They could no longer support a revolutionary literature except by opposing the watered-down cultural position of the Communists. As news of the Spanish Civil War and the Moscow Trials reached New York intellectual circles, the editors became even more discouraged, and they suspended publication of the magazine in late 1936.

When *Partisan* reappeared in 1937, it was essentially a new magazine, with several new editors including literary critic F. W. Dupee, artist George L. K. Morris, and Dwight Macdonald, as well as Rahv and Phillips. The Communist press claimed that Rahv and Phillips had swiped a loyal magazine, but this was hardly the case. In effect, the editors had moved leftward in their politics (if only temporarily), as they openly sympathized with Trotskyism and a form of international revolution (Macdonald was a member of the movement for a short period). The American Trotskyists were delighted, if a bit suspicious, for they had acquired important allies among New York intellectuals. A number of important writers, either Trotskyists or independent radicals such as James Burnham and Sidney Hook, began to publish in the magazine.

If Communist intellectuals had been more perceptive, they might have noted a curious continuity in the interests of Rahv and Phillips. The editors had felt they were helping to create a radical culture at the outset of their venture, but, by the end of the 1930s, the context of this pursuit had changed so much that their commitment led them increasingly into political isolation and cultural elitism. Moreover, the Moscow Trials made anything like overt political commitment seem like the gravest of risks. Only those intellectuals who preserved their political independence could survive. This theme, in effect, proposed that the intellectual withdraw from active politics. What it meant at first for the magazine was that it would commit itself to no political movement (except vaguely to Trotskyism where Trotsky himself was seen as a kind of symbol of the alienated but activist modern intellectual). The magazine's most important commitment, however, was to the essentials of the independent intellectual life.

An effect of this new position was the magazine's reconsideration of modern literature. Rahv and Phillips had long been interested in defining and creating a radical literature. Before 1936, they felt that this might be proletarian literature: plays, novels, and poems which expressed overt radical political ideas. By 1937, however, they had done an about-face. Now they felt that radical literature meant radical technique and literature which uncovered the social, and particularly the psychological, dilemmas of modern intellectuals. Thus writers in *PR* began to discuss the nature of modern avant-garde literature and such authors as Henry James, Kafka, Eliot, Proust, and Joyce.

This literary position embroiled the magazine in a political and cultural fight. In 1937, the Communist movement had enlisted the support of a number of enthusiasts for American literature, especially traditional writers such as Mark Twain, whose works were at that point undergoing a revival. *PR* represented a more European cultural orientation, while the League of American Writers and its allies were increasingly nationalistic. The sniping which both sides took at each other reflected a broader split at this time between American intellectuals over the source of their cultural allegiances.

With the Hitler-Stalin Pact in 1939 and the outbreak of war, cultural nationalism (now devoid of any alliance with Communist intellectuals) increased. Although Rahv and Phillips continued to oppose this cultural nationalism, they were at the same time moving toward support of America's participation in the war. However, Dwight Macdonald continued to oppose the war and to call for a world revolution. Although he left the Trotskyist movement in 1940, he did so largely because that movement gave qualified support to a Soviet foreign policy which Macdonald could not approve. For almost two years, Macdonald on one side, seconded by Clement Greenberg who was temporarily an editor, opposed the American war effort, while Rahv and Phillips gave it qualified support. This split remained a working agreement to disagree until 1943 when Macdonald left *PR* to found, with Nancy Macdonald, the antiwar journal, *Politics*.

During these years of the late 1930s and early 1940s, *PR* reflected the heart of a debate among New York intellectuals over the nature of the world war and the intellectual issues at stake. Once again the cultural position of the magazine illuminated its political shift as the editors deepened their discussion of the alienation and, paradoxically, the responsibilities of the modern intellectual. After Macdonald left the magazine in 1943, the editors focused more of their attention on cultural matters. Although American politics and culture were at that time no more conducive to the production of great literature and art than they had formerly been, there was, they argued, not much point in maintaining a stiff political opposition.

Moreover, by the 1940s another element—anticommunism—had become the preoccupation of the *Partisan*. Their own experience in the Communist intellectual movement probably made this inevitable. The Soviets, with their bureaucracy, their suspicion, and their intolerance, had wreaked havoc upon their own intellectual life. The American Communists argued that the Moscow Trials were a positive step in opposing fascism. Equally bad, they supported a vulgar sort of nationalistic revival in the United States after 1936. *PR* could not support an independent intellectual life or promote authors such as Kafka and Joyce without bringing down upon themselves the criticism of such Communist critics as Mike Gold. But the *Partisan* also made anticommunism into a sort of *sine-qua-non* for intellectual life during the war and during the beginning of the Cold War. Writers such as Sidney Hook, James Farrell, and James Burnham pursued the issue of anticommunism with a good deal of vehemence and heat.

This political position was accompanied by a further development of the cultural politics of the magazine. After 1944, a number of writers, particularly Arthur Koestler and William Barrett, a philosopher from Columbia University, wrote extensively on the neurosis of the modern intellectual. The older position of the magazine, essentially an existential one, had been that the writer was by definition a stranger to his society. Now, however, the conflict was seen as an internal one. For many writers, the essential character of the modern intellectual was his neurosis—his internalization and obsession with the incompatibility between himself and society. This position, together with the politics of the *Partisan* hinted at a conservative adjustment of *Partisan Review* to American life.

The nature and extent of this adjustment were most fully elucidated in 1952 in a symposium called, "Our Country and Our Culture." The predominant theme of the essays in the symposium was that intellectuals, though perhaps alienated from society, ought still to consider the virtues of living in America, while so much else of the world was in physical and ideological shambles. To the editors, no real force for radical change appeared to be alive in the world. It was therefore important to make the best of a mediocre possibility. In this final development alienation came to count for less; it merely represented the gulf between mass culture and the culture of intellectuals.

As the *Partisan* made its peace with American society, it largely gave up its interest in politics except insofar as they might intrude into the life of intellectuals. For the next two decades the magazine continued its distinguished record of publishing new authors and important cultural essays. During these next years, too, the editorial board changed, first with the addition of Richard Poirier in 1963 and then with the resignation of Philip Rahv in 1969. In 1963 the magazine was given editorial offices and support by Rutgers University where it is now published.

College Park, Maryland, 1973

Black & White

LOS ANGELES, 1939-1940

The Clipper: A Western Review

LOS ANGELES, 1940-1941

GUY ENDORE

TODAY a magazine with the staff and contributors to match the quality of those who worked with *Black & White* and *The Clipper*, would probably sell for fifty cents or more an issue, would more readily manage to secure some sort of national distribution, and would command a decent amount of advertising. But *Black & White* came out on a shoestring at the ragged end of the depression and never really got out of the red. Even with such names as Dreiser, Steinbeck, Priestley, and others of similar importance on its cover, it failed to achieve a circulation out of the hundreds. "I don't think I ever printed a thousand copies of any issue," Saul Marks, the printer, told me.

The idea for *Black & White* was conceived in 1938. At that time it was the custom of Saul and Lillian Marks, owners of the Plantin Press of Los Angeles, to visit Wilbur and Ida Needham at their little bookstore in Santa Monica, and spend the evening yelling at each other about all the great disputes of the day, over plates of spaghetti and glasses of wine.

Saul had learned the art of fine printing in Warsaw, had emigrated to the United States in 1921 and opened a little shop in Detroit, and then years later, in 1931, had started his now highly esteemed press in Los Angeles. As for Wilbur, he reviewed books for the Sunday edition of the *Los Angeles Times* under Paul Jordan Smith, in addition to helping his wife run the bookstore.

Wilbur felt constricted and restrained by his inability to write as he damned-well pleased about the books he reviewed, and often brought up the idea of letting himself go in some sort of sheet or broadside that hopefully Saul would print for nothing or for no more than the cost of paper. It was still the era of worldwide unemployment, the era of the rise of fascism and Hitlerism, the time of Spain's agony and the threat of World War II, and Wilbur was full of things that were bursting to be said.

Thus, gradually, during these bull sessions, the leaflet idea expanded into a plan to get out a monthly magazine. "We began to think of something that would reach not only leftwingers and liberals but also those who were still walking the tightrope in between. Peace and civil rights and the defense of minorities and the poor were to be our principal objectives," Wilbur recalls. And Saul remembers a decision to be "basically humanist with a moderate Marxist bias, but with never any sacrifice of literary standards."

However, when it came to preparing the first issue, Wilbur found that he had overestimated the time he could spare, and underestimated the out-of-pocket expenses, and he therefore called upon his friend Byron Citron to do the spade work. "Byron did a magnificent and heroic job," Wilbur declares. "Nothing less than heroic work could have brought that magazine into being."

An impressive list of associate editors and contributors lent their names and their talents to that first issue. There was Lawrence Clark Powell (now retired after being head of the UCLA library and dean of the library school), and Haakon Chevalier (translator of Malraux), and Edwin Corle (well known for his books on Western themes), Carey McWilliams (biographer of Ambrose Bierce and California historian who now edits *The Nation*), and Donald Ogden Stewart (famed humorist and playwright now living in London), as well as Ella Winter (Donald's wife, the widow of Lincoln Steffens and herself a notable student of the human condition).

Byron Citron, the first editor of *Black & White*, is now a construction engineer, but at that time he was still a student at UCLA. He and his friend Ed Mosk, who is now a lawyer but who was then still studying at USC, not only struggled valiantly to get out a magazine with no bankroll and few subscribers, but also collaborated on articles such as one on Buchman and moral rearmament which appeared in the third issue.

Wilbur was delighted to see his dream coming true and immediately contributed to the first issue a review of the reviews of John Steinbeck's

Grapes of Wrath, but at the same time he wasn't too pleased with the contents of that issue as a whole. It was all good stuff, articles about Hollywood, the WPA, Harry Bridges (who was then fighting off the whole American press, plus all of the legislators and the courts of the United States), yet it was all good strong stuff, but somehow it didn't seem to add up right.

"Scarcely any poetry, not one short story nor a single piece of art work," Wilbur recalls. "And when the second issue came out and wasn't very much different, I felt I had to drop whatever I had in hand and take over. I was determined to infuse a little more life and spirit into my baby. And I did. And from then on, until I again had to drop it, our issues began to sparkle with the variety of its contents: fearless factual articles, crisp editorials, good modern poetry and art, excellent short stories, plus hard-hitting reviews. All our issues are still readable and even exciting despite a quarter of a century that has passed. How many other old magazines can pass that test?

"We had an editorial note that said: '*Black & White* welcomes new writers, but is as yet unable to pay for the material.' But that didn't stop us from getting work from everywhere. Professors from various colleges sent in contributions. So did writers from the motion picture industry, social workers out in the field, and such people as Mike Quin, the longshoreman turned writer. And even a retired Negro policeman from the L.A. force, Jess Kimbrough.

"For me," Wilbur adds, "the best measure of our success was the virulent condemnation that Martin Dies gave us in his annual report as head of the House Un-American Activities Committee. He gave us six columns of artfully contrived vituperation, innuendoes and cleverly twisted half-truths. Evidently our little magazine had begun to count on the American scene."

But seven months without income was just about all that Wilbur could take. He turned over the magazine to an editorial board and dropped out, while continuing to watch from a distance. For after all it was still his baby, and he wasn't too sure that it was developing the way it should.

Issue number 3 contains a little item describing Needham as entering the editorial offices of *Black & White* and presenting the magazine with an article entitled "Who Spoils Your Breakfast?," which the editors found so hot they rejected it unanimously, with this comment: "Needham evidently doesn't like newspapers; and he is especially aller-

gic to those published in Los Angeles and Hollywood. If we allowed him
to regurgitate all over the pages of *Black & White*, the magazine would be
little more than a specimen of all the breakfasts Needham had spoiled for
him in the last twenty years.''

The story then goes on to give Needham's reply to an offer by the
editors to tone down his article to a printable condition. ''Why you
spineless eels!'' roared Needham. ''Tone it down? It isn't halfway strong
enough as it stands, and it stands only on one leg. Try and tone it down
and I'll do some toning down for the rest of you! Take the article on the
platter as it is, or throw it down the drain.''

The editors conclude: ''We threw it down the drain.''

It's more than barely possible that Needham wrote that item himself,
perhaps to explain why some of the virulent diatribes he had originally
intended to write for *Black & White* never appeared there, neither while
he was editor nor when he turned over the editorship to an editorial board.

With Wilbur's disappearance from the masthead the title of the
magazine was changed to *The Clipper*, but the first page inside bore the
subtitle: ''Formerly *Black & White*,'' and apparently the policy had not
changed noticeably, the contents still presenting the same variety and of
the same high quality. Saul Marks had this to say of Wilbur's going: ''I
thought it was for the best because Wilbur was too partisan. It seemed to
me that he was hampering the publication's growth.'' And Lester Koenig
agrees: ''Needham tended to lock us in the straightjacket of doctrinaire
thinking.''

Obviously some big political and editorial dispute was going on behind
the scenes. I am not sure of what it was, and with a lapse of over 25 years
that is understandable. Besides I disliked those seemingly endless arguments that were so unavoidable in that terrible period of our earth's
history. By that time I was myself being listed as a member of the
editorial board along with Sanora Babb (now Mrs. Jimmy Wong Howe,
wife of the well-known cinematographer), Cedric Belfrage (author of
Away from it All, a travel book that had a worldwide success), Wolf
Kaufman (a prolific journalist and radio-writer), Lester Koenig (now the
producer of Contemporary Records), Meyer Levin (author of *The Old
Bunch*, who has since written several bestselling novels about Israel), and
John Sanford (poet and novelist now residing in Montecito).

But though listed as a member, Sanora Babb had this to say of me when
I asked her recollections: ''Yes I can recall the excitement of our editorial

planning, but nothing specific. You I remember very well: quiet, wise and deep. And I have never forgotten one dead-serious, alarmed, absurd meeting, a special one, too, an interview with you on your heretical behavior: the study and practice of yoga! I believe your reply was that you were in hopes that the exercises and food disciplines might help your sciatic nerve pains! I suspect they did. They helped me. You see I remember all the wrong things."

My feeling is that what took place was an effort to make *The Clipper* the organ of the League of American Writers and thus give it more of a straightforward political direction. I do remember once in New York, where the League of American Writers was headquartered, I had a violent argument, with whom I don't recall, about *The Clipper* being sponsored by the league. But apparently the New York people had ambitions for a paper of their own and did not intend to sponsor one published in Hollywood.

I know, too, that Wilbur Needham nourishes some vague sort of grudge against the league, but I cannot get from him anything meaningful or distinct. So I can only point out that for three issues *The Clipper* appeared as "published by the Black & White Press," and then to this phrase was added, "under the auspices of the Hollywood Chapter, League of American Writers." (Wilbur Needham notes "that . . . *Black & White* was never run by or connected with the League of American Writers. *The Clipper* may have been . . . ."—Editor). Eventually, in August 1941, it was published by *"The Clipper Press,* a non-profit literary, educational organization . . . ,'' but still under the auspices of the Hollywood Chapter of the League of American Writers. And thus it continued for four more issues, when it ceased publication.

What was the meaning of all these changes? They reflect, if I may interpret them, the turmoil of a period when it was a difficult and heartrending business to take a political stance that would be both principled and smart. For years American intellectuals and artists had been foiled over and over again in efforts to align this nation against Japan's invasion of China, against Mussolini's arrogant military adventurism, against the Nazi anti-Semitic insanity. Over and over again, the American creative set had been revolted by the shabby treatment that England and America and even France had given to the legitimate government of Spain while she was perishing under the blows of Franco and his fascistic allies. Over and over again they had seen England

alienate Russia and finally openly snub her while sacrificing Czechoslovakia to the vulture Hitler at the Munich conference table.

American artists and intellectuals could not of course foresee the sharp
and unexpected blows that would eventually drive Russia and England
and America and China into each other's arms and compel them willy-
nilly to fight fascism all over the world. Many of them, if not most of
them, could only see the desolation of this period when there was
apparently no way one could induce the great democracies to form any
kind of union that might have nipped the Rome-Berlin-Tokyo Axis in the
bud and prevented a world conflagration. The reactionaries and the
bureaucrats seemed everywhere in power and determined to let the Axis
take over the world rather than do anything that might save Russia from
being devoured by Hitler, while Russia, under Stalin, seemed determined
to make nothing but wrong moves that would make those who looked to
her for salvation, tear their hair out in despair.

It is significant that in this harrowing period *Black & White* and *The
Clipper* adopted a policy that all the editors can now look back on with
pride. Thus Agnes Smedley could write in our August 1941 issue about
the famine and diseases affecting China under the Japanese attack:
''Where are all those vitamin extracts of which we have heard so much in
Western lands? Where is the American and British medicine? Where is
the quinine to wipe out the scourge of malaria that kills countless people
here each year? And above all, why is it that we must constantly hear the
roar of Japanese planes run by American gasoline; why must Chinese
soldiers be torn to bits by American ammunition? Why must Japanese
troops be transported on American trucks with American gasoline, to
fight the Chinese army which is holding the fort for democracy in the Far
East?''

And thus Carey McWilliams could speak out in the June 1941 issue
about the ''confusion and horror and despair spreading throughout the
world these days. I had a feeling of great compassion when I read the
farewell note which Virginia Woolf left for her husband: 'I have a feeling
I shall go mad,' she wrote. 'I cannot go on any longer in these terrible
times.' ''

It would be my opinion that for ''these terrible times'' *The Clipper*
adopted the only possible correct stance: our editorial board stood for
culture and compassion. And that is why the issues are so readable to this
day. In an era when there was so much ranting and crude propaganda

obviously sprung from dogma, the pages of *Black & White* and its successor are seen to be remarkably free of the disease of the day.

Instead one finds a beautiful piece such as that of Frank Scully in his "Death of a Genius" (March 1941), where he records his impressions as he finds himself the lone visitor to the funeral chapel where lie the remains of F. Scott Fitzgerald. "You went down a long corridor where everything was carpeted and silent as death. The William Wordsworth room was open to you. And there lay American genius surrounded by his friends.

"Not a soul was in the room. Except for one bouquet of flowers and a few empty chairs, there was nothing to keep him company except his casket."

Such is the policy of compassion and culture. You will find it exemplified in Dreiser's brief note on the passing of Sherwood Anderson (May 1941) and in his longer piece on the still living Upton Sinclair (September 1940) whom he salutes as that rare manifestation: "a thoroughly honest writer." You will find it in Wilbur Needham's attack on Thomas Wolfe (July 1939) and in Larry Powell's laudatory piece on Steinbeck (June 1939).

And in such moving short stories as Sanora Babb's "Young Boy, The World" (September 1939), Jess Kimbrough's "Humpy" (January 1941), and Lew Amster's "Mister Kiss" (December 1940), which are listed with no disrespect to the equally meritorious work of Bezzerides, John Steinbeck, Gordon Kahn, and Samuel Ornitz, who in the last issue of the magazine published a fine extract from his novel, *Bride of the Sabbath*.

The high standards of our work are shown in the fact that Lewis Jacobs chose two motion picture reviews from our publication for his anthology, *Introduction to the Art of the Movies*. One was Cedric Belfrage's review of *Citizen Kane*, the other was Meyer Levin's review of *Tuesday Brown*. Apparently Lewis Jacobs was not aware that there never was such a picture as *Tuesday Brown*. The whole thing was a spoof concocted by Meyer.

Cedric Belfrage recalls for me in a recent letter the two first studies that he, as a Britisher, made of our funerary shenanigans: "The American Standard of Dying" and "Forest Lawn Beckons You" (October and November 1939). Cedric is convinced that all the talking he did about this subject when he went to serve England during the war, resulted in Evelyn

Waugh picking up the same subject, with the result that Cedric's own book, *Abide with Me*, when it appeared, was totally swamped.

It was the American entry into the world war as a result of Pearl Harbor that stopped our magazine. Sanora Babb, in whose apartment we used to hold so many of our editorial meetings, recalls the men going off to war, and herself going out to solicit money for the War Chest, and teaching women how to drive ambulances. One of our contributors, Robert Meltzer, assistant director on Chaplin's *The Great Dictator*, was to die in combat. Curiously his story-article (January 1941) begins with a note: "The following fragment is from the miscellaneous papers of Robert Meltzer, a young writer whose unexplained disappearance early in 1941 . . ."

And so our paper died.

Los Angeles, 1968

Part Eleven

PERSONAL JOURNALISM

AS journalism—as dutiful reporting and objective analysis of events—American radical periodicals were generally never as "good" after the Bolshevik crisis as before. The organs of the fractious parties were necessarily the principal tools in the sectarian tempests that occupied so much of American radicals' attention. And, in the case of the Communist journals at least, the exigencies of following a rigid line subject to revision without notice marred and inhibited those journals at their best.

The exception to the journalistic weakness of the post-1919 radical press was in the curious but tenacious tradition of personal journalism. Burdened with all the usual handicaps of radical publications, these publishing ventures also suffered from the lack of organizational subsidies and the burdens of regularly producing an issue with a staff that frequently numbered only one. Perhaps because the laws of natural selection were so harsh in these circumstances, those personal publications that did manage to establish themselves were excellent indeed. They provide the sources for a tradition of American radicalism which, because it was nonorganizational, left no other sources and was, therefore, frequently overlooked in the histories.

This strain of social dissent and criticism is, in some ways, more vital intellectually than the parties were. The parties came and went, however golden their particular moments. To look solely at them for the history of

American radicalism is to see a dramatic flood and ebb that is not the entire story. Extremely successful publishing ventures like *I.F. Stone's Weekly* in the 1950s indicate the continuity and durability of the radical tradition in even that apparently arid era.

Dr. Robinson's Voice
in the Wilderness
NEW YORK, 1917-1920

CHARLES LEINENWEBER

THE United States' entrance into World War I came as a distinct shock to most American radicals. In response, the traditionally gradualistic Socialist party—the major center for American radicalism—produced an antiwar manifesto of astonishing militancy. Convening by chance just one day after war had been declared, the party proclaimed its "unalterable opposition to the war," and branded it as a "crime against the people of the United States and against the nations of the world." The party promised unyielding opposition to conscription and mass action to end the war. As party leader Morris Hillquit explained, war had come so suddenly that Socialists "had no time for calm deliberation." Caught up in horror and surprise, they broke through the restrictions of their narrow, legalistic socialism.

Many Socialists, along with independent radicals who moved around the periphery of the Socialist camp, were enraged by Woodrow Wilson's betrayal of his antiwar line. Previously, even party left wingers, who could rarely be accused of too much admiration for capitalist politicians, had at times praised Wilson. In August 1916, the left-wing *International Socialist Review* attacked a reformist party newspaper for calling Wilson a militarist. The *ISR* charged: "To howl suspicions of militarism against a president who has kept the working class of America out of war during a hair-trigger period is a species of treachery to the working class. . . ." Key writers for the important left-wing magazine, the *Masses*—including Max Eastman and John Reed—openly endorsed Wilson.

The war took author and editor Dr. William J. Robinson by surprise, as it did many other American radicals. Also like the others, Robinson was enraged by Wilson's betrayal of his antiwar following. An independent radical with close personal ties to the Socialist party, Robinson decided to strike back against the war and Woodrow Wilson with his own journal. He founded *Voice in the Wilderness* in September 1917—some five months after the United States entered the war—out of personal funds. Throughout the journal's episodic career, which came to an end in January 1920, Robinson remained editor, staff, and virtually sole contributor.

Robinson was peculiarly suited for such a demanding, one-man effort. He was unswerving in his radical pacifism, and, by his own admission, he was a loner. Robinson was constitutionally incapable of working with other people and this, more than his politics, explains his refusal to join the Socialist party. Moreover, Robinson was already a writer and editor of vast experience. Prior to *Voice in the Wilderness*, he had launched more than a half dozen journals and written more than a dozen books. His books and journals ranged through literature, birth control, sexuality, and scientific medicine. He conceived of his every effort as a message to the world.

Unfortunately for Robinson, the Wilson government proved ill disposed toward the message of *Voice in the Wilderness*. The Post Office Department confiscated the first issue, declaring it "unmailable." Robinson then asked if he could send it out in sealed envelopes as first-class mail, but again the Post Office refused. When Robinson brought in the next issue a month later, the Post Office informed him that because the first had not been mailed as scheduled, he had lost his second-class privileges. Once again, they would not let him use first-class mail and confiscated all copies. A third issue appeared in extremely emaciated form, heavily censored by the government, but even that was confiscated. Robinson managed to produce one more issue, in December 1917, but it met with the same fate as previous ones. Under this heavy layer of repression, *Voice in the Wilderness* was silenced. Robinson ceased publication for seventeen months, resigning himself to mailing out occasional bulletins. These, too, were seized.

In seeing his journal literally snuffed out by the government, Robinson experienced another shock. Just as the war had taken American radicals by surprise, so, too, did the subsequent repression. In a naive way, most radicals had believed in the efficacy of American democracy—not only in the democratic political arena, but also in the government's desire to protect freedom of speech and press. Even while mounting his preparedness campaign, Wilson had paid considerable lip service to civil liberties. Now, suddenly, he was turning against those who had cheered his words most passionately.

Robinson, of course, was only one of thousands of victims of the repression. Similarly, his journal was only one of the many radical periodicals suppressed. In dozens of cities and towns throughout the nation, offices of the Socialist party and Industrial Workers of the World were raided by police and mobs, their literature and files destroyed, and their members harassed and beaten. Similar tactics were used to crush the People's Council, the only massive liberal antiwar movement, and drive it out of existence. Official repression took the form of indictments and convictions under the Espionage Act. The Espionage Act was used freely against radical pacifists at large, Socialist party and IWW leaders, and radical publications. The *Masses*, the *International Socialist Review*, the *American Socialist*, and *The Appeal to Reason*, were among the most important publications to fall before it.

Robinson could scarcely have used *Voice in the Wilderness* to fight repression, since the journal itself had been suppressed. Once he was able to resume publication, however, in June 1919, Robinson mounted a sharp attack on the government. By then it had become apparent that repression was to be a permanent feature of American politics. Long after the armistice, Woodrow Wilson still refused to release political prisoners. While they languished behind bars, a new impetus to repression was being added—the anti-Red hysteria. Robinson understood repression as a consequence of the militarization of government during the war and the continuing rule of plutocrats. In many respects, this was the closest he ever came to class analysis of American society.

During the wartime repression, the vast majority of American Socialists held firm to their internationalist or pacifist convictions. This was true of the party's Right as well as its Left. However, a small number of Socialists deserted to Wilson's war camp. These were mostly intellectuals—well known and highly visible—including Charles Edward Russell, William English Walling, John Spargo, Upton Sinclair, W. J. Ghent, and J. G. Phelps Stokes. Except for Sinclair, these deserters became "renegades." They not only supported the war, but they supported the government's repression of their former comrades. The renegades offered their services to investigating committees, endorsed the Espionage Act, and utilized the capitalist press to accuse party members of cowardice and treason. During the important 1917 mayoralty campaign in New York, the renegades branded Socialist candidate Morris Hillquit as a "champion of German Kultur," who was "giving needless aid and comfort to the enemies of democracy the world over. . . ."

Perhaps even more than did Woodrow Wilson, these renegades incurred the wrath of Robinson. To him, they were "moral skunks" who "will never be forgiven, will never be readmitted into the ranks of decent men, of honest radicals." Interestingly, several of the more vociferous renegades—including W. J. Ghent and J. G. Phelps Stokes—had been close friends of Robinson prior to their defections. In a lengthy correspondence with Stokes—whose wife, ironically, had been imprisoned for her opposition to the war—Robinson explained that the renegades' worst crime was their unseemly alliance with the capitalist press.

Robinson considered the capitalist press to be "mankind's greatest curse." He confessed to being heartbroken at seeing ex-radicals, who had previously recognized it as a prostitute press, writing in its columns. Robinson devoted a substantial portion of every issue of *Voice in the Wilderness* to attacks on the press. Unlike the staff of the *Masses*, Robinson was never humorous when writing about the press. In fact, it could be said that he was never humorous when writing about anything that angered him. With impassioned outrage, he characterized the press as "the lowest rung in the ladder of falsehood, misrepresentation, dishonesty and mental degradation." He believed editors and publishers to be kept men, poisoning the minds of the people and brutalizing their souls. The capitalist press—represented in vilest form by the *New York Times*—served only the plutocrats. It had been instrumental in generating support for the war and the repression, in creating reactionary mobs, and in spreading slanders about the Bolshevik Revolution.

To the capitalist press, Robinson counterposed a small collection of newspapers, magazines, and journals that he believed represented the forces of humanitarianism. Prominent among them were the various Socialist publications and his own *Voice in the Wilderness*, but also included were the liberal magazines—*The Nation, The Dial*, and even the wavering *New Republic*.

In general, Robinson made no qualitative distinctions between liberals, on the one hand, and radicals or Socialists, on the other. His own radicalism, although extremely pointed when it came to criticisms of the war or of the press, was elusive in nature. In seeking allies, Robinson looked only for those qualities of humanitarianism and honesty that he admired most. Thus he could write with equal enthusiasm of the liberal People's Council, the Socialist party, the IWW, and the Russian Bolshevik party.

Voice in the Wilderness contained no domestic social or political program whatever. This alone may account for Robinson's reluctance to perceive differences within the Left. Perhaps the closest Robinson came to formulating a program was in a call to tie certain reactionary politicians, generals, publishers, and labor leaders in a bundle to be "gently deposited at the bottom of the sea."

Robinson's failure to develop a program was unquestionably the most serious weakness in *Voice in the Wilderness*. In consciously rejecting all "tenets, dogmas, programs or platforms," Robinson's critical philosophy remained only half developed. The best example of this appeared in one of the last issues of *Voice in the Wilderness*. Following a lengthy and scathing indictment of the established order, Robinson concluded with a vapid whimper:

> I believe we need a radical change—a political, industrial, social, religious and moral change—a change in the relations between individual and individual, between nation and nation.
>
> We need more love and more light—more kindness, more intelligence, more understanding, more forgiveness.

Robinson, in short, was a utopian with no vision of utopia.

On questions of foreign policy, Robinson was more concrete. In a sense, it was easier to develop a program of foreign policy because the alternatives were clear. Robinson demanded that the United States withdraw its troops from Europe and, later on, from Russia, and demanded that the United States recognize and aid revolutionary regimes in Russia, Hungary, and Mexico, and cease aiding counterrevolutionaries everywhere. Robinson condemned the Treaty of Versailles as criminal and demanded that a just settlement be instituted.

Even though he had developed concrete suggestions for foreign policy, Robinson still made little attempt to understand war or imperialism. His *Voice in the Wilderness* was much more a cry of pain than an analytical journal. This is understandable in the context of American radical and Socialist theory as a whole. The analyses of the war by radical theoreticians—even by such respected figures as Louis Boudin—showed great variety and uncertainty. The war was seen variously as a traders' war, a militarists' war, a nationalists' war, a munition manufacturers' war, a war between feudalism and capitalism, and so forth. There were even a few theories of war as an inherent predisposition of men (but not women) and in the nature of all mankind.

The only well-thought-out analyses of war and imperialism to appear in the American radical press were translations of articles by European revolutionaries. Brilliant contributions by the ultra-leftist Anton Pannokoek appeared regularly, but ultimately the work of Karl Liebknecht had a more profound impact. When war first broke out in Europe, it was Liebknecht's steadfast opposition that inspired American Socialists and rekindled their hopes for the world Socialist movement. In time, Liebknecht's theoretical analysis of the war—not merely his example—began to penetrate American Socialist consciousness. This was most noticeable in 1919, when a major portion of the party's left wing began to move toward revolutionary communism and attempted to differentiate themselves from the Right. Robinson was totally unaffected by Liebknecht as a theoretician. In the pages of *Voice in the Wilderness*, Liebknecht remained an exemplary antiwar hero.

During the period following the Bolshevik Revolution, the right and center wings of the Socialist party supported the regime of Lenin and Trotsky. In many ways, Robinson's attitude toward revolutionary communism was similar to theirs. He was extremely friendly toward the Revolution and through his little journal, supported it with great enthusiasm. He believed that Lenin and Trotsky eventually would be recognized as the greatest historical figures of the twentieth century. But, as with the war and similar questions, Robinson showed little understanding of either the Bolshevik Revolution or revolution in general. He looked upon revolutionary Russia as a noble, isolated "experiment" and viewed Hungary in a similar way. Robinson failed to recognize the need for the Revolution to be extended throughout Europe, if only to survive.

Like the party Center and Right, he believed that any attempt to set up a revolutionary Communist party in the United States was both unnecessary and ludicrous—unnecessary because of the electoral process and ludicrous because it could not possibly gain support. Within the Socialist party, the center and right wings ultimately dealt with the emerging revolutionary Left by expelling them—some two-thirds of the membership. Robinson, writing before the expulsions but while the fight was brewing, was not so harsh. He disagreed with the revolutionaries, to be sure, and thought their rhetoric to be a menace to the movement. Revolutionary bombast, he argued, would only bring more repression. But all the while, Robinson believed that the revolutionaries were not really serious. Despite their flaming oratory, he felt they were fundamentally reformists, like himself. Developments within the Communist party during the next two decades proved Robinson to be a shrewd judge of character.

Berkeley, California, 1969

Upton Sinclair's

PASADENA, CALIFORNIA, 1918-1919

STANLEY K. SCHULTZ

IN April 1918, when the United States had been at war with Germany for a year, the first issue appeared of *Upton Sinclair's; A Monthly Magazine: For a Clean Peace and the Internation*. In his introductory statement of purpose about "this magazine in embryo, trying to be born," Sinclair disclaimed any egotism in the choice of title. Sham modesty, he explained, was untimely in a day of crisis. "I have a certain trade-mark," affirmed the new editor. "Wherever I have travelled over the world, I have met plenty of prejudice, but I have met no thinking people who did not know my trade-mark, and what it stands for. It stands for Social Justice." Sinclair diagnosed the world as suffering from a disease upon which he was expert. He claimed to know the germ and to have ready the serum. He offered his magazine.

Over the following ten months the Socialist novelist and essayist published ten issues of *Upton Sinclair's*. He also printed two supplements—the first in April 1918, and repeated in May, the second in November of the same year. Then in February 1919, *Upton Sinclair's* came to an abrupt halt. The magazine had not sold well, nor had it carried advertising as a source of income. Searching for another vehicle of expression, Sinclair turned to longtime friends on the staff of *The Appeal to Reason*, another Socialist periodical, published in Girard, Kansas. That magazine had given Sinclair his first "break" as an author when it had serialized his novel *The Jungle* fourteen years earlier. Now *The Appeal to Reason* agreed to take over Sinclair's small subscription list and provide him with space for a regular column. Sinclair wrote his first column in the February 1919, issue and continued writing regularly until December 31, 1921, when *The Appeal to Reason* ceased publication.

In its announcement of the merger, *The Appeal to Reason* (February 8, 1919) trumpeted the "extraordinary impression which the little publication made" by listing some of those readers who wrote letters to the editor—H. G. Wells, Eugene Debs, H. L. Mencken, Col. Edward M. House, Havelock Ellis, Count Leo Tolstoi, Sinclair Lewis, Frank Harris, and Luther Burbank. But to measure the importance of the periodical by its correspondents was somewhat misleading. The magazine hardly provided a forum for free debate. In the marketplace of ideas *Upton Sinclair's* had only one product to sell.

From a makeshift office attached to his home in the quiet streets of Pasadena, California (then largely a millionaires' suburb of Los Angeles), Sinclair wrote, edited, and mailed his new magazine. In contrast to other contemporary Socialist periodicals like the *Masses* and *The Appeal to Reason, Upton Sinclair's* primarily was a one-man operation. Except for an occasional poem by George Stirling or Maxwell Anderson and sonnets or editorials by his wife, Mary Craig Sinclair, the editor provided all the contributions himself. The closest he came to printing a major piece by anyone else was in December 1918, when he refused an article from Marxist writer John Reed, stating that "it would fill half the magazine."

Sinclair had too much to say to allow other writers space in his columns. The magazine, therefore, was an intensely personal journal, a catalog of the editor's likes and dislikes. He supported the Single-Tax campaign in California state health insurance programs, a national land tax, federal conscription of wealth (80 percent of incomes over $5,000); indeed, he covered most of the liberal and Socialist schemes of the day. As journalist H. L. Mencken put it, in an article quoted by Sinclair (July 1918), a single issue of the magazine "contains fully a third of all the sure cures now current. . . . The rest, I daresay, will appear in later numbers; the recall of judges, Fletcherism, the Gary system, internal baths, the initiative and referendum, sex hygiene, . . . osteopathy. If Sinclair overlooks any of the larger and juicier ones—any, say above the rank of vorticism and paperbag cookery—I shall make him return my dollar."

The chief concern of Sinclair, however, was the European war. He devoted much of his space in columns about the proper response of Socialists to the war. In addition to writing new articles for his magazine,

Sinclair reprinted past pieces and excerpts from earlier books by himself. He also used his periodical to serialize two books that he then had in process—*The Profits of Religion: An Essay in Economic Interpretation* and *Jimmie Higgins*, a novel about the legendary, tireless, faceless worker in Socialist party causes and his reactions to the war.

When Sinclair began publication, a host of other left-wing, Socialist, and radical periodicals—which almost universally condemned the Wilson administration and the war—already had occupied the scene, and some had departed. Established magazines like *The American Socialist*, *The Call*, the *International Socialist Review*, and the *Masses* had died a death of government attrition. While they lived, such periodicals had offered literary podiums to scores of liberal and radical journalists, artists, and intellectuals. The *Masses*, for example, had presented an impressive array of talent, an inventory of the leading literary figures of the day. Contributors had included Randolph Bourne, William English Walling, Bertrand Russell, George Creel (ironically), Vachel Lindsay, and Ernest Poole, as well as writings by its distinguished editors Max Eastman, John Reed, and Floyd Dell. But the editors of the *Masses*, like others whom their domestic enemies had labeled "traitors," "agitators," "free lovers," "anarchists," "revolutionaries," and "red Socialists," had experienced heavyhanded repression by a government dedicated to making the world safe for democracy. The United States Post Office Department had revoked the mailing privileges of many Socialist magazines and newspapers, including the prestigious *Milwaukee Leader* under the editorship of Victor Berger, a former member of the U.S. House of Representatives. In at least thirty-three different cities the Department of Justice had raided headquarters of the Industrial Workers of the World, displaying a cheerful disregard for such elementary legal guarantees as search warrants.

For Upton Sinclair such a state of events and such an atmosphere of intolerance presented difficult personal choices. As a pacifist, a libertarian, and (as he recalled in his autobiography, *American Outpost*, 1932) a Socialist in spirit long before he knew that Socialists existed, Sinclair should have been found in the camps of the persecuted. But he had other signal fires to light. For at least two basic reasons the self-proclaimed champion of underdogs had chosen to offer a magazine supporting Woodrow Wilson and American entry into World War I.

In a split within the American Socialist party over the question of the war, Sinclair found both an opportunity and an obligation to air his views in his own periodical. The party never had been united. The entire spectrum of political and social thought in America had colored the movement. But the outbreak of European war in 1914 had driven the crucial wedge into party loyalty. Most Socialists, and nearly all of the top leadership, had opposed the war thoroughly. In the 1916 presidential campaign the party platform had demanded that the United States not enter the war unless by a referendum vote of the entire populace. The proposition had appeared ludicrous to a number of conservative Socialists, who then defected to Woodrow Wilson in the election. In March 1917, an emergency convention of the party had met in St. Louis to discuss its stance on the then accomplished fact of American participation in hostilities. The official party position emerged in the form of the St. Louis Proclamation. This document indicted the war, maintained that American entry could not "be justified even on the plea that this is a war in defense of American rights or American 'honor,' " identified the capitalist class as the fomenter of conflict, opposed military conscription, and promised continued Socialist opposition.

For Sinclair, as for other Socialist intellectuals such as Charles Edward Russell, John Spargo, Algie M. Simons, W. J. Ghent, J. G. Phelps Stokes, William English Walling, and Gustavus Myers, this was too much. Spargo charged the party with being essentially "un-neutral, un-American, and pro-German." Russell reportedly demanded that all Socialists opposed to the war be driven from the country as "dirty traitors." Sinclair was more tolerant than most, but he deserted the party along with the rest. With Germany's continued attacks on Russia following the Bolshevik Revolution in the fall of 1917, many Socialists and former party members gave grudging support to Wilson's peace program. With Eugene Debs (who maintained party ties), Sinclair affirmed that Wilson's Fourteen Points were "thoroughly democratic and deserve the unqualified approval of everyone believing in the rule of the people, Socialists included." Although Debs and other party members steadfastly denounced military actions, Sinclair gave unstinting support to the American war effort. In the war he beheld potential for furthering his cause of "Social Justice," and no such temporary allegiances as membership in the American Socialist party would stand in the way of his personal crusade.

While internal battles within the ranks of American Socialists encouraged Sinclair to present a magazine voicing Socialist support of the war, an even more important reason lay within the man himself. Given his character and personality, his personalized duty to obtain "Social Justice" for all men, it was not surprising that *Upton Sinclair's* was largely the product of one man's mind.

Like most individuals, Upton Sinclair was several personalities. But unlike many other men, in Sinclair the contradictions ran deep. By ancestry and birth a southerner, in his personal and public morals he became as staunch a Puritan as ever had burned a witch. He ardently championed Prohibition, refusing to drink even such stimulants as coffee or tea. He never used tobacco and always demeaned others who did. He avoided sexual relations with his first wife after the birth of their child because another pregnancy would have meant the financial death of passionate hopes for his writing crusade. By temperament a "loner," Sinclair married, divorced, and married again. A self-proclaimed commoner and friend of the "have-nots" of America, Sinclair chose for his second wife Mary Craig Kimbrough, daughter of a southern plantation owner who patronized and exploited his Negro tenant farmers. By career choice a dedicated crusader seeking to rid the world of poverty, Sinclair condemned many individuals for being self-interested; yet he took pride in the price his fulminations against capitalism could command in the literary marketplace. He never missed an opportunity to advertise himself and his works.

Quite early in his career, Sinclair professed his purpose in life and at the same time painted a striking self-portrait. In the May 14, 1903, issue of the *Independent*, a popular magazine of the day, Sinclair asserted his "fiery, savage hatred of Wealth, and of all that Wealth stands for." Determined to free himself from any taint of debasing materialism, he promised that in America "there shall be one man standing before this people with heart as white as snow; . . . one man to whom jewels and fine raiment, wines, tobaccos and rich food, horses and carriages and servants and houses and ornaments are foul ordure from which he has swept clean his soul; one man who lives altogether for the Spirit, for worship and love and beauty, and the service of mankind."

Throughout one of the most prolific writing careers in American history, Sinclair rarely swerved from that course. He persisted in measuring his countrymen by the yardstick of his own self-righteousness. And he remained certain, as he confessed later in his *American Outpost*, that

"there are a great many Americans with a new dream in their hearts. . . .
Some day we shall hear from them, and see the sprouting of the seed we
have been scattering all these weary years."

Sinclair was a utopian idealist and, psychologically, a man without a
country. He was not anti-America; he reverenced the democratic principles that Americans long had professed. But he despised the failure of his
countrymen to practice their preachments. Sinclair's homeland was not
America—it was "Humanity." His motto was not the jingoistic "my
country right or wrong"; it was "Truth" and "Social Justice" as he
conceived those intangibles. To that homeland he gave undivided loyalty
with all the zeal of a religious convert.

Together with such other contemporary Progressives *qua* Socialists as
muckraking journalist Charles Edward Russell, urban reformer Frederick
C. Howe, and debunking historian Gustavus Myers, Sinclair believed in
the basic integrity and fundamental honesty of "the People." Were the
common men and women of the nation made aware of the true "facts"
about capitalism and that most damnable of all institutions—private
property—they would foster a peaceful revolution. Sinclair gave all his
energies to the promotion of that revolution.

As a writer during the opening decades of the twentieth century he
resourcefully cataloged the failures of democracy. Throughout the long
parade of his social criticism, fiction and nonfiction (both of which often
were semiautobiographical), he revealed his sense of shock, anger, hurt,
and bewilderment at the practices and politics of Americans. Like Jurgis,
protagonist of his most famous novel, *The Jungle* (1906), Sinclair believed himself to be living in an American capitalist jungle in which
strong devoured weak, in which an insatiable greed for property and
power drove men to become predators upon humanity. It was a theme he
repeated in such other works as *The Moneychangers* (1908), *The
Metropolis* (1908), *Love's Pilgrimage* (1911), and *King Coal* (1917), as
well as in later works, including his own magazine. He was a vicious
polemicist who seldom allowed courtesy or personal regard for others to
vitiate the attacks he carried out in the name of "Social Justice." But
beyond polemics, Sinclair attempted at least two practical experiments to
transform his theories into realities.

The first was an effort at founding a utopian community in the American tradition of Brook Farm and Fruitlands. In the fall of 1906, with the
$30,000 he had earned from the unexpected success of *The Jungle*,

Sinclair established a cooperative colony of middle-class intellectuals. Helicon Hall, located on a several-acre farm near Englewood, New Jersey, which ultimately housed between fifty and sixty adults and ten children. The joint-stock venture, praised by men like William James and John Dewey but vilified by many newspapers as a "love nest," lasted but a few months. On March 7, 1907, a mysterious fire (possibly of incendiary origin) burned Helicon Hall to the ground. With the fire went both the young Socialist's manuscripts and his dreams for a cooperative commonwealth.

The second experiment came eleven years later with Sinclair's effort to create his own "true Socialist press" in *Upton Sinclair's*. Responding to the problems of war abroad, of "Social Justice" at home, and to the split in the party, Sinclair believed that the time was ripe for disseminating the "real Truth" to the American public.

"So I come again with my message of Social Justice," Sinclair announced in the inaugural issue of his magazine. "If you really want to do away with the horrors of Armageddon, you have to abolish exploitation, you have to drive poverty from the earth; you have to change the ideas and ideals—not merely of German Junkers, but of American gentlemen, business-men, merchants and masters of affairs." To this end, Sinclair explained the importance of American participation in the war. While as a pacifist he despised all forms of violence among men, he conceded that the "hideous slaughter" might lead to a world in which "aristocratic plunderers in different nations" no longer could exploit the masses and trample underfoot all human rights. One country, Germany, was to blame for starting the war; one country, America, might claim the glory of ending hostilities and of leading the world to social harmony.

Sinclair wrote that he took the German Socialists at their prewar word that only a military defeat could destroy the power of the Prussian ruling caste. He hoped that a victory for Wilsonian democracy would eliminate forever aristocratic authority in all countries. "Here is the prayer of a Socialist and Pragmatist," the editor wrote in his issue of August 1918. "May this destruction of goods, this slaughter of the world's manhood not cease until its work has been completed." Posterity could then reflect that "the War which ended War cost twenty million lives, but it was worth it; it cost two hundred billion dollars, but it was worth it." What difference did it make, Sinclair asked, whether men were killed upon battlefields or in sweatshops, mills, and mines; what did it matter whether wealth bought weaponry or brothels, saloons, and gambling dens?

To achieve benevolent ends, the humanitarian approved inhumane means. It was difficult to see the pacifist for all the warmongering rhetoric.

Sinclair asserted that "a Clean Peace" is the most important work now confronting the world." He described a "Clean Peace" as the peace program of President Woodrow Wilson, one "very close to the formula of the Russians: Self-determination and self-government." If the liberals of the world would only make clear what they wanted and then support the president, such a peace was possible.

"The greatest words in the world just now," Sinclair claimed, "are the Clean Peace and the Internation. . . . Merely to make the words familiar is to bring nearer the great goal." The "internation" as Sinclair saw it was a necessary international government guaranteeing freedom and self-government everywhere in the world. He credited Wilson with sharing this goal. "He has been fairly pleading with us," Sinclair emphasized, "to give him a public sentiment for a just and enlightened peace." The president, however, was helpless without the force of public opinion. By every utterance, capitalist newspapers in America showed their desire to balk Wilson's intentions of "real Democracy." Socialists, liberals, radicals—all men of goodwill—must unite behind Wilson (and Sinclair) in striving to achieve international order and a clean peace.

In his issue of May-June 1918, Sinclair called for a reunification of all American Socialists, together with comrades in other countries, to work toward the realization of the Wilson peace program. Denouncing as a "great calamity" the famous St. Louis Proclamation, he claimed that President Wilson was counting upon such propaganda as he, Sinclair, was writing so that common men throughout the world might rally to the cause.

Throughout the brief life of the magazine, Sinclair continued to agitate for his proposals. In his last issue (February 1919), he reviewed the situation. America had responded "with noble enthusiasm" to the summons to make the world safe for democracy. But now that the war had ended, the fine promises were fading before the onslaught of capitalistic and aristocratic greed. Lloyd George had sold out the British people; Allied armies were crushing the Soviets in Russia; the German leaders were forbidding government by the workers in Berlin. Still, Sinclair pressed on. Less enchanted with Wilson than he had been ten months earlier, Sinclair was still willing to praise Wilsonian idealism. He delighted that ''into this pit of snarling beasts comes the Spokesman of Democracy: Woodrow in the Lion's Den, weaponless, save for his typewriter and his tongue.'' If only he would, Wilson yet might use his moral power. Sinclair wondered, however, whether the president would ''let himself be hoodwinked and see the stage swept clear for worldwide civil war between capitalist reaction and Bolshevist fury?'' Wilson, it was hoped, still might place himself at the head of the masses of the people and march them into the new world of freedom and justice. The clean peace and the internation might yet be recognizable goals, thought Sinclair, even though he had altered the subtitle of his magazine from the idealistic ''for a Clean Peace and the Internation,'' to ''for Social Justice, by Peaceful Means if Possible.''

For his support of the war and the Wilson administration, critics from the political Left and Right denounced the editor. With characteristic aplomb, Sinclair faithfully reprinted letters damning him. Also, characteristically, he more than counterbalanced these with letters of praise. Using his magazine as a soapbox, Sinclair carried on political and social dialogues with correspondents whom he never allowed the final word. Sinclair answered the charges of ''Sherlock Holmes at War'' (Sir Arthur Conan Doyle) that ''if Germany were paying you highly, you could not serve her better than you are doing by spreading both class and international jealousy at such a time'' by pointing out that in none of the Holmes stories was there any hint that the criminal might have a social excuse for his crime or that the institution of private property might be at fault (August 1918). To conservatives who criticized his defense of ''traitors'' like Eugene Debs, the editor responded that the principle of free speech must be preserved. To Socialists who denounced him for begging for clemency from Wilson for political prisoners instead of firmly asserting constitutional right, Sinclair explained that in wartime extreme measures probably were necessary and pointed to the handicaps under which the president operated.

Sinclair's support of the war had forced him into an intellectually tenuous position. His attitude about free speech was equally ambivalent. He supported both those citizens who denounced the Wilson administration and the government that in turn repressed them. Sinclair defended Mrs. Rose Pastor Stokes, wife of Socialist railroad president J. G. Phelps

Stokes, who had gone to prison for suggesting that "the government is for profiteers." He pleaded for fairer treatment for Max Eastman, Floyd Dell, and other staff members of the *Masses*. The government had barred several issues of the semi-Marxist magazine from the mails and had twice brought the editors to trial under the Espionage Act of 1917. Sinclair urged clemency for Eugene Debs, as well as for a host of pacifists, conscientious objectors, and others who opposed the war effort (October, November 1918).

Still, Sinclair also argued that unqualified free speech was not an absolute social right. In suppressing dissent in a time of war hysteria, the government actually protected the lives of those rebels whom angry mobs might otherwise tar and feather, or lynch. Further, the government faced not only internal dissatisfactions, he explained, but systematic and enormously powerful attempts by the enemy to stimulate such dissatisfaction. Sinclair affirmed that the administration was compelled to restrain those hopelessly irreconcilable extremists "who claim the right to oppose the war and the draft here and now." He promised when the war was over to try to win free speech and a free press in America. For the time being, however, he merely petitioned President Wilson to reduce the bitterness of radicals and opponents of the war not yet imprisoned and that of the prisoners themselves by removing them from inadequate city and federal jails to a modern prison-farm colony (September, October 1918).

Sinclair also hedged his response to the Russian Revolution. He rejoiced when Alexander Kerensky came to power and hoped that Russia would postpone its proletarian revolt and remain in the war. But when the Bolsheviks persisted, Sinclair declared the action inevitable and dashed off a telegram to President Wilson urging him to withstand Allied pressures for intervention. In a jingoistic spirit he observed that "if we wait, the Soviets must ultimately ask our help" (August 1918). On the home front, Sinclair vehemently protested government censorship of informative materials about the revolution. He called attention to the action of the Post Office Department forbidding the circulation of a pamphlet by Lenin, *The Soviets at Work*, a technical account of the internal organization of what the editor labeled "the new Russian democracy" (February 1919). He expressed his indignation at the hysterical anti-Soviet propaganda "now being fed to the American people by our Wall Street newspapers and magazines." After the president had failed to take his advice against intervention, Sinclair wrote again, warning that the Soviet movement could not be put down by Allied armies and that attempts to do so only would result in Soviet governments in all Allied countries in a short time (January 1919).

Though he was in heartfelt sympathy with "a tormented people, enslaved and degraded through many centuries," Sinclair nevertheless proclaimed: "I am not a Bolshevik, and I have opposed the Bolshevik movement." He explained that he had never advocated a violent revolution in any country where the ballot had been won. "I have never advocated a 'dictatorship of the proletariat.' " Believing that the Soviet overthrow of the Constituent Assembly in January 1918, had been a frightful blunder, Sinclair suggested that the Allies intervene to the extent of returning the Assembly to power and of keeping the peace until a representative election throughout Russia could be held. For once uncertain of the proper response of Socialists to a Socialist revolution, Sinclair thought that perhaps American radicals should try simply to influence their government against using its troops to restore the old landowners (November 1918; January 1919).

Above all, Sinclair feared the possibility of a Bolshevik revolution in the United States. There were, he asserted, Bolsheviki in America, including a half million Jews from New York City's East Side, ready to take possession of Wall Street and Fifth Avenue. These American proletarians would foment a bloody revolution that, in the long run, would defeat any possibility of real "Social Justice." Sinclair hoped instead that Americans could "contrive a new kind of revolution—a democratic revolution, in which men of all classes may unite in the abolishment of wage-slavery, with its curses of poverty, prostitution, crime and war" (September, October 1918; January 1919). In the face of threatened violence at home—if not abroad—the utopian again became the pacifist.

The February 1919 issue of *Upton Sinclair's* gave no hint that it would be the last. But Sinclair had fallen prey to the *bête noire* of all the "little" radical magazines in America—a lack of capital and of subscriptions. He had priced the periodical consistently at 10 cents a copy. With the July 1918 issue he had lowered the packaged subscription price from ten subscriptions for $5 to six for $3 while keeping the single-subscription yearly price at $1. As inducements he had offered cut-rate deals from time to time and also had promised a free copy of one of his books to any new subscriber. But it was in vain. After merging with *The Appeal to*

Reason, Sinclair affirmed in its pages (February 15, 1919) that the "lobbyists of Wall Street" had been responsible in part for the demise of his magazine. For the rest, failure probably had come because, as Sinclair wrote of himself, "he told all the truth so well, that he managed to get even more abuse from Tories and exploiters than he got from pacifists and rebels."

Despite his self-pleading, Sinclair had failed to make a go of his venture for the same reason that many other contemporary "little" radical periodicals went under—public apathy. In wartime and in the hectic months of peace immediately following the war, many citizens were unwilling to give financial support to journals that challenged the fundamental tenets of American capitalist society. Whether such magazines, like *Upton Sinclair's*, favored or opposed American participation in the war itself made little difference. For all of its damaging blows to the principles of free speech, public hostility toward the Socialist and radical periodicals was not as destructive as public indifference.

In Sinclair's case, at least one additional factor contributed to the death of his magazine. His dedication to the truth as he conceived it and his habit of castigating individuals on every side of a problem made his writings appear inconsistent and shallow to many readers. Sinclair himself recognized this problem. In the March 1, 1919, issue of *The Appeal to Reason* he observed: "I was never very happy supporting it [the war], and sometimes I was hot, and sometimes I was cold, and sometimes I was 'Mr.-Facing-both-ways.' " Some years later the journalist H. L. Mencken captured this facet of Sinclair's personality even more accurately. Writing to Sinclair in 1936, Mencken admitted: "that you have done more or less hollering for free speech, but how much of it did you do during the war, when free speech was most in danger? My recollection is that you actually supported Wilson." Mencken continued: "In political controversy there is such a thing as give-and-take. . . . You are far, far better on the give than on the take. No man in American history has denounced more different people than you have, or in more violent terms, and yet no man that I can recall complains more bitterly when he happens to be hit. Why not stop your caterwauling for a while, and try to play the game according to the rules?" (Sinclair, *My Lifetime in Letters*, 1960, pp. 322, 324).

But Upton Sinclair could not stop "caterwauling," nor could he refrain from rhetorically standing on both sides of a fence and then blaming the fence itself for his awkward position. The nature of the man and his often misdirected quest for a democratic "grail" would allow him to take no other course in life. Despite his egoism, his zealousness, and his torturous self-justifications, there was something admirable about a man so self-confident that he could print with an equal lack of guile the jibes and praises of foes and friends alike. There was something appealing about a man so assured of the innate humanity of other men that he could forgive the very evils he himself uncovered and could look hopefully toward a brighter future. *Upton Sinclair's* not only marked the tensions, frustrations, and inconsistencies of one brand of American socialism during a wartime crisis for socialism around the world, but it displayed as well a revealing chapter in the life of one of America's most representative "radicals."

Madison, Wisconsin, 1969

Good Morning

NEW YORK, 1919-1921

DANIEL AARON

LIKE other magazines impulsively conceived, inadequately financed, and espousing unpopular views, *Good Morning* had a short life. It was not an unhappy one, however, because its contributors and supporters were an unlugubrious set of people whose disenchantment with World War I and the aftermath had not convinced them that Americans would never laugh again.

"Now is the time to start a magazine," Ellis O. Jones, formerly editor of *Life* and one-time passenger on Henry Ford's Peace Ship, announced to a group of rebel artists and writers in 1919. Arthur Henry Young (1866-1943) agreed. Better known by his abbreviated signature, "Art Young," he was one of the artists who helped to found the magazine in that year, and his report of its rise and demise provides the fullest and most authentic account of its short history.

Most of the backers of *Good Morning* had written or drawn from the *Masses* until the government silenced that gaily truculent organ of dissent because of its opposition to the war. Some of them still served on the staff of the *Liberator*, founded in 1918 to sustain somewhat guardedly the cause of revolt. But Young, who with Max Eastman, Floyd Dell, John Reed, and a few others had been twice tried and acquitted under the Espionage Act of 1917, now felt that he and his fellow artists deserved some recompense for their work:

> I had considered it a privilege to draw for the *Liberator*. But a few of us on the staff who had always been ready to contribute for nothing began to feel that it wasn't quite right that engravers, paper dealers, and desk-editors should have their pay or the magazine

would not go on, while those who did the creative work had to forgo compensation. That was and still is a condition accepted by those who contribute to radical magazines which are not self-sustaining. Yet one's individual economic responsibilities sometimes call for a more fruitful arrangement.

Hence he was receptive to the suggestion to "awaken the socialist spirit anew" among the war-weary liberals and radicals and at the same time to earn a little money.

Meeting at Allaire's restaurant, an "old-time hang-out of the literati," the founders discussed possible names for the magazine. Here is Art Young's recollection of the proceedings:

> Then I said, "Why not call it by some familiar name—some name that we hear every day——?"
>
> Ellis chimed in with: "Like 'Good morning, have you used Pear's Soap?' " which was an advertisement long familiar to the public.
>
> "That's it," I said, "Let's make it *Good Morning*." There were no dissenters, and I began to sketch out a top for the editorial page (technically known as a masthead)—with a jovial figure personifying the rising sun as our emblem.

But the organizers still had to raise money—at least $10,000 according to the estimate of a knowledgeable journalist. Art Young, already in his early fifties "and a bit battered and sad to look at in my mirror," was willing to undertake the job of canvassing prospective donors. Both the public and himself, he reasoned, needed "a new hold on life," himself particularly. Three months later, after hard soliciting, he had managed to scrape up less than half of the required amount, but ignoring the warnings of practical advisers, Young and Jones decided to publish the first number without the necessary cash reserves. On May 18, 1919, ten thousand copies of *Good Morning* were quickly sold. It looked as if the editors had won their gamble as congratulatory letters from friends poured in promising support. Five months later it was clear that *Good Morning* would not escape the embarrassments awaiting all such shoestring enterprises.

Art Young, now in charge following the resignation of Ellis Jones, found it harder and harder to raise enough money to pay for paper, office expenses, and distribution costs. And none of the timeworn devices to restore ailing magazines—banquets, dances, and other promotional efforts—succeeded in reversing *Good Morning*'s decline. He could count on some voluntary help, but even with the occasional handouts from friends, it was Young who had to write most of the editorials, supply most of the cartoons, and make up each issue. After October 1919, *Good Morning* faltered, skipped a few numbers, appeared as a semimonthly, and then folded in October 1921. A final effort—a popular antiwar edition issued under the name of the Good Morning Publishing Company—sold well but not enough to encourage continuation.

It was evident, as Art Young wrote later, that he and his associates lacked the "certain hardness" and "pile-driving energy" successful publishing demanded. Yet *Good Morning* deserves a second look not only because it catches the mood of the liberal-radical generation between the collapse of Wilsonian peace hopes and the start of the Harding era, but also because it is a personal monument to one of America's most original cartoonists.

The men who dreamed up a magazine in Allaire's restaurant told each other that "satire and ridicule can be more effective weapons than solemn statistics and shrill denunciations." Lincoln Steffens, fresh from the peace conference at Versailles, agreed. He urged Young to "keep *Good Morning* going. There's nothing to do now but laugh—laugh like Hell!" Certainly the magazine found plenty to laugh at: xenophobes, superpatriots, war-profiteers, labor-fakers, prohibitionists, professional Bolshevik haters, hair-splitting lawyers, *New Republic* liberals, Woodrow Wilson, Mitchell Palmer, Warren G. Harding—everything and everyone, in short, that typified what *Good Morning* called "the chaos of hypocrisy" and "educated stupidity." Names already familiar to readers of the *Masses* and *Liberator* appeared in *Good Morning* (McAllister Coleman, Howard Brubaker, Clement Wood, Edna Millay, Louise Bryant, Robert Minor, William Gropper, Hendrik Van Loon, Alfred Dehn), but what kept it from becoming merely a pale imitation of its predecessors was the graphic wit and humor of Art Young.

He had come a long way since the days when he pilloried the Populists, approved the hanging of the Haymarket anarchists, and vilified Governor John P. Altgeld for pardoning those of them who escaped the noose. When Altgeld died in 1902, Art Young already felt deep misgivings about his earlier views. Eight years later he was a militant Socialist who now refused to draw cartoons in support of ideas he no longer believed in. All the while he had been refining his technique, moving from a style reminiscent of Thomas Nast (whom he had known briefly) to a simpler and more economic one. As his social convictions sharpened, many of his drawings and cartoons became more pointedly and radically political, but he continued to satirize bourgeois fatuities with customary geniality and to temper his indignation with humanity and humor.

Good Morning is loaded with examples of Art Young's most powerful and original work, some of it reprinted from *Puck, Life, Metropolitan*, and *Masses* but much of it new. Introduced for the first time is his cartoon series, "The Wisdom of the Poor Fish," that droopy-headed and goggle-eyed apologist for things as they are, the voice of defeatism and compromise uttering abject platitudes. An unforgettable cover for the May 22, 1919 issue depicts one old bum sprucing up his pal after a night in the park: "Gee Bill, you look like Hell." Bleary-eyed tycoons in "The Prohibition Question" wonderfully register degrees of drunkenness; the swinish guzzler in "The Last Supper" (Young's brutal yet comic per-sonification of capitalism) tilts perilously over an abyss as he satisfies his gluttony. Appearing intermittently are Art Young's impish fantasies, "Post Cards from Hell."

Pervading these and other drawings is a kind of old-fashioned social democracy, suggestive of an earlier egalitarian America, and a covert sympathy for human foibles. Young's plutocrats are usually more ridiculous than evil. If the "Brutal Legalism" of a Mitchell Palmer provokes his rage, the sweating capitalist labeled "Commercial Aristoc-racy" who is digging his own grave does not. The pharisaical Woodrow Wilson who jailed Eugene Debs comes in for some knocks but not the moribund president rejected by his former supporters: "The rabble too have discarded their 'heroes,' " Young remarks, "but they are slower to act about it and more decent."

Not all of Art Young's drawings and jokes in *Good Morning* are political, of course, and his charming animal cartoons, spoofs of modern art, and graphic commentaries on assorted American types indicate the further dimensions of his interests. But at this time he regarded himself primarily as a reformer who proclaimed through his art the message of "Socialized Living" preached by the great reformers from Christ and Plato to the Bolsheviks. His principal subject was "Man under capitalism," a Chaplinesque figure—"tricky, blustering, cowardly, boastful, fawning, generous, pathetic, and ever hopeful.'' This was also Mark Twain's view of ''the damned human race,'' and there is something autochthonously American in Art Young's satire that reminds us of the great humorist whom he so much admired.

He never, however, shared Mark Twain's ferocious pessimism, even during the bleak 1930s when the causes he believed in and defended barely survived. The Art Young who edited *Good Morning*, the hater of cant and cruelty and injustice who tried to reprove and improve his countrymen but no one person in particular (''And who am I to be the monitor of another's actions?'')—was forever casting ''the mantle of charity'' over the victims of his satire. What distinguished *Good Morning* from most of the shriller radical magazines of its own day and later was not its objective, ''the surrender of capitalism,'' but its ebullient tone, its dedication to ''life'' and ''laughter.'' It demonstrated a truth, insufficiently recognized in certain quarters today, that social satire can be mordant without becoming either sour or cantankerous.

Northampton, Massachusetts, 1968

Debs Magazine
CHICAGO, 1921-1923

DANIEL WALDEN

WHEN World War I broke out, most Americans were opposed to the entry of the United States. Within two years, not only had more than $1.5 billion worth of bonds been sold, but "preparedness" had emerged as the wedge by which universal military training entered the scene, and American "neutrality" had become a pejorative term. To some, Kaiserism versus democracy was the question; to others, the perpetuation of wartime prosperity was the issue. According to the U.S. ambassador to England, "Perhaps our going to war is the only way in which our present prominent trade position can be maintained and a panic averted." One month later the United States formally declared war on Germany. A day after the declaration, on April 7, 1917, the Socialist party's convention began to meet in St. Louis.

The convention drafted a resolution declaring the party to be "unalterably opposed to American entrance into war" and affirming the party's opposition "to the system of exploitation and class rule which is upheld and strengthened by military power and sham national patriotism." Specifically, the declaration of war was branded as "a crime against the people of the United States and against the nations of the world." Some two months later, the Espionage Act was passed, making it a crime to speak or otherwise act against the war. Through the ensuing year more than 1,000 men and women were prosecuted and more than 130 were sent to jail. One of the last arrested, on June 16, 1918, after a particularly strong antiwar speech, was Eugene Victor Debs.

Debs, born in 1855, was brought up in Terre Haute, Indiana. Influenced by his Alsatian father's cultured background and antislavery feelings, unblessed by the sanctions of organized religion, his mind developed freely. Quitting high school in 1870, he was soon firing a freight locomotive and a member of the Brotherhood of Firemen and Enginemen. In his mid-twenties he accepted the job of secretary-treasurer of the brotherhood and editor of its journal. In 1885 he was elected to the Indiana state legislature. Seven years later he helped organize the American Railway Union, the pioneer industrial union of all railroad crafts, and led a successful strike. Just a few months later, unfortunately, the Pullman strike was a fiasco. Ever optimistic, Debs wrote: "No strike has ever been lost, and there can be no defeat for the labor movement." Even jail did not dampen his spirit.

Springing back politically, Debs organized the Social Democratic party of America in 1897. Baptized in the roar of conflict, seeing that "in the gleam of every bayonet and the flash of every rifle the class struggle was revealed," he had been ideologically influenced by Edward Bellamy, Laurence Gronlund, Karl Kautsky, Victor Berger, and Karl Marx. Debs referred to Marx as "the incarnation of the spirit of the oppressed, of the downtrodden of all the earth. . . . that great intellect, that towering genius, that colossal man." In turn he then founded the Social Democratic party and in 1901 the Socialist party. Under its banner, committed to the death against the principles of "reactionary trade unionism," he upheld industrial unionism and the class-struggle union. "Everything depends on solidarity," he said in 1925, one year before his death. "Power comes through unity."

Debs' antiwar stand was crystal clear. Deriding the European Socialists who supported the war in 1914 and the American Socialists who followed suit in 1915, he wrote: "I am not opposed to all wars. . . . I refused to obey any command to fight for the ruling class, but I will not wait to be commanded to fight for the working class." In other words, as he put it in Canton, Ohio, in 1918, laying down the gauntlet for the Justice Department agents in the audience, "I may not be able to say all that I think, but I am not going to say anything that I do not think." For, he emphasized, "I would rather a thousand times be a free soul in jail than to be a sycophant and coward on the streets." Opposed to Prussian militarism as well as "the Junkers of the United States," he saw the repressive wave of the future in the "very gentry who are today wrapped up in the American flag, who make the claim that they are the only patriots, who have their magnifying glasses in hand, scanning the country for some evidence of disloyalty, so eager, so ready to apply the brand to the men who dare to whisper opposition to Junker rule in the United States.'' He ended on a challenging note: ''Be true to yourself and you cannot be a traitor to any good cause on earth.''

Indicted for violating the Espionage Act, Debs went on trial early in September 1918. On September 11, affirming his distaste for both violence and the present social system, he reminded the jury that ''In all the history of the world the people have never yet declared a war.'' Indeed, applying his aphorism to the new Soviet state, he noted that the hour had struck for change, the Czar had been overthrown, and though he admitted the Bolsheviks might fail he believed that ''they have written a chapter of glorious history.'' Similarly, at home, he knew that a change was due in the interests of the people: ''American institutions are on trial here before a court of American citizens. The future will tell.''

Unmoved by his plea the jury returned a verdict of guilty as charged. Just before sentence was passed, Debs said: ''. . . while there is a lower class, I am in it; while there is a criminal element, I am of it; while there is a soul in prison, I am not free.'' The judge sentenced him to ten years in prison; the conviction was upheld by the Supreme Court on March 10, 1919, four months after the end of the war. On Palm Sunday he was taken to Moundsville, West Virginia; two months later he was transferred to the federal penitentiary at Atlanta, Georgia. On December 25, 1921, Debs was freed by President Harding. A free man but no longer entitled to the sovereignty of his citizenship, Debs was now a citizen of the world.

As early as 1897, Debs had said: ''I am for Socialism because I am for humanity.'' On that ticket he ran for the presidency five times—in 1900, 1904, 1908, 1912, and from prison in 1920, when he got more than 900,000 votes. Approved by acclamation at the party's 1920 convention, he still maintained his independence by criticizing the party's platform for not putting more stress on industrial organization. At the same time, chiding Victor Berger for red-baiting and others for factionalism, he wrote in *Debs Magazine* in 1922: ''I have known many comrades in all these parties. I have high regard for them. They are as honest as we are.'' Therefore, he added, ''We must stop all this petty wrangling.''

The fact is, as the *Debs Freedom Monthly* put it in August 1921, ''the most important issue today is the immediate and unconditional release of Eugene V. Debs and all political prisoners.'' Given this statement of purpose it was hardly surprising that each issue of that year would demand first ''the release of the political prisoners,'' followed by the demand for a new deal in industry. Through the pages of Irwin St. John Tucker's new journal these themes were reiterated, as were the condition of the hungry, the cause of war, the fate of the black and white oppressed. Some of the articles were a bit fulsome. Judah Magnes' piece, "America's Only Saint" was only one cut above a description of Debs as "America's greatest soul." On the other hand, the bulk of the articles reflected the times and the Socialists' response.

From the first issue in August 1921 the program was clearly delineated. The release of Debs and all political prisoners headed the eight-point list. The other demands related to the restoration of free speech, press, and assembly; collective ownership and democratic ownership of industry; recognition of the Soviet government; opposition to militarism and war; full employment for workers; support of workers in bettering their conditions; and the return of idle lands to the people, with use as the sole criterion. After all, these were the years of the "Red Scare," when "saving the country from the Bolsheviks" meant smashing the unions, the radicals and progressive-minded, and the "foreigners." From the passage of the Espionage Act in June 1917, and the Sedition Act in May 1918, the chase was on. Hostility and revenge were in full supply. In fact, with the entry of the country into the war a wave of antiforeign hysteria swept the nation. Directed at first at minority groups—presumed to be sympathetic to the Central Powers—the venom was soon redirected to the elimination of all those who were in some way against the war. The open-shop campaign nationally and the Supreme Court's antilabor attitude were corollaries. At the same time the split inside the Socialist party, out of which came a pro-Bolshevik wing, made matters worse.

In almost every issue the names of Irwin St. John Tucker and Eugene Debs predominated. Tucker, whose antiwar pamphlet *The Price We Pay* linked American participation in the war with the House of Morgan loans to the Allies, was the editor. Debs was the central source of news, the point of it all, a major contributor who was eventually to be listed on the masthead as chief contributing editor.

Of course, many of Debs' pieces were not written expressly for the *Debs Freedom Monthly*. On the other hand, it was one of the small number of sources where he was printed at all. His Cleveland speech, given just before he went to prison, was run in the September 1921 issue. Speaking candidly, he admitted his opposition to the system. Attempting to "get in touch" with his audience he noted that the ruling class was trying to suppress "the rise of the workers, the peasants, the soldiers, the common man, who for the first time in history said, 'I have made what there is, I produced the wealth; I want to be heard.' " On the race question, consistent with his belief as early as 1908 that this "is not a race question but a class question," he affirmed the rights and opportunities of all peoples. On war he stated succinctly that "They make war; you do not." Pointing out that "they" also make the peace, he commented sarcastically that "They are going to make the world safe for democracy, and that is why I am going to the penitentiary." He ended by reminding his listeners that "We need to get together. . . . The world is against us if we are not for ourselves."

Time and again the plight of the hungry was demonstrated. Very often Debs was used as the model for the argument against political prisoners. Norman Hapgood, for example, once wrote that the case against Debs flowed from the Socialist leader's "theory" that "it is permissible for him to believe all killing wrong and to state his belief." The necessity for this country to understand the Soviet Union was also a subject of prime importance. Debs' "Long Hearted Russia" late in 1921 and Isaac McBride's "Millions Starve in Volga Valley" in 1922 were the prelude. The "Solidarity Number" of May 1922 began a more serious approach to a deep-seated and vexing problem. To support the Russian Revolution without surrendering the American Socialist identity, the workers' unique identity, as Debs put it in the spring of 1922, was the hardest task of all. "Divided the workers will gain nothing. United, the world and all its treasures are theirs."

Meanwhile the great railroad strike of 1922 saw a million men on strike, mine workers gained a partial victory in their struggle, and Jean Longuet (Marx's grandson) spoke with Debs at an International March to Victory banquet in Chicago. And early in 1922, *Debs Freedom Monthly* became *Debs Magazine*, a month after his release from prison, when it became obvious that a change of name and a new statement of aims were due.

Convalescing and writing at home, Debs was faced with momentous decisions. Constantly pressed by his friends, he lashed out once in a while pleading that he was "sick and worn." But once back in harness he announced his decision to remain in the Socialist party; never fond of factions, he refused to attack friends with whom he differed. His article on his imprisonment reminded readers that he had been broken by two years in jail, and that "A prison is an incubator for vice and crime."

Writing for *Debs Magazine*, for the *Liberator, The Appeal to Reason*, and the *New York Call*, he overtaxed himself. Speeches and visits in Chicago, New York, and the University of Wisconsin further depleted his strength. His correspondence and his article writing diminished correspondingly. Then in the fall of 1923, almost overcome by nervous exhaustion, Eugene Debs was forced to return home. *Debs Magazine*, which came into existence as *Debs Freedom Monthly*, collapsed at the same time. As David Karsner put it, it seemed that American socialism had begun with Debs' imprisonment in Woodstock in the 1890s and ended in the Atlanta penitentiary.

Very probably, as one insightful reporter wrote of Debs to Ray Ginger, "With his head he never understood Marx, but with his heart he instinctively felt the answers that the Great Karl pondered and labored and buried in verbiage and statistics." He died in 1926. The work that he did, his belief in people, and his lifelong sincerity and conviction linger on.

University Park, Pennsylvania, 1969

The Modern Quarterly

BALTIMORE AND NEW YORK,

1923-1932, 1938-1940

The Modern Monthly

NEW YORK, 1933-1938

SIDNEY HOOK

IN the history of the American radical movement *The Modern Quarterly* and *The Modern Monthly* together represent one of the major expressions of an independent American revolutionary Marxism. It began almost by accident, as an enterprise of a young man in Baltimore trying to storm his way into the literary world under the slogans of revolt—in politics, economics, culture, and especially sex. It acquired significance by reason of the profound social changes that followed hard on the end of the Prosperity Era. It began to exercise influence by virtue of the writers the magazines attracted as contributors, and especially because of the fierce opposition it evoked from the Communist party and its front organizations.

The career of *The Modern Monthly* and *The Modern Quarterly* cannot be dissociated from that of their editor, V. F. Calverton, who played a rather unique role in crystalizing the development of a radical American intellectual movement whose traditions have outlived both Calverton and his detractors. Calverton achieved whatever success he had not in consequence of his own ideas or personality but by providing a center and rallying point for independent radicals, who, sympathetic at the time to the ideals of a Socialist society, found the Socialist party full of goodwill but too ineffectual, and the Communist party too sectarian and parochial, pistol-whipped by the Kremlin watchmen of orthodoxy into political idiocy. Calverton himself was an entrepreneurial rather than a revolutionary type. He loved the excitement of ideas, caught them on the fly, read widely but not carefully, and was prepared to embrace, or at the very least to give a hearing to any idea that flaunted or outraged the status quo in America. He had a strong journalistic sense and was aware that opposition was more arresting, extremism more attention-getting, than the balanced analysis of the liberals and moderate Socialists of his time —whom he unfailingly and unjustly castigated as the worst supporters of the existing system.

Among the most remarkable features of Calverton, and in part an explanation of his success, were the range of his interests and his complete lack of vanity. They were not altogether unrelated. Whether it was the stage or the cinema, the dance or music, philosophy or science, the social sciences or the sexual sciences, workers' education or the education of children, the black revolution or the revolution of women, Calverton wrote and talked with gusto about them, offering a Marxist sociological interpretation of their changes in form and content.

What he wrote was usually very crude, and expressed in a hurried pedestrian style. Reading him was intellectually painful to the individuals whom he attracted to his magazine. Although they shared his critical social position, they found that he vulgarized Marxist or sociological interpretations, oversimplified issues with breezy generalizations based on a few dubious facts, and ignored logical difficulties. Nonetheless his work was a challenge to them and to others to do more subtly and with more circumspect scholarship the things Calverton tried to do, namely, to relate problems and changes of thought, values, and practice to developments of the social scene, the movements of classes, and the clashes of class struggles. Despite Calverton's crudities, he was at least attempting to apply the dogmas of Marxism, which until then had functioned merely as sterile incantations in the official Communist literature, to the problems and predicaments of the day.

When I speak of Calverton's lack of vanity I refer to the *sangfroid* and apparent goodwill with which he would take criticism. He radiated a willingness to learn that bordered on avidity, a readiness to make concessions that would often disarm criticism and calm intellectual impatience. Most of the time it was not what Calverton himself did and said that was important, but what the individuals, in the wide circle of those whom he enlisted as collaborators, contributed to the pages of his periodicals, or to the almost daily meetings at his home and office.

The result was that Calverton's periodicals and habitat became a kind of open forum for radical debate on all sorts of issues—not only an open but an exciting forum, made all the more important because it was free of party dogma and control. It was the only thing of its kind in the United States. Calverton was free of any tincture of fanaticism. It is a tribute to him that some of the regular attendants at his meetings were not even Socialists, but individuals who enjoyed the argument and the free play of ideas that whirled around him and his guests. One could in the course of a season meet almost every heretical or independent thinker in the radical movement. In the early years, on occasion even Communist party figures like Mike Gold or Joseph Freeman appeared, but this was before the Kremlin ordered a massed offensive against Calverton and other "social-fascists."

The reader interested in *American* radicalism, rather than in the history of radicalism in America, will find in *The Modern Quarterly* and *The Modern Monthly* ideas and points of view that reflect indigenous American social thought, sympathetic to, but not uncritical of Marx, and progressively more critical of the Stalinist Soviet regime and its dominant mythologies. The American Workers party in part emerged from the discussions initiated in its pages. The publications of the Kremlin took note of the contents of these periodicals and often polemicized against them. The influence of *The Modern Monthly* grew until the eve of World War II, which produced a rift between Calverton and his more important contributors. The magazine did not survive Calverton's sudden and premature death.

The odd thing about the campaign launched against Calverton and his periodicals by the Communist party is that it was unprovoked by Calverton. Indeed, from the standpoint of revolutionary politics, Calverton was prepared to accept the leadership of the Communist party, and every political dictum of the Kremlin. All he wanted was to serve in his own way on the cultural front as a spokesman for the Communist cause. All the "important questions of politics" he was willing to leave to Foster and then to Browder. And, indeed, up to 1930, he was a frequent and trusted contributor to the *Daily Worker* and the *New Masses*! What occurred about that time indicates the extent to which purely personal resentment and envy of Calverton's growing reputation as a Marxist critic of life and literature played a role in the judgment of political excommunication against him.

It is difficult for individuals who have not lived through the 1920s and 1930s to recapture the intellectual and cultural mood of those years. In passing, one should warn against the unreliability of the reports of some of the activists of the period. Political autobiography has become a species of historical fiction.

The great watershed, not only in economics and politics but in the intellectual life of the country, was the depression. This became more apparent as the social consequences of the depression developed. Thousands among the professional and intellectual groups of the country began to experience a revulsion against the "system," and not always because their personal fortunes were affected. Among many it was inspired by genuine idealism, and in some by a sense of guilt because of previous unconcern with social and political issues. This gave rise, with various degrees of fatuity, to a great naiveté about what was going on in the Soviet Union. At the very time that the Stalinist terror was getting under way, the concern of American intellectuals was fixed by Soviet propaganda on "a planned and planning society" in which all the evils which seemed endemic to the American economy had disappeared. Walter Duranty's lying dispatches from the Soviet Union had not yet begun to be challenged.

Just as striking as this awareness about the new hope from the East was a kind of fetishism about the words "revolution" and "revolutionary," and a tendency to accept extremist attitudes and doctrines. "Marxism" was in, and it began to crowd out "psychoanalysis" and the new sexual morality among advanced thinkers. The mood of the time was expressed in books (and articles) like Robert Briffault's *Breakdown*, in which it was soberly maintained that when the social revolution came English would have to be abandoned for a new language free from class prejudice.

At the beginning, the minuscule Communist party and movement in the United States did not profit from the disaffection among intellectual and professional groups. The main reason was that it was invisible, torn by factionalism and sectarianism concerning issues that had arisen in Moscow as Stalin moved against the Left and Right Opposition. The representatives of the Communist party, with the exception of some talented artists whose political sophistication was exhausted by sympathy for the underdog, were jargon-ridden, grubby little bureaucrats, with no mass base in industry or the general population, much more anxious to keep their orthodox standing in the Church of the Elect, which worshipped at the altar of History as interpreted by the Encyclicals of the ECCI (the Executive Committee of the Communist International), than to lead movements of social change.

Whatever political talent existed in the Communist movement of the time was found in the opposition movement within its ranks. At the onset, therefore, the great sympathy for the Soviet Union was combined with an almost equally great reluctance to become associated with the intellectual and cultural projects of the Communist party. Those professionals and intellectuals who retained some smidgin of political common sense were bewildered when they became familiar with the bizarre, concrete political programs and slogans of the Communist party. These were formulated for it in Moscow or by the representatives of Moscow on the scene. They were puzzled, for example, by phenomena like Communist advocacy of "self determination for the Black Belt," with the right of secession from the United States, or by the fact that one of the electoral demands of the Communist party in the *mayoralty* campaign for New York was: "Hands off China."

In time, however, the necessity for political faith created its own object and the inanities of the Communist party were overlooked. Since there was no other organization that could provide a realistic political education for those who had become emotionally alienated from the existing system, and who hungered "to do something," even if it was no more than attending meetings, raising money for good causes, or distributing literature, the professionals and intellectuals gradually flocked to the front organizations which the Communist party set up. Whatever doubts they had about the details of politics they gladly surrendered, the better to enjoy the euphoria of their faith. The standard response of the intellectuals to the political inanities and insanities of the Communist party of that time was: "We are not experts about these matters. Who are we to tell Foster what's wrong with dual trade unionism, or contest Stalin's theory that socialists are 'the twins' of fascists, or develop our own ideas about the conquest of political power in America. Our task is to support the political leadership, not to ask questions." These words and others like them were bettered by Kyle Crichton (Robert Forsyth), who spoke for a majority of the members of the League of Professional Groups, a front group established by the Communist party. In the spring of 1933, he replied to criticisms of the Communist party made by Herbert Solow, myself, and others.

Some of the contributors to *The Modern Quarterly* and *The Modern Monthly*, however, were seriously interested in politics, schooled in Marxist theory, and aware of the disastrous consequences of sectarian Communist practice. They tried to influence the thinking of those disillusioned with traditional American politics but who had not yet swallowed whole the new Communist faith. At the outset, even though they were critical of the Soviet Union, they subdued their criticisms of the internal Soviet regime in order to win a hearing among those who had no objections to the social philosophy of communism, which was hardly distinguishable in some versions from socialism, but who had strong objections to the Communist party.

Candor requires me to say that although Calverton opened his pages to the serious critics of the political theory and strategy of communism, his heart was not in such criticism. Had the Communist party continued to collaborate with him, *The Modern Quarterly* would have turned into something else. But it was not to be. There were a few figures in the American Communist party, among whom Joseph Freeman was the most notable, who became at first annoyed and then indignant at the intellectual role Calverton had assumed. It was intolerable to them that someone with such modest talents, who had taken no political risks and whose greatest flair was—so it appeared to them—for self-aggrandizement, should be regarded as the leading Marxist literary critic in America. These men had thrown their lot in with the Communist party in the mid-1920s and had suffered an almost complete isolation from the mainstream of American culture. They felt themselves more gifted than Calverton and more subtle in their interpretations. They were certainly more aware of the political dogmas of the party and the dangers of running afoul of them. They respected and even agreed with some of the political critics of the Communist party, so long as the criticism was only oral and in private. They had lived in the hope that someday, when the myth of permanent American prosperity was exploded, there would be a new birth of revolutionary American culture under *their* leadership. Calverton appeared to them as an interloper, all the more dangerous because of the catholicity of his approach, and because his policy of editorial freedom attracted to his magazine critics and thinkers of national reputation.

There was no question about Calverton's political piety. He was pathetically eager to work out some *modus vivendi* with his scornful Communist critics that would not divest him of his periodicals. But Calverton had become a symbol of the new unorthodox revolutionary approach. His reputation and influence were increasing. He had to be destroyed.

The attempt to destroy Calverton was motivated by the charge that around him, and behind him, were a group of intellectuals interested in organizing their own political party and movement. This would prevent the Communist party from benefiting by the radicalization of the American *intelligentsia*. A new radical political party would also put the Communists on the defensive against the political criticism of independent radical minds who objected vigorously to any attempt to manipulate indigenous American movements of social protest in the interests of the Soviet Union.

The campaign against Calverton was mean and ugly. It opened with an article entitled "The Fascism of V. F. Calverton" in the *Communist*, the official organ of the Communist party, by its titular head, William Z. Foster. Foster was obviously not the author of the article but he signed it in his new role, shortly to be taken over by Browder, of a kind of commissar of Communist cultural affairs. After all, if Stalin could play the part of arbiter in deciding the philosophical and cultural disputes of the Soviet Union, why could not the little brothers of the Comintern emulate the role of Big Brother?

Actually, Foster was unfit for the task both by training and inclination. He was a superb trade-union functionary and a master of organizational detail, with a factory worker's impatient view of theory and theoretical disputes as just so much "hair-splitting." He knew how to organize a strike although he did not have the eloquence to inspire one. I recall a meeting I chaired at which he spoke before some students at New York University. He confessed to me that he would rather dig ditches eight hours a day than deliver a lecture. And as he and the audience suffered through the performance, one could readily believe him. Foster was never more than a tool in the hands of the Kremlin to dislodge a less tractable leadership.

The second attack on Calverton was also delivered in the *Communist* by a party hack, A. Landy, who sought to find a systematic expression of "Social-Fascism" in the rather vague and commonplace Marxist views of Calverton. At most, these views could be faulted for their confusion, which actually stemmed not from Calverton's lack of revolutionary ardor but from its excess. He recognized the difficulties of orthodox Marxism and was quite aware of the fact that modern anthropology had made Morgan's and Engels' simple schemes of social evolution obsolescent. Calverton was not willing, however, to abandon the orthodox Marxist doctrines of the class struggle, historical materialism, and economic development, and he sought to save them by a theory of "cultural compulsives" according to which "the truth" of ideas in the social sciences depended only on the class or vested interests of those who stood to gain political power by the dissemination of these ideas.

Neither Foster's nor Landy's attacks carried much weight outside the Communist party itself. Not only were they inherently absurd, they were unread except by the faithful. But they were sufficient to reinforce Moscow's criticisms of the American Communist party's work on the cultural front. One of the organs of the Communist International, *International Literature*, probably spurred on by A. Trachtenberg, took the *New Masses* to task for not mobilizing radical opinion against Calverton and Eastman.

Nothing loath, the *New Masses* carried out its political assignment. Since its audience was more literate than that of the *Daily Worker* and the *Communist*, it made no attempt to convict Calverton of "fascism," but sought to destroy his personal reputation by charging him with widespread and deliberate plagiarism of other people's ideas. The chief author of the article was David Ramsey (born Hymie Rosen), an untalented youngster whom Calverton had befriended, and who had passed himself off as a Ph.D. in physics victimized by reactionaries at Johns Hopkins. (It was subsequently reported that he had never even earned a bachelor's degree.) All the article established was that some of Calverton's literary habits were sloppy, his quotations sometimes garbled, and that the purpose of the exposure was not the safeguarding of the purity of the American revolutionary movement, but character assassination of someone whose modest literary efforts had been awarded the prize of public attention by the burgeoning radical *Zeitgeist*.

After these attacks Calverton's criticism of the political fatuities of the

American Communist party became outspoken. He joined in a quiet way the American Workers party (which A. J. Muste, head of the Brookwood Labor School, J. B. S. Hardmann of the Amalgamated Clothing Workers, Gerry Allard of the Illinois Progressive Miners Union, James Burnham, and I, among others, had organized), but took no active political role. The influence of *The Modern Monthly* continued to grow. But the influence of the Communist party, especially after the Kremlin ordered it to drop its sectarian Third Period tactics and to break out the colors of the Popular Front, grew much more rapidly. The hypnotic attraction of the Soviet Union and its revolutionary rhetoric was too much for many of Calverton's friends and contributors. An amazing number confessed to him, sometimes orally and sometimes by letter, that now that the Communist party had declared him to be a counterrevolutionary, they could no longer collaborate with him, even though they knew the charge was poppycock. Quite a few whose names appeared in the pages of the periodicals in the early years, after 1934 transferred their talents and allegiances to Communist party front activities.

Towards the end of the 1930s *The Modern Monthly* became more and more the personal organ of Calverton rather than the spokesman of any political group. The *Partisan Review*, which had broken away from Stalinist control, began to attract independent radicals, especially in the universities, who could not swallow the Stalinist line. Its editors had never protested the unconscionable treatment Calverton had received from their erstwhile comrades. They also had a stronger sense of the autonomy of the literary and artistic experience in relation to the political and social conditions under which it found expression.

When World War II broke out, Calverton refused to see it as anything more than a clash of rival imperialisms. Like many others in the Socialist and independent Communist movements, he clung to the view that the militant revolutionary Socialists had taken during World War I: the enemy of the workers was in their own country. Some of us argued that the victory of Hitler and fascism would destroy the possibility of democratic socialism anywhere, whereas their defeat would at least give democrats and Socialists another chance to reform and reconstruct the world. But we were unable to convince Calverton that the attitude of neutralism, justified in World War I, was suicidal in World War II. There was little to choose between the rival imperialisms of World War I, and even the victory of the Central Powers at the time would have had no worse consequences than the victory of the Allied Powers. (The world would at least have been saved the experience both of bolshevism and fascism.) But the victory of Hitler and fascism spelled a new barbarism.

Although Calverton was not convinced, I firmly believe that had he lived until Pearl Harbor, and possibly even before then, he would have followed those of us who urged that Socialists give critical support to the war against fascism. For despite his weakness for large and extreme views, Calverton had a stock of political common sense on which he would draw when the chips were down.

Although his style was sometimes fierce and denunciatory, and although he sought, unsuccessfully, to out-Mencken Mencken, Calverton's personal manner was gentle. He admired many things and people, perhaps too uncritically. Although he engaged widely in polemics, he did not have the heart of a fighter. He never enjoyed a battle, and would go a long way to insure peace. Despite his detractors he was not immodest; he was always eager to learn, sometimes pathetically so. What stands out about him, and dwarfs many of the faults he shared with others, was his generosity of spirit, and his respect for the positive qualities and virtues in those he knew—whether friend or foe.

New York University, 1968

Politics

NEW YORK, 1944-1949

DWIGHT MACDONALD

POLITICS was born toward the end of the hot war against Hitler's Germany and it died soon after the beginning of the cold war against Stalin's Russia. It criticized both wars intemperately, insistently, interminably and, I think, correctly. It began as a "democratic socialist" magazine with a Marxist slant and an antiwar position based on hopes for "Third Camp" popular revolutions after the war—in Europe and Asia; even the editor didn't expect anything to happen here. (See "Why *Politics*?" in the first issue.) It ended disabused of revolutionary hopes, through with Marxism as a guide to radical politics, bored with socialism as irrelevant, or worse, to basic change, and skeptical of the kind of mass democracy most fully developed in the United States and the USSR. (The differences are important, of course, but so are the similarities; too close for comfort; and now there is Mao's China to be uncomfortable about.)

Under the pressure of unexpected events, unexpected to the editor anyway, the magazine's "line," never very firmly anchored, meandered through some exotic country that was not on the Marxist maps he had, more or less, relied on at the start of the trip. The Old Left natives became increasingly restless, muttering their ritual exorcisms: Mere Speculation, Pure Idealism (pejorative in their patois) and, most potent: Petty-Bourgeois Moralizing. But history refused to follow the Marxist script (sabotage?) and the meanderings through the marshlands of anarchism and pacifism became, *faute de mieux*, the mainstream of the magazine. The end of the line: Even the weariest river winds somewhere safe to sea. Or rather to the swamps of petty-bourgeois moralizing—stagnant compared to the dynamic torrent of Marxist doctrine; but much safer.

"It was a time of troubles," I wrote in *Memoirs of a Revolutionist*

(1957), ''the terrible last years of the war, the Nazi death camps and the atomic bombings and then the grey dawn of 'peace' when the reality behind the illusions of the antifascist crusade began to emerge, with Stalin's Russia smoothly taking over the role of Hitler's Germany. All of this demanded attention, reporting, exposure, analysis, satire, indignation, lament.''

It is true that *Politics* was a one-man magazine—I was the sole owner, publisher, editor, and, putting it mildly, the most prolific contributor —but not the whole truth. On the practical side, it was a one-woman magazine: my then wife, Nancy, was business manager, as she had been on *Partisan Review* when I was an editor there from 1938 to 1943. Without her talents and energy, the magazine would have been improbable if not impossible. Her chief assistants should also be mentioned—the business manager is the Unknown Soldier of the little magazine world: Dorothy Brumm for the first three years and after that, seriatim, Bertha Gruner, Anna Matson, and Judy Miller.

Nor was it as much of a one-man show editorially as it looks on the record. The name, for instance, was an inspiration, but not mine. All I could think up were clinkers like *Radical Review* (not knowing it had been used in 1917, and it wasn't much then) and, actually, *New Left*. Then C. Wright Mills, who had just emigrated to the University of Maryland from his native Texas, got in touch with me, or perhaps it was vice versa—we were both looking for trouble—and suggested that since the magazine was to deal with politics why not call it just that? Which I did. (A prime editorial virtue is receptivity to the ideas of others even when they are better than one's own.) It was a perfect name, boldly simple yet complexly connotative, and it looked great in type.

Again for instance, there was the list of possible contributors I drew up when I was planning the magazine in the fall of 1943, after I'd resigned from *Partisan Review* because the disagreement on the war had become paralyzingly acute between me and the other two active editors, Philip Rahv and William Phillips. It was not an inspiring list. Almost all the names I could think of—or rather we, for, like Mills, others were involved, no editor is an island entire of itself—were the familiar ones of the Old Left, anti-Stalinist section. All good men, honorable men, and sound politically. Maybe too sound—was it worth all that trouble to get out another edition of so well-established a text?

We needn't have worried. Few on the list ever wrote for the magazine, or were asked to—mutual suspicions flared up at once, well-founded on both sides—and as soon as the magazine began to appear, unforeseen writers came forward. Of the eight most copious contributors—five or more articles—only Paul Goodman belonged to the Old Left, and he was a member in bad standing because of anarchistic deviations. He was also the only American—myself always excluded from these tabulations —the seven others being the late Andrea Caffi ("European"), Nicola Chiaromonte, Lewis Coser ("Louis Clair"), the late Peter Gutman ("Peter Meyer"), the late Victor Serge, Nicolo Tucci, and George Woodcock. (By nationality: Russian-Italian, Italian, German, Czech, Russian, Italian and English.) A curious and perhaps significant fact, when one considers that the three major articles which made the most impression at the time, and are still best remembered—again excluding my own—were by Europeans: Bruno Bettelheim's "Behavior in Extreme Situations," Albert Camus' "Neither Victims nor Executioners," and Simone Weil's "The Iliad, or the Poem of Force."

There were some memorable articles by Americans, of course—Paul Goodman wrote three or four, and there were perhaps a dozen others, including pieces by James Agee, Daniel Bell, John Berryman, Robert Duncan, Conrad Lynn, C. Wright Mills, Meyer Schapiro, and George Schuyler—but in general *Politics* was, as they say in the movie world, a co-production. Mostly an Italian-American co-production, the American being me and the Italian being my dear friend, Chiaromonte, who was a close collaborator from the beginning as contributor, adviser and talent scout: he got his friend, Caffi, to contribute from Paris (Bobbs-Merrill is bringing out a volume of Caffi's essays shortly); he brought in Tucci, just resigned from the Italian embassy in Washington, who did a regular column, "Commonnonsense," making fun of practically everything in the highest style and spirits; he discovered Weil's "Iliad" in the wartime *Cahiers du Sud*; and through him I met Constantine Nivola, who did three handsome covers (January and July 1945, and November 1946).

The first issue sold out 3,000 copies so quickly that we ventured to reprint (and expensively reset; we'd forgotten to ask the printer to hold the type) another 2,000, which were also sold. We had underestimated the novelty appeal of any Vol. 1, No. 1, also the journalistic vacuum caused by the liberal press's giving up on serious criticism of the war and of Stalin's Russia, as embarrassing an ally for Roosevelt's crusade for the

Four Freedoms (*from* want, *of* speech, and . . . what were the other two?) as Czarist Russia had been for Wilson in his Promethean struggle To Make The World Safe For Democracy. Maybe we should swear off Crusades and just let everything slide.

By 1945 the magazine had reached a circulation of 5,000, about evenly divided between subscriptions and newsstand sales, and there it stuck, pretty much until the end. The deficits averaged $2,000 a year. They were met partly out of my savings from six years on *Fortune*, mostly from a trust fund of Nancy's. The range was from a low of $958 in 1945 to almost $6,000, which was three times as much as we could afford to lose. Our printing costs had doubled in four years, mostly because of the wage increases the powerful New York printing unions had won. As a friend of the working class, I couldn't object. But as a publisher, I couldn't continue.

By current standards of Left journalism, 5,000 isn't much. But that was way back in the cottage-industry period, before dissent was taken up by the mass media and rationalized, in the Weberian sense, into a mutually profitable industry. There wasn't much coverage of the Left, or its journals, in the daily press, no "take-outs" in the news-magazines, very little "in-depth" reportage in the monthlies and weeklies, and no TV interviews or panels, in fact no TV. But even in those primitive, pre-electronic, days, when Marshall McLuhan was just another contributor of *Politics*, even then, 5,000 wasn't brilliant. Not even if the paying customers are multiplied by five—or should it be ten?—to account for all the old *Politics* readers I've met in the last twenty years. I sometimes think there must have been an underground railroad of free loaders which circulated each copy until it disintegrated in the hands of the eighty-fifth reader somewhere in Nepal.

But whatever the total readership, paid and unpaid, it was more than enough for my purposes, which were to write to and hear from my peers. It was a lively, responsive, irritable and articulate audience, mostly male (81 percent), college graduates (90 percent), urban (66 percent lived in cities of over 100,000). They were also young: 65 percent were under thirty-five; 22 percent were students and another 22 percent, symmetrically, were in the armed forces. (There was never any trouble getting the magazine to the latter, by the way, nor, as far as I know, any military censorship.) They wrote a lot of letters-to-the-editor, more than I could answer—5,000 is really too big a circulation for a serious magazine. Many of them I printed, especially the unfavorable ones: the Letters column still is lively reading.

The first aim stated in the editorial program outlined in the first issue was "to create a center of consciousness on the Left, welcoming all varieties of radical thought." The center wasn't achieved but variety was. My editorial "formula" was to have none. I tried to judge manuscripts not by whether their politics agreed with mine but by how well they made their points: the quality of the style, logic, and research.

Finally, I tried to stick to a rule of thumb in political criticism: that the policies of governments should be judged by their effects and not by the reasons advanced to justify them. And to apply the rule to "us" as well as to "them," whether it was their bombings of Polish, Dutch, and English cities or our far more extensive aerial massacres—something like ten to one in tonnage of bombs dropped—of the civilians of Hamburg, Berlin, Dresden, Tokyo, Hiroshima, Nagasaki, and other "enemy" cities; or the tacit collaboration between the *Reichswehr*, definitely theirs, and the Red Army (ours? theirs?) in destroying the Polish resistance fighters in Warsaw (see October, November, December 1944, and March 1945); or the open collaboration between Churchill's "us" and Stalin's "us-them" at Teheran and Yalta in the incorporation of Eastern Europe into the Soviet empire. For the ultimate collaboration between "them" and "us" see "The Jews, the *New Leader* and Old Judge Hull" (January 1945), which describes one of the few operations our State Department has carried out efficiently: the long, determined, and finally successful maneuvers of Assistant Secretary Breckenridge Long—to whom Hull, and Roosevelt, had entrusted the handling of the Jewish refugee "problem"—and other high officials in State to deny refuge to the Jews of Europe in the early war years before the death camps began to operate, when a great many could have been saved had Mr. Long—and his superiors—not deliberately blocked the door of American sanctuary.

New York City, 1969

Hannah Arendt writes of *Politics*:

When I was asked to write a brief note on *Politics* I was tempted to yield to the rather pleasant melancholy of "once upon a time" and to indulge in the nostalgic contemplation that seems to be the appropriate mood for all recollection. Now that I have carefully reread the forty-two issues which appeared from 1944 to 1949—more carefully, I am sure, than I read them more than twenty years ago—this mood has vanished for the simple reason that so many of its articles, comments, and factual reports read as though they were written today or yesterday or yesteryear, except that the concerns and perplexities of a little magazine with a peak circulation of something over 5,000 have become the daily bread of newspapers and periodicals with mass circulation. For the issues, far from being outdated, let alone resolved, by the enormous changes in our everyday world, have only increased in urgency.

This is true for draft card burning, black power (then called "Negroism"), and mass culture; for the military and political futility of "massacre by bombing"; for the military-industrial complex (a "permanent War Economy" was proposed in January 1944 by Charles E. Wilson, then head of the War Production Board, and the atomic bomb was hailed by Harry Truman as "the greatest achievement of the combined efforts of science, industry, labor and the military in all history"); for the breakdown of democratic processes in the democracies (England and the United States); and it is, of course, true for the Cold War which, however, in its beginning "reflected a genuine horror at Russia's record in Europe" (George Woodcock) and was not merely the result of big-power politics. It is especially true for issues that lay dormant for long years, such as the question of responsibility for the horror of Nazi death camps, which came to the fore only much later, in the late 1950s with the new series of war crime trials that culminated in the Eichmann trial in Jerusalem, or for the restoration of the status quo in Europe after the liberation from Nazi occupation. The series of articles on Greece, beginning in January 1945, and running through the whole year, is still an excellent introduction to what happened in that country in 1967. For it seems that only now are we beginning to pay the full price for the annihilation of all European underground movements against fascism and Nazism, which succeeded because it was one of the very few items on which the Allied powers wholeheartedly agreed.

The half-forgotten tragedy of Warsaw, which the magazine followed with such close and moving attention during the two months when Polish resistance fighters rose up against the German *Wehrmacht*, only to be promptly betrayed by the Red Army and finally massacred by the Nazis, was no less a condition for ruling East Europe than the defeats of the French, Italian, and Greek underground movements were for turning the clock back in the West to political regimes whose bankruptcy had been among the most effective causes not, perhaps, of the rise of Hitler but certainly for his conquest of Europe. As Nicolo Tucci said in November 1944: the victors' "job is that of transforming . . . a place of terror and hope into a place without terror and without hope."

I have picked my examples of the magazine's astounding relevance for contemporary political matters almost at random; in fact, there are only two issues of major importance today of which I can find no trace in its back numbers— the rapid disintegration of the big cities and the alarming rise of "invisible government." It has been said of the old *Masses* (1911-1917)—the only magazine I know which bears a certain resemblance to *Politics* and fulfilled a similar function thirty years earlier—that it "seems to have been written in anticipation of a cosmic event which never occurred and in blessed unawareness of the one that did." But whether or not it was "History which destroyed [the *Masses* editors'] frame of reference and made the objects of their concern seem fanciful and unreal," the point of the matter is that the exact opposite is true for *Politics*.

Leaving history aside, which of course may well have had its hand in the matter, praise is due exclusively to the editor of this one-man magazine, to his extraordinary flair for significant fact and significant thought, from which followed his flair in the choice of contributors. It is one thing to announce that one wants "to print work by younger relatively unknown American intellectuals" and by even less known "leftist refugees," and another to find those who twenty years later will be very well known indeed. Dwight Macdonald's discovery of Simone Weil is the most striking instance; but who then knew the names of Victor Serge, C. Wright Mills, Nicolo Tucci, Nicola Chiaromonte, Albert Camus, or Bruno Bettelheim? For if this was a one-man magazine, it never was the magazine of one man's opinion, not only because of the great generosity and hospitality which made it possible for many voices and viewpoints to have their say but, more importantly, because the editor himself never was a one-opinion man or, perhaps, had ceased to be opinionated when he felt the need to have a magazine of his own.

That Macdonald "is continually changing his mind" (James Farrell) is well known, but what is perhaps less recognized is that this is among his virtues. No one, of course, who is willing to listen to reason and to reality can help changing his mind, but most of us do this imperceptibly, hardly being aware of our changes, whereas Macdonald in a veritable furor of intellectual integrity and moral honesty sets out to hunt down his "mistakes," without ever changing the record in the slightest, his technique being to annotate his earlier articles with refutations of himself. God knows, this is something much more noble than "flexibility."

Politics always prided itself on being radical, which—following a remark of the young Marx—means "to grasp the matter by the root." In line with this aim, stated in the first issue, the editor began to free himself of all formulas—"my 'formula' being to have none," as he put it later—more specifically, of the Marxist formula with its faith in History and Progress. When this process of liberation was completed, after the bombing of Hiroshima, which occurred at the end of the magazine's second year of existence, he set out for the discovery of new roots in the realm of theory, on the one hand new "Ancestors" such as William Godwin, Proudhon, Bakunin, Alexander Herzen, Tolstoi, etc., and "New Roads in Politics" on the other. The new post-Marxian mood—all contributors were former Marxists—was strongly anarchist and pacifist, and its most important contribution was Macdonald's own series of articles, later published as a book, *The Root is Man*. The new creed, if such it was, consisted of a radical humanism for which man was not merely the root, the origin of all political issues, but the ultimate goal of all politics and the only valid standard of judgment to be applied to all political matters.

I personally think that these attempts at arriving at a new political theory have worn less well than comments and reports, but who could not be struck by the fact that this mood of a few lost writers on the Left of twenty years ago today has become the dominant mood of a whole generation firmly convinced in word and deed that "all the genuine problems are moral in nature"—as David Bazelon critically remarked about the New Roads writers with respect to socialism. Radical *humanism* obviously does not follow from being radical, from grasping the matter by the root; like every 'ism it could even stand in the way of being radical, that is, it could prevent looking for the root in every matter as it presents itself. After a few years experience, Macdonald reformulated his first program and now, in 1946, wished to do no more than "to seek out the long-range trends in the welter of daily phenomena." In this context, the word radical assumes a different meaning. It now points to the fearless, unbiased search for those facts in everyday affairs that contain the roots for future developments. In this respect, *Politics'* radical record is admirable; it was indeed so close to the future that the whole enterprise often looks like a premature dress rehearsal.

In order to avoid misunderstandings, especially by Marxists or former Marxists who equate political intelligence with prophetic powers, I hasten to admit that Macdonald's batting average for short-time predictions was not too good—a failing he shared with Karl Marx who, around 1858, was afraid lest *Das Kapital* not be finished before the outbreak of the revolution. Most of these "mistakes" were irrelevant—for instance, his belief in 1944 that the liquidation of the British Empire was "remote." Some were more serious, especially his failure to understand the complex nature of World War II which to him, as to the entire American Left, was simply an "imperialist" war. But this estimate belongs still to his preradical, ideological leftist period, and the chief reasons why he did not revise it after his break with Marxism was his new turn to pacifism, in addition to his conviction that "the Soviet System was an even greater threat to what I believe in than Nazism was," a very debatable statement because it identified the Soviet System with bolshevism (Lenin's one-party dictatorship) and bolshevism with Stalinism. Macdonald was clearly wrong when he wrote, three months before Hiroshima, "To say that civilization cannot survive another such war is a truism; the question is whether it can survive this one."

The German "economic miracle," the rapid recovery of Japan, the rebuilding of Russia after Stalin's death have all demonstrated that *up to a point* the modern means of production function nowhere better than where the modern means of destruction have first created a kind of *tabula rasa*—provided that the population of the country is sufficiently "modern" and that the production process is not obstructed by the perverse power considerations of a totalitarian dictatorship. (Today it is England, hardly touched by destruction in the war in comparison with Germany, but profoundly unwilling to change her old ways of life, whose fate is in the balance.) And subsequent events proved Macdonald equally wrong when, under the direct impact of Hiroshima, he thought, "We Americans are coming to be hated with an intensity formerly reserved for the Germans." It is, I think, fair to say that, although he once mentioned "the German atrocities in this war [as] a phenomenon unique at least in modern history," he underestimated throughout the horror as well as the outrage inspired by the Nazi extermination factories.

What in retrospect is so remarkable about all this is not the mistakes but, on the contrary, in spite of them and sometimes even because of them, the fact that he could be so uncannily right in detecting "the long-range trends." It may have been a mistake to be against World War II (except on religious grounds, which are always valid because they are non-political); but did not the end of the war, the dropping of atomic bombs on Hiroshima and Nagasaki, give justification to his misgivings? With the development of nuclear weapons, has not modern warfare indeed begun to threaten with extinction not only civilizations but mankind? And though it was clearly premature in 1945 to fear that Americans would be hated like Germans, it was as though somebody cried 'Wolf' when the animal was still so many miles away that no one even believed in its existence. But when twenty-two years later the animal has arrived and Macdonald can write with entire justification, and in words befitting the genuine patriot he is and always has been, "In the last two years, for the first time in my life, I'm ashamed to be an American," then one can only admire the political instinct of this citizen of the Republic who, albeit without being fully aware of it, sensed in Mr. Truman's outrageous jubilation about the Bomb a decisive departure from that "decent respect to the opinions of mankind," which is, as it were, built into the very foundations of this Republic.

Politics, then, which counted so many non-Americans among its contributors, was radical in the sense of going back and reviving much that belongs to the very roots of the American tradition as well as much that belong to the roots of the radical tradition everywhere—the tradition of nay-saying and independence, of cheerful "negativism" when confronted with the temptation of *Realpolitik*, and of self-confidence: pride and trust in one's own judgment. These qualities distinguish the radical, who always remains true to reality in his search for the root of the matter, from the extremist, who singlemindedly follows the logic of whatever "cause" he may espouse at the moment.

In *Politics*, this closeness to reality proved itself, simply and spectacularly, when the magazine decided to embark upon the package project to the liberated countries at the close of the war. Here, the editor wrote, was "something which those who have criticized the magazine's 'negativism' must admit is positive and constructive.'' I suspect he wrote this sentence with tongue in cheek, unaware of how literally right he was. Who in Europe at this time would have believed that there existed such a thing as ''international fraternity,'' to which Macdonald appealed, after the fierce political infighting on the Left? (In order to be helped at all you had to belong to some party or, at least, to some splinter group.) But here was a small, independent journal, and its appeal to its readers was such a success that ''sometimes it seems that *Politics* is a house organ for the package project rather than a magazine of its own.'' It was just solidarity with those who had suffered, and nothing else.

It is this radical mentality as such that has remained alive in these pages rather than theories or prophecies, which, right or wrong, are lamentably irrelevant in the long run because no prediction can ever really anticipate, and no theory really fit, what will be once it has happened. This attitude can be tested on almost every page of *Politics*, and especially on those where phenomena are presented and analyzed which have no place in the leftist frame of reference. Thus, Macdonald understands that ''just as war releases the productive energy of industry from the bonds of property and profit, so it also allows expression to some very fine traits of human nature which have little outlet in peacetime society.'' And while, after having left the Trotskyists, he still believed in ''the yardstick of basic values'' with which ''to measure month-to-month developments''—all he had left after parting with Marxism—he soon was fearless enough to admit that this yardstick was no less suspect than the verities of the Left, ''that our ethical code is no longer *experienced*, but is simply assumed, so that it becomes a collection of mere platitudes.''

It was against this sensitivity for the long range, that is, for the crucial issues ''in the welter of daily phenomena,'' which enabled him to raise the ''moral'' question in our present political predicaments so early—the question of ''How may we tell Good from Evil?'' The crucial, always hidden in the complicated and complex welter of appearances, is simple and, once discovered, painfully obvious. Nothing is rarer and more precious than the ability to hit upon it. *Politics'* marksmanship in such matters was very high, not merely among the writers, the editor and his contributors, but also among its readers. It was a sergeant, stationed in Germany in 1945, who said, ''In modern wars there are crimes not criminals. In modern society there is evil but there is no devil.'' And what could go more directly to the heart of the matter than Mary McCarthy's remark, after the assassination of Gandhi, about political murder in our time: "It is Gandhi who can be killed or Trotski or Tresca, men *integri vitae scelerisque puri*, while Stalin remains invulnerable to the assassin's bullet"; or Dwight Macdonald's word at the same occasion, perhaps the most fitting epitaph of the man and certainly to be inscribed into the hearts of all true lovers of equality: "He seems to have regarded the capitalist as well as the garbage-man as his social equal."

Politics lasted six years, three as a monthly, one as a bimonthly, and two as a quarterly. It died in 1949 of "the gray dawn of peace," of a time "without terror and without hope." What now came was the political apathy of the 1950s, the arrival of "the silent generation," whose imminence Macdonald must have already felt early in 1948 when he began "feeling stale, tired, disheartened and, if you like, demoralized." This end is not without tragic overtones. The man who had chosen "politics," this "most unpopular term," to name his magazine, with the intention to restore to it its ancient dignity, gave up in despair of politics rather than *Politics*. The silent generation, in due time, gave way to the civil rights movement, but the period of a deceptive calm took its definite end only with the assassination of Kennedy. Nearly five years later, *Politics* has found no successor—except, perhaps, *Ramparts*.

While it existed, it was less a one-man magazine than a one-man institution, providing a focal point for many who would no longer fit into any party or group. The feeling of companionship among its readers had something almost embarrassingly personal about it, and it was precisely this personal note that inspired confidence, not in the rightness of any opinions so much as in the reliability of those who wrote for it. Something of this atmosphere is still alive in the extensive letters-to-the-editor columns, many of them attacking and all of them carefully answered, sometimes at considerable length. Among the things that made this magazine an institution—and I think a unique one—was that Macdonald regarded his readers, if he cared to print them at all, as his intellectual equals.

New York, 1968

In Fact

NEW YORK, 1940-1950

ROBERT SOBEL

IN FACT was the next-to-last major experiment in personal journalism in the serious press, and its creator, George Seldes, was one of the few remaining "crusading journalists" of the period between World War I and World War II. Only *I. F. Stone's Weekly* outlasted it in this school of journalism, which Seldes has called more in the tradition of "press newsletter" than newspaper or magazine. Both Seldes and Stone were adept at uncovering obscure stories, exposing corruption and conspiracies, and challenging the morals and abilities of newsmen and editors on other larger and more popular journals. Seldes, in his prime in the 1930s and 1940s, reveled in sensational disclosures and did not mind being characterized as more a prosecutor than an impartial judge.

In Fact did not offer balanced analysis or impartial judgments; it was clearly biased, and Seldes never attempted to mask these biases. It was written with a definite audience in mind, and one such group did exist in 1940, when the first issue of the press newsletter was printed. The readership declined late in the decade, and as new issues cropped up and a new reform movement appeared—a movement more subtle than the old—interest flagged in what Seldes had to say. The last issue of *In Fact* appeared in 1950. In his farewell editorial, Seldes remarked "Our Enemy is Fascism" and concluded "The Curse is Apathy." To most of his readers, however, the enemy was no longer fascism but communism, and Seldes' problem was his inability to interest a new generation in old problems.

Seldes was born in 1890, grew up in the reform tradition of progressivism, and for the rest of his career considered monopoly, Wall Street, and "the interests" as the enemy of American progress. The rhetoric of progressivism placed the people on the side of righteousness and the plutocrats on the side of the devil; although in practice many progressive leaders were subtle and even devious, their words offered dualism and hopes of utopia. Young men like Seldes would, for the rest of their lives, fight evil and protect the innocent, crusade against injustice and expose the malefactors, without ever seriously considering the complexities of life, the intertwining of good and evil, their own limitations insofar as impartial analysis was concerned, and the possibility that they were often doing more harm than good. Like others of his generation, Seldes sought causes worthy of his lance and, when he found them, he fought hard and long. In his autobiography, aptly entitled *Never Tire of Protesting* (New York: Lyle Stuart, 1968), Seldes wrote of his joy during the Spanish Civil War: "It seemed that everything evil in the world was on one side, and all the opposites on the other. For once in history, for one people at least . . . there was something fine and noble burning in the eyes of everyone and audible in the shouts of *pan y liberdad* (bread and liberty) which filled the streets of beleaguered Madrid." Seldes lost his job with Hearst through his partisanship for the republican cause and his opposition to Franco, whom the Hearst publications supported. But this was all right; he had gone down in a good cause—and with glory.

In the late 1930s, Seldes sought a proper medium for his expressions. For a short time it seemed that *Ken—the Insider's World*, an exposé magazine started and controlled by *Esquire*, might be the answer. Seldes wrote articles for *Ken* about the American Legion's connections with big business. When they were printed the pieces drew sharp opposition. The magazine folded soon after, as a result—according to Seldes—of pressures from "the Morgan interests" which threatened to boycott *Esquire* unless *Ken* either changed its tune or was eliminated. As was typical in such cases, Seldes charged big business with having vast powers over every aspect of American life, and this attitude was usually behind Seldes' several failures.

A new venture, a slick weekly known as *Friday*, also failed, and once again "lack of advertising," presumably from big business eager to crush a critic, was the cause.

Early in 1940 Seldes and Bruce Minton decided to found their own magazine. The two men and several friends would put up approximately $500 apiece; Seldes thought that with $3,000 he could put out several issues of a four-page newsletter. A partner offered to sell subscriptions to

American Federation of Labor and Congress of Industrial Organizations union locals, and Seldes wrote the prospectus, in which he called *In Fact* "a fortnightly publication of facts, news and exposes," written—as the first issue indicated—"for the millions who want a free press."

Volume I, No. 1, appeared on May 20, 1940. In it were stories attacking the Associated Press for being anti-Negro, the *New York Times* for being pro-British, big business for attempting to draw America into World War II, and the Catholic Church for a variety of reasons. This set the stage for the next decade. Seldes had a wide range of interests, and with the aid of his friends was able to cover a great deal of territory. For example, he was the first writer to expose the connections between cigarette smoking and lung cancer, and the attempts on the part of tobacco companies to keep the news out of the papers. His major concerns, however, were two: the power of the Catholic Church and its alleged drive to bring fascism to America, and the corruption of the American press. Scarcely an issue went by without a major blast at either the newspapers or the Church.

In Fact got off to a shaky start, but subscriptions picked up and within a few issues the publication appeared to be successful. But now Seldes and cofounder Bruce Minton began to quarrel. Seldes insisted on criticizing all political groupings, while Minton hoped *In Fact* would become a more pro-Communist publication. Seldes won the struggle, and Minton left after the eleventh issue. Less than five years later it was learned that Minton had been a secret member of the Communist party. An attempt was made to smear Seldes, but accusations of his having Communist leanings fell flat.

At its height *In Fact* had 176,000 subscribers. Then, in 1948, subscriptions and renewals began to fall off. Seldes had always boasted of the loyalty of his readers, noting that most were trade-union members, liberals, and people aware of the dangers to themselves and democracy from "the interests." According to him, the journal declined as a result of attacks from both Left and Right. He refused to join the pro-Soviet American Council on Soviet Relations, and with his refusal the left-wing crusade against *In Fact* picked up momentum. Then the FBI began an undercover campaign against the journal and Seldes accused the FBI of monitoring his mailing list. By 1950 there were only 56,000 subscribers, and Seldes was able to continue publishing only by using the profits from the sale of his many books. Finally, on October 2, he was forced to admit financial pressures had done him in, and *In Fact* ceased publication. Notwithstanding the fact that pressures had always existed in publication, and that such a newsletter was bound to receive more than its share of them, Seldes' judgment regarding the falling off in subscriptions was probably inaccurate. After all, *I. F. Stone's Weekly*, similar to *In Fact* both in political leaning and format, existed for a longer time than Seldes' organ. This is so because Stone, unlike Seldes, was able to adjust to new conditions and isolate new issues, thus maintaining reader interest and a reason for existence. Toward the end, Seldes continued to play upon his twin themes of Catholic power and big-business control of the press. These were important issues in the early 1940s, when *In Fact* was at the height of its circulation and influence. Social injustice, the problems of the depression, the antifascist crusade, and the power of the interests, seemed old-fashioned and not relevant after 1948. The signs were there for all to see. The beginning of the Cold War, the rapprochement with Germany and Japan, the ability of the economy to maintain itself after the war and not lapse back into a depression as many social critics of capitalism thought it would, and the isolation of communism, and not Catholicism, as the major danger to the American Left, were facts of life Seldes either did not perceive or to which he could not or would not adjust.

By 1948 he appeared more a relic and fossil than a vital newsman. In much the same way as Henry Wallace failed to capture the nation's imagination by recalling the spirit of the 1930s and the world war's crusade against fascism in that year's presidential election, so George Seldes was unable to maintain his readership by breaking lances against enemies of the past. Others mounted more effective campaigns against McCarthyism, racism, and related problems. The world was a far more complex place in 1950 than it had been a decade earlier; it was more difficult to tell the "good guys" from the "bad guys" in the Cold War than during the Spanish Civil War. Seldes' audience realized it even though he did not, and so his influence declined. With the passing of *In Fact* there ended a glorious, well-intentioned, crusading, and often effective chapter in the history of American journalism.

Hempstead, New York, 1969

I. F. Stone's Weekly

WASHINGTON, 1953-1971

DONALD J. MURPHY

I. F. Stone's Weekly first appeared in January 1953, when the Cold War abroad and McCarthyism at home were luridly changing the American intellectual and political climate from that known by the activist generations of the 1930s and 1940s. I. F. Stone as an editor was both an enthusiast for and observer of the crusades of the independent Left in America during a period that seemed to end despairingly with the defeat of Henry Wallace in 1948. With his new journal, Stone waged intellectual guerrilla warfare throughout the 1950s against the ascendant Cold Warriors, political witch-hunters, and their assorted bureaucratic allies. Even before he launched his *Weekly*, he had taken aim at the strident Cold War policy of Truman and Acheson, and at the domestic Red Scare they were encouraging, without completely controlling.

From the vantage point of the early 1970s, the most striking aspect of the first decade of *I. F. Stone's Weekly* was the editor's prescient understanding that Cold War diplomacy and McCarthyism were not aberrant, temporary trends, but mutually reinforcing developments. Stone noted that the Cold War provided momentum for the spread of the Truman administration's "containment" policy from Europe to Asia; under Eisenhower, John Foster Dulles extended the strategy of United States policemanship into the Middle East. As the global anti-Communist policy continued, and the Communist bloc frequently hardened its own diplomatic positions, new American military strategies—such as "tactical" nuclear war, "sharing" nuclear weapons, and various scenarios based on the new ICBM—heightened the arms race, deadlocked negotiations, and increased tension. The Cold War policies of Dulles and the Pentagon, based on the myth of a monolithic Communist conspiracy abroad, furthered the political witch-hunts at home. Stone, unlike many liberals committed to or ambivalent about the Cold War, assailed not only the menace of Senator Joseph McCarthy, but also consistently exposed the broader and more significant threat to constitutional rights from other congressional and state inquisitors, the FBI, and the Eisenhower administration's loyalty-security program. McCarthyism, he argued, was a national plague, with its origins in the Manichean approach to the Communist world. Such were the major themes of *I. F. Stone's Weekly* in the 1950s.

Born in Philadelphia in 1907 of Jewish parents, I. F. Stone (Israel Feinstein) began working for newspapers in Philadelphia and nearby New Jersey towns while still in his teens. In the course of a journalistic career that included periods with the New York *Post* and Philadelphia *Record* in the 1930s, *The Nation* in the 1930s and 1940s, and a variety of small liberal and radical New York journals like *PM*, the New York *Star*, and the New York *Daily Compass* in the 1940s and early 1950s, Stone managed to do ". . . everything on a newspaper except run a linotype machine." The independent spirit that would later shape *I. F. Stone's Weekly* was already apparent in the youthful journalist; by the early 1930s he had dropped out of the University of Pennsylvania and Norman Thomas' Socialist party. Neither an academic career, which he anticipated would be too stifling, nor Socialist party politics, which he found too sectarian, satisfied his quest for intellectual freedom and relevance. The decision to found an independent paper of his own in the early 1950s expressed this same "come-outer" nonconformism. Stone acknowledged one important model of independent, shoestring, radical journalism influencing the style and format of his own paper. George Seldes' *In Fact*, a four-page tabloid like Stone's, briefly succeeded during the late 1930s and early 1940s as an experiment in committed journalism, until Seldes defended Tito against Stalin and consequently lost his financial support from left-wing unions and organizations.

Whatever his objections to the universities and left-wing politics, Stone had a much more fundamental argument with the "Lords of the Press." Although he believed that freedom of the press still operated in American society, even during the worst days of McCarthyism, he attacked the atrophy and moral timidity of the big American dailies and other bulwarks of establishment journalism. From his long experience as

a reporter, Stone concluded that the "communications industries"—most obviously TV and radio, but also the press—communicate
"very little news." Reporters in Washington for the larger dailies and
wire service groups, he contended, were frequently manipulated or
co-opted by the government agencies they were assigned to cover. In
capitalist America, their employers, the publishers, were most concerned
with selling; hence, advertising overshadowed news and opinion. Except
for a few newspapers, like the *New York Times*, the press carried surprisingly little news; moreover, it was also timid in editorial opinions. Where
it was emboldened to take an occasional stand, as some of the big papers
did on behalf of civil liberties, it did not go beyond this to question the
arms race and the Cold War. "Most U. S. papers stand for nothing. They
carry prefabricated news, prefabricated opinion, and prefabricated cartoons," Stone complained.

In his four-page mini-journal, I. F. Stone sought with remarkable
success to isolate and report relevant news overlooked or slighted by the
big papers. For news, he ". . . tried to dig the truths out of [published
government] hearings, official transcripts, and government documents."
At this art he might have surpassed in skill all the American "muckrak-
ers" of this century. Stone also gave his *Weekly* a clear, committed,
independent, and radical perspective. The journal, at least in the early
1950s, found its readers among subscribers of the dissenting New York
newspapers that Stone had previously worked. Its circulation grew from
5,000 in 1953 to 20,000 ten years later. With the onset of massive
American intervention in Indochina, Stone's reputation as a journalistic
prophet of that calamity significantly increased his readership and gave
his views a wider national impact, especially among American intellectuals.

The fundamental insight that America's post-1945 anti-Communist
foreign policy created and sustained a government apparatus and ideology for choking off dissent—"McCarthyism" in a word—was the most
significant theme of *I. F. Stone's Weekly* in its first years. Stone's
concern with the links of war and repression was continued down through
the Vietnam War of the 1960s and 1970s, although by then the political
context and institutional sources of these phenomena had changed. In
foreign affairs, Stone advocated coexistence with communism in an era
of nuclear weapons; a "pragmatic" approach to revolutions—Russian,

Chinese, Vietnamese, Algerian, Cuban, and those to come; the inevitability of socialism but not necessarily communism (to Stone, a perverted form of socialism largely created by viciously repressive regimes which preceded it); and the need for an American leadership "prepared to talk in sober, mature and realistic terms of the real problems which arise in a real world where national rivalries, mass aspirations, and ideas clash as naturally as the waves of the sea." The United States, he believed, had become the leader of a world counterrevolution after 1945, and the inevitable and tragic consequences of this role was the erosion of its own liberal, constitutional order at home.

Linking Stone's critique of American foreign and domestic policies from the 1950s, at least, to the present is his underlying commitment to the *legal* framework for peace and freedom. While his was a lonely voice calling for a realistic understanding and detente with the Soviet Union during the 1950s, he was as uncompromising a critic of the lack of legally guaranteed freedoms in post-Stalin Russia as he was of the lawlessness of McCarthyism at home. His attack on American foreign policy, moreover, was related to his fears that America was merely the most dangerous of an atavistic type, the nation-state. The nation-state as a political unit was irrational and obsolete in a world of nuclear "overkill" and "menaced by the religious fanaticism of competing, oversimplified and delusive ideologies." In the 1960s and early 1970s, Stone continued to warn against a spreading "international anarchy," with the United States as a leading exemplar of the pattern in Vietnam. A reinvigoration of international organization (the UN) and international law, and the expansion of scientific, cultural, and economic exchange across ideological frontiers were not utopian demands for Stone, but desperately needed reforms in an increasingly unstable world. While "revisionist" historians called into question Woodrow Wilson's liberal internationalism, journalist Stone found an essential validity in Wilson's vision. Likewise, somewhat oldfashionedly, Stone affirmed that seam of the American liberal tradition which reasserted English revolutionary legality at the time of the nation's birth and found expression in the concepts of a balanced national government as defined by Madison and the Bill of Rights as defended by Jefferson, to perpetuate that tradition. Peace, freedom, and reform, all organically linked together, are the three principles of Stone's liberal "usable past." His radicalism derived from his uncompromising commitment to those ideas, and his intelligent grasp of their relevance to a continuation of what the Founding Fathers called "republican virtue."

The first issue of *I. F. Stone's Weekly* appeared in January 1953, just as Dwight D. Eisenhower's first administration began. I. F. Stone shared the widespread liberal and radical skepticism about Eisenhower's talents, the big business interlock on his administration, and the incredible Philistinism of the country at that moment. Nevertheless, he recognized that Ike was more open to pressure for reducing the tensions of the Cold War than the Truman-Acheson team which had launched both the Cold War and its own pre-McCarthy antisubversive drive at home. With characteristic political realism, Stone called on the Left and liberals alike to rally around the slogan "Back Ike for Peace." He warned that an escalation of the Korean stalemate was a distinct possibility; reactionary Republicans favored that course, and Big Labor, with its own Cold War commitment, would doubtless go along with them. Stone's hope shrewdly rested with the more moderate Republican and big business elements, who were increasingly worried about the economic costs of the war and the arms buildup generated by the Truman administration. Throughout the 1950s, Stone looked to these moderate conservatives as the only effective domestic check to those segments of the political and military elite leading the Cold War policy. With Stalin's death and the end of the Korean War, Stone called for further steps by Washington towards peaceful coexistence in 1953.

Whatever slight thaw in Cold War tensions Stone discerned under Eisenhower were in spite of the presence of the man Ike installed as secretary of state, John Foster Dulles. In a biographical sketch written in 1953, Stone devastatingly attacked Dulles' record in the 1930s as Sullivan and Cromwell's sophisticated apologist for fascist aggression. The same Dulles who pleaded for patience and acquiescence in the brutal Japanese and German expansion in the 1930s, on the theory that the League of Nations was underwriting a too-rigid international status quo, sanctimoniously spoke of the "liberation" of Eastern Europe in 1952. The underlying consistency of Dulles, Stone hinted, was his concern for stabilizing Germany and Japan as bastions of conservative capitalism against the Soviet Union. In 1953, he was once again looking to a conservative Germany and Japan as anti-Communist bulwarks under American sponsorship. Yet Dulles, eight years after a war started by German and Japanese aggression which he "consistently misconceived and misrepresented,'' was unanimously nominated by the Senate Foreign Relations Committee to direct American foreign policy! Stone's suspicion of Dulles never abated during the 1950s. Whether in Latin America, Asia, Europe, or the Middle East, Dulles' hand was ever present in extending and perpetuating the Cold War, nearly always working through local reactionary oligarchies. By 1955, Stone was calling on Eisenhower to fire him as an obstacle to Ike's movement towards negotiations with the Soviets at Geneva. Even when Dulles was dying in 1959, Stone resisted the maudlin sentimentalism of much of the press, calling him ''cold, arrogant, and ruthless,'' and, while wishing him recovery, demanded his retirement.

In early 1955, Stone illuminated a new and ominous development in the shaping of America's increasingly global anti-Communist foreign policy: the willingness of Congress, especially the Senate, to abdicate its constitutional power to declare war, clearly manifested in the Formosa Resolution. The brinksmanship of Dulles, supported by hawks like Admiral Radford, Senator Knowland, and the ''China Lobby,'' was now invoked to dare Communist China to invade Quemoy and Matsu, two tiny islands near the Chinese coast. When the Senate voted, with two dissenting votes, to approve a sweeping delegation of its warmaking powers to the president, Stone denounced it, calling it ''the first blank check for preventive war ever signed by an American Congress.'' In Stone's view, the Senate had ''degenerated into the role of a rubber stamp for the State Department.'' Moreover, he argued, this degeneration was a logical result of the ''bipartisan'' foreign policy pursued since the start of the Cold War, a process which threatened ''. . . to create a one-party state in the making of foreign policy.'' Congress, Stone complained, had made ''four fatal commitments'' in 1954-1955. The SEATO Pact, German rearmament, the Formosa Resolution, and the U.S.-Chiang Mutual Security Pact were approved ''with less consideration than is often accorded local harbor improvements.'' The only witnesses before the Senate Foreign Relations Committee hearings on the Formosa Resolution and the pact with Chiang were Dulles and Radford; no opponents of these measures were heard. With the Senate seemingly approaching the Supreme Soviet in its tendency to approve all executive policies by acclamation, Stone urged those Americans still committed to democratic control of foreign policy to rally support for the Morse-Lehman Resolution, which aimed to significantly limit the scope of the Formosa Resolution, with an eye to Senate recovery of its warmaking powers and negotiations on the future of Formosa. By May 1955, Stone was slightly more hopeful. Eisenhower, in a complete reversal of the drift towards war with Red China, had Dulles announce that the United States would, after all, open talks with the Chinese, as both sides accepted a cease-fire on Quemoy and Matsu. Stone credited Ike with halting the growing influence of Knowland and the China Lobby over American foreign policy. Once again, a moderate peace faction within the establishment, led by Senator Walter George, big business Republicans, Wall Street, and both wings of the Democratic party this time, supported the turn away from war.

Stone reacted to Eisenhower's heart attack in September 1955 by calling it a "world calamity." He linked Ike with FDR as a president committed to world peace—an improvement over Truman in that regard. Recalling his "Back Ike for Peace" slogan of 1953, Stone once again located the major pro-peace bloc within the moderate-conservative, big business wing of the Republican party, supported by moderate and conservative Democrats, especially the powerful southern Democrats headed by Senator Walter George. The Republican big business spokesmen, George Humphrey and Charles E. Wilson, wanted to reelect Ike in 1956 on a popular program of lower taxes, a balanced budget, and a sound dollar; to do that, they had supported Ike's moves towards peaceful coexistence since 1953. On the other hand, Stone warned that a Democratic sweep in 1956 was an "appalling" prospect; the Democratic-aligned Cold Warriors of Big Labor, the Catholic Church, and the aircraft industry were more dangerous to progress towards peace than the Republicans. Even Adlai Stevenson was unreliable on the peace issue.

In the spring of 1956, I. F. Stone visited the Soviet Union and Poland. Even before this journey, Stone recognized in Khrushchev's epochal speech to the twentieth party congress an historical development: the formal emergence of Soviet "revisionism" in violation of strict Leninist (and certainly Stalinist) ideology. Specifically, Stone saw Khrushchev admitting the incompatibility of peaceful coexistence with the Leninist theory of violent revolution. The Soviet Union now seemed ready to officially abandon the latter idea as too dangerous in the nuclear age. From his observations in Moscow and Warsaw, however, Stone concluded that the de-Stalinization *within* the Soviet Union was being undermined by Khrushchev and the new "collective leadership" itself.

Despite denunciations of Stalin's crimes, the Soviet leaders, Stone felt, had no real intention of dismantling the totalitarian police state apparatus. Stone recognized that his earlier hopes for significant liberalization of Soviet political and intellectual life were unfounded. Soviet criminal law, he found, had not been revamped to provide explicit legal guarantees of individual rights, despite calls for major reforms immediately after Stalin's death by high party officials. When, in the fall of 1956, the Soviets used brutal force in Hungary to crush a meaningful de-Stalinization, Stone acutely noted the irony (and degeneracy) of a worker uprising against a "workers' state" and the use of Soviet military power to destroy the Hungarian workers' councils, themselves latter-day soviets.

Despite his realistic support for Eisenhower's efforts to relax international tension, Stone was never under the illusion that Ike was capable of dynamic leadership in this quest. During Eisenhower's second term, Stone's doubts about Eisenhower increased. With Ike on the golf links, Dulles ill, and Press Secretary James Hagerty seemingly "America's ranking active statesman" in the midst of turmoil in Eastern Europe and the Middle East, in December 1956 Stone sardonically concluded that "the leadership of the 'free world' was resting."

Eisenhower and Dulles by 1957 were perpetuating the Cold War in Europe by rearming Germany and continuing to pursue the mirage of German unification. In the Middle East, the basic U.S. policy was to extend the Cold War and aggravate the instability of that volatile area by the heavyhanded imperialism of the "Eisenhower Doctrine." This was, Stone saw, a warmed-over Truman Doctrine to replace the departing British with a new American sphere of influence that would protect growing American oil interests. Stone saw in the intervention of U.S. Marines in Lebanon in July 1958, the administration's willingness to risk world war. Moreover, the move further crippled the congressional and democratic control of foreign policy previously sapped by the Formosa Resolution; Eisenhower and Dulles consulted neither Congress (as promised by the "Eisenhower Doctrine"), NATO, nor the UN. When a single Democratic Congressman, Henry Reuss, objected to this lack of consultation, House Speaker Sam Rayburn of the loyal opposition gaveled him down with the words: "In times like these we had better allow matters to develop rather than make remarks about them." Those "matters," Stone noted, might have been thermonuclear!

The Eisenhower administration ended in 1960 amid the frustration and humiliation of the U-2 incident and the breakup of the Paris "Summit" of May 1960, tension over Berlin, the rise of revolutionary "Third World" movements directed against American interests, most dramatically in Cuba, and, perhaps most menacing, an arms race spiraling out of control. Stone exposed the almost complete unwillingness of the Eisenhower administration to take new initiatives for peace while it increasingly piled up its stock of nuclear weapons. The Eisenhower "open skies" proposal for aerial inspection by both the United States and the Soviet Union to guard against surprise nuclear attack, one of the few American initiatives, had little support from the Pentagon and less from the Russians, who consistently rejected all such proposals. The development of the ICBM, fitted with nuclear warheads, in 1957 destroyed the "open skies" concept completely, and promised a dangerous escalation of the arms race. Yet both the economically developed and especially the underdeveloped nations desperately needed the resources increasingly diverted to this futile competition. From 1954 on, Stone called for a nuclear test ban as the first goal of peace supporters. The basis of this agreement, Stone believed, was the self-interest of both superpowers and their willingness to compromise. Only after the Cuban missile crisis demonstrated the dangers of diplomatic immobility combined with nuclear threats did the two powers reach a limited test ban agreement. Stone repeatedly called attention to the larger insanity of the arms race momentum, including such delusions as "tactical" nuclear weapons and "sharing" (surplus) nuclear missiles with NATO countries. In the Kennedy administration, Stone found equally futile and provocative schemes: the bomb shelter campaign, McNamara's "counterforce" doctrine, and the antimissile missile.

The most persistent domestic concern of *I. F. Stone's Weekly* during the 1950s was the defense of the Bill of Rights, and the possibility of social reform that depended on those freedoms. His *Weekly* first appeared when Senator Joseph McCarthy was near the apogee of his power, and ready to turn against the very Republican leadership he had aided so effectively by his earlier charges of "twenty years of treason." Stone feared that McCarthy wanted to create an informal dictatorship within the existing political system, based on a network of informants within the national government. Based on these informants, McCarthy, from his new chairmanship of the Senate Government Operations Committee, would then proceed to simultaneously smear the Left, the liberals, and practically anyone else who refused to cooperate with him, to further publicize himself, and to become the dominant power in American politics. Unlike many liberal critics of McCarthy, Stone understood, however, that McCarthy was merely the most immediately dangerous symptom of the political elite's own simplistic anti-Communist demonology which fueled the Cold War. When McCarthy fell from power after the Eisenhower administration and congressional moderates and conservatives turned against him in 1954, Stone understood, if other liberals did not, that McCarthyism was far from dead.

Stone, throughout the early and mid-1950s, assailed the blindness and cowardice of the Senate, the administration, the press, and other members of the political elite for failing to curb McCarthy and McCarthyism. The Senate, he noted, had reports from its own committees critical of McCarthy's corrupt financial dealings and his abuse of legislative powers; yet, it permitted him to go unchecked in his increasingly scatter-gun investigations until 1954. Only when he openly challenged the Defense Department and the Army did the establishment turn against him. Stone shrewdly noted that McCarthy was only effectively destroyed because he was endangering a victorious Republican administration and party. Had the Democrats remained in power in 1952, Stone cogently argues, the Republicans would not have restrained him. Still, I. F. Stone did not wash his hands of the fight against McCarthy. He brilliantly contributed to the movement that ended in McCarthy's censure at the end of 1954. He called attention to the opportunity, with the Republicans in power, with opposition to McCarthy's wild forays growing, with the Cold War ebbing slightly, to cut the demagogue down.

The long-run crusade against McCarthyism as a broader political disease originating in Cold War ideology preoccupied Stone long after 1954. Among Stone's specific contributions to the campaign against McCarthy was a brilliant, scornful portrait of the senator in late 1953. Stone imaginatively captured McCarthy's symbolic significance in the "haunted fifties" when he described the Wisconsin senator as a man with a "grey jailbird complexion . . . gravelly voice, bored, impersonal and inexorable like the detective hero in a soap opera." If the melodramatic qualities of McCarthy and his sordid entourage caught Stone's eye, he never missed McCarthy's more significant links to the network of professional anti-Communists of HUAC, and whose real head, he argued, was the FBI Director, J. Edgar Hoover. It was Hoover's files and former FBI agents who first fed HUAC's earlier "subversive" hunts and later McCarthy's. As the senator rose to power, Hoover personally befriended and publicly endorsed him, comparing McCarthy to Hoover himself as an anti-Communist "fighter" and patriot. Stone recognized that while McCarthy fell, Hoover, with his "files" on alleged "subversives," remained as an immensely powerful McCarthyite in the government.

Stone's most perceptive criticism of the McCarthy phenomenon came when the Eisenhower administration, including Vice-President Nixon, finally turned against the Wisconsinite in March 1954. Senator Ralph Flanders, an Eisenhower Republican from Vermont, attacked McCarthy in an important speech on the Senate floor. But, as Stone showed, the logic behind Flanders' speech was pure McCarthyism itself. Flanders painted a lurid and false picture of a world Communist conspiracy encircling the United States, which was somehow all part of the "age-long warfare between God and the Devil for the souls of men." Flanders, like Secretaries of State Acheson and Dulles, thought and acted upon a Manichean conception of the world divided between the "free world" and a diabolical international communism. Until the Cold War ideology was shattered and peaceful coexistence recognized as mankind's only hope, neither the free society promised by the Bill of Rights nor the reform movements periodically necessary to renovate it would survive. Once again, Stone revealed his radicalism in the very clarity and uncompromising character of his commitment to the best ideals of traditional liberalism.

During the 1950s, *I. F. Stone's Weekly* regularly called attention to the precariousness of constitutional rights under the assaults of the political witch-hunters. In 1953, Stone revealed the understanding of history that informed his journalism in a militant piece endorsing Albert Einstein's call for defiance of congressional committees inquiring into political beliefs, even at the risk of imprisonment. Stone brilliantly traced the Anglo-American historical roots of the First and Fifth Amendments, around which—particularly the First—he called all Americans to rally. The legal position Stone advised paralleled Einstein's, and was just as uncompromising. First, Stone argued, the First Amendment prohibited government investigations whose purpose was to "expose, disgrace, and pillory holders of opinions.'' This was the fundamental line of defense. Second, a congressional committee had no right to act as a "roving grand jury for the discovery and punishment of individual crimes.'' This referred to the success of congressional inquisitors in undermining the Fifth Amendment which left the power of indicting and trying criminal cases to the courts, not the Congress. Congressional investigation was a legitimate power, Stone insisted, provided it strictly respected the Bill of Rights. But the usurpation of power by the congressional committees revived the very dangers that caused John Lilburne, in 1637, to refuse to cooperate with the Star Chamber which was investigating his alleged heresies and wanted him to inform on his fellow dissenters. The arbitrary, illegitimate power of the Star Chamber was the *raison d'être* of the Fifth Amendment, Stone concluded. With Stone's encouragement (but not that of the *New York Times*), Einstein's call for refusal to waive First Amendment rights, even at the risk of contempt citations and jail, found a response. Marxist author Harvey O'Connor, citing both the First Amendment and the illegitimate scope of McCarthy's investigations, defied McCarthy, and, after being cited for contempt by Congress, later won vindication in the courts.

I. F. Stone exposed other threats to civil liberties in the 1950s. He exposed the sweeping scope of the witch-hunt in such instances as the deportation and denaturalization drive by the federal government against foreign-born radicals and their families. Stone attended a conference of the "Popular Front"-spawned American Committee for the Protection of the Foreign Born, and, in describing its dreary upstairs meeting hall in Chicago, the absence of young people, and its willingness to fight back against repression, he captured the tragic isolation of the Old Left by the 1950s. Another bureaucratic, rather than congressional, threat to First Amendment rights was the federal loyalty-security program, begun by Truman and expanded by Eisenhower. Indeed, some of the worst abuses of civil liberties in the 1950s arose in this program, and its many imitations on the state level. As Stone showed, the legal rights of individuals in "security risk" cases were almost nonexistent.

Stone grasped the crucial importance of the Supreme Court in protecting civil liberties and civil rights, or in acquiescing in their violation during this period. Chief Justice Vinson, appointed by Truman in 1946, presided over a Court that permitted congressional committees to undermine First Amendment rights by refusing to hear cases like that of the

Hollywood Ten, where the First Amendment right was the central issue. It also upheld the "conspiracy to advocate" language of the Smith Act and the Taft-Hartley anti-Communist oath for labor officials. The Vinson Court, as Stone argued, was a Cold War Court, dispensing "counter-revolutionary constitutional doctrines, revising Madison in the spirit of Metternich." The appointment of Earl Warren struck Stone as a hopeful event promising a decision against Jim Crowism and perhaps a new majority to uphold civil liberties. Stone considered Warren a "happy accident" in the party of Nixon and Knowland. In the sphere of civil liberties, the Warren Court, on the whole, fulfilled Stone's hopes. In May 1957, McCarthy died, and the Warren Court, with a new liberal majority, seemingly interred McCarthyism in a series of decisions that same spring. In the *Watkins* decision, the investigatory powers of HUAC and, to some extent, too, the Senate Internal Security Committee, were curbed in the name of the First Amendment. In the *Sweezy* case, the power of state witch-hunters was likewise restrained on First Amendment grounds. The Warren Court was turning the clock back to a broad construction of the First Amendment that it vindicated against latter-day witch-hunters. Stone rejoiced and thought the new American Inquisition was "irreparably crippled." Senator Eastland and Congressman Walters, he wryly suggested, should have investigated "Constitution-carrying Republicans" instead of Communists.

By 1959, Stone was forced to take a less optimistic view of the Supreme Court. He bitterly denounced the Court's *Barenblatt* and *Uphaus* decisions as restoring much of the sweeping discretionary powers of congressional and state witch-hunters which had been curbed two years before. The "balancing" theory of Felix Frankfurter, Stone maintained, was the basis of the majority's opinion. This perverse doctrine, he argued, was predicated on the major premise that abridgment of First Amendment rights was constitutional if it was reasonable, and on the minor premise that regulation of Communists was reasonable. Because of this decision, Stone noted later in 1959, southern civil rights activists like Carl Braden and Frank Wilkinson, and peace activist Willard Uphaus faced jail sentences for invoking the First Amendment. A further blow came in 1961, when the Court upheld the Mundt-Nixon law, a pernicious and sweeping statute requiring organizations labeled "Communist action," "Communist-front," and "Communist-infiltrated" to register with the government or face imprisonment of their leaders and membership. The Supreme Court, Stone implied, was only slightly less vulnerable to McCarthyite logic than the Executive and Congress when dealing with First Amendment freedoms.

The most momentous Supreme Court decision in the 1950s, of course, was the ruling that racial segregation in education was unconstitutional. Stone welcomed it as a vindication of American democratic vitality, but he became increasingly anxious about a looming racial crisis as the decade passed. He correctly assailed Eisenhower's inept and vacillating nonleadership on the question of school desegregation. Eisenhower's fumbling, in turn, greatly aided the growth of southern white resistance. Although Stone perceptively analyzed the similarities of southern racism and the racism of French colonials in Algeria and whites in South Africa, and saw, too, the social sickness of the South, his originality in these views is less marked than his commitments to peace and civil liberties. He visited Little Rock and the Arkansas delta country in the fall of 1958 and was appalled by southern white racism, especially among the middle-class whites he met. It is unfair to criticize Stone for not recognizing what hardly any other northern intellectual discerned in this decade: namely, the significance of the massive continuing Negro migration to the big northern cities. Stone's statement that the South was ''a Whig and racist survival in an America otherwise steadily more egalitarian'' in the 1950s had truth in it at the time, but egalitarianism outside the South in the 1950s was more a matter of rhetoric than of substantive economic and social gains for the Negro, especially for the most recent migrants from the South.

In his analyses of American politics in the 1950s, I. F. Stone found little to his liking. As one who remembered some of the vitality of the New Deal era of the 1930s, Stone frequently bemoaned the irresponsibility, complacency, and co-optation of liberals, intellectuals, and the labor movement (especially the leadership), groups that once questioned the status quo in varying degrees. Each group in the 1950s made its terms with the Garrison State or the Cold War. As Stone repeatedly stressed, the labor movement was more wedded to the arms race and big military budgets than big business itself, and its support for the Cold War was far more uncritical. In the business recession of 1958, Stone noted that both political parties were bankrupt of creative ideas. The Republicans favored classic deflation, at the expense of labor, and the Democrats favored a continued WPA of arms spending, although that had failed in the past. Stone's own ideas were not very radical, but he did suggest more national planning within a ''mixed'' economy. He cautiously hoped that the Republicans under Eisenhower could reach a major settlement with Russia, and then pave the way for the Democrats to abandon the Cold War and transform the Garrison State into a planned ''mixed'' economy based on prosperity and peace. Neither the Kennedy nor the Johnson administration, tragically, chose to take the route Stone recommended.

Murray Kempton has ventured the interesting thesis that I. F. Stone, while certainly a radical, is also ''our very last Old Whig.'' According to Kempton, Stone shares with the younger Edmund Burke and the Old Whigs ''their hatred of wars and their passion for private liberty, their assurance that it would all come out right in the end.'' If this is an important clue to Stone's *Weltanschauung* and that of the journal he published from 1953 until, for reasons of health, he terminated in 1971, historians must also look for Stone's roots in the American liberal and radical traditions. Fear of war and empire as avenues to arbitrary, irresponsible power and the extinction of the right of dissent were also a profound part of the early American Whig tradition, out of which came Stone's hero, Thomas Jefferson, and the Constitution and the Bill of Rights itself. This American tradition of opposition to war, usurpation of power by any branch of government, and to any compromise of constitutional rights was often reasserted by critics of war and empire through the next two centuries. Where I. F. Stone is somewhat unique is in his assertion of this historic stance in the age of the Garrison State. His journalistic career in Washington began in 1940, when ''Dr. New Deal'' faded away to be replaced by ''Dr. Win the War.'' A new power structure emerged in post-1945 America, increasingly responsive to an expanding military-security bureaucracy that included the Pentagon, the CIA, and the FBI. With the cooperation of older institutions of the power structure—the executive and legislative branches, and the press—an imperialistic foreign policy in the name of anticommunism and repression of internal opposition in the name of ''security'' transformed America into the armed camp long feared by pre-1940 vintage antiwar and libertarian liberals and radicals. To fight the degeneration of democracy, to sustain the traditional liberal and radical struggle for peace, civil liberty, and social reform in the era of the Garrison State was the purpose of Stone and his paper.

Although Stone is in the American liberal-radical tradition, he is also a truly cosmopolitan man with a sense of history. His reports, in *I. F. Stone's Weekly* during the 1950s, on post-Stalin Russia and on the Cuban revolution in the early 1960s reveal a broad historical understanding of those upheavals. In these reports, he seemed to attempt a reconciliation of Marx and Jefferson. That is, he understood and defended the social and economic aims of the Russian and Cuban revolutions, but he bemoaned the absence of political freedom in both societies, especially marked and deplored in Russia.

I. F. Stone's Weekly during the 1950s was far more often a source of accurate than false prophecies about the direction of American politics and policies. That Eisenhower was not as susceptible to the Cold Warriors as his predecessor, nor, for that matter, his three successors in the presidency in the 1960s; that Congress was moving the country towards war and disaster by effectively abdicating its warmaking authority to the president, as in the Formosa Resolution and Lebanon episodes; that Earl Warren turned the Supreme Court away from the Cold War while the other two branches were committed to it; that Khrushchev in 1956 would lose control of de-Stalinization; and that the arms race was out of control—all these were brilliant perceptions by a journalist with an unmatched grasp of relevant facts. Not accidentally, the *Weekly* was among the first and the few to understand the evolving United States policy disaster in Indochina; the Tonkin Gulf Resolution, for Stone, was a re-run of the Formosa Resolution and the Eisenhower Doctrine, only more mendacious in origin and catastrophic in its consequences. Murray Kempton has suggested that *I. F. Stone's Weekly*, and the other writings of its editor in the 1950s, are indispensable to a proper understanding of that period. Stone and his journal are indispensable, indeed, for a comprehension of the last 25 years of American history.

Turin, Italy, 1973

Part Twelve

POSTWAR PERIODICALS

THE last significant political act of the Old Left was its participation in the presidential campaign of Progressive party candidate Henry Wallace in 1948. Appropriately, the role of the radicals in that campaign symbolized the effect of sectarian animosities and the Communist movement on the American Left.

Domestically, Wallace stood for a continuation of the New Deal spirit and reforms but he did not establish appreciably better credentials for this job than the Democratic incumbent, Harry S. Truman. What distinguished the Progressive party and provided its chief reason for being was Wallace's contention that American aggressiveness toward the Soviet Union, and not Soviet policy, was primarily responsible for the emerging Cold War. Wallace and the Progressives called for a conciliatory and cooperative foreign policy—a continuation of the wartime alliance—in order to secure the peace and thus permit continued reform at home. The Communists supported Wallace, not so much because of the merits of his position, but because such an endorsement would best serve the national interests of the Soviet Union.

The Socialists, on the other hand, were equally "other-directed." Their line on practically every question was similarly shaped by what the American Communist party did: they opposed it. So, in 1948, in thoughtless knee-jerk reaction to the Communist support of Wallace, they opposed him, even though he represented the most "leftist" of the candidates and even though this meant support of a bellicose and belligerent foreign policy (many of the Socialists were pacifists). Socialist leader Norman Thomas distinguished himself as one of the noisiest and most persistent red-baiters of the former vice-president.

Wallace's campaign failed miserably, and with it passed the last important active part played by the Old Left in American politics. With the deepening Cold War, Korea, and McCarthyism, the Old Left tailed off in the 1950s into nothing but a memorial moraine. The Communists opposed the war in Korea, for instance, but it did not really matter: they were so impotent that no one paid attention. Even in this time of anti-Red hysteria, there was little talk of the old Sedition Act. Communist leaders were harried and persecuted, and membership dropped steadily, until, it has been feasibly argued, the party would have been gone completely by 1960 had it not been for the regular dues payments of those numerous members who were FBI agents and informers. With the exception of a few party functionaries, certainly no one had a greater interest in the maintenance of the crippled party than J. Edgar Hoover. Since the war he had built his bureau's request for appropriations on the increasingly illusory Red menace.

The Socialists were also irrelevant to postwar conditions. They had sacrificed their revolutionary program when the New Deal accomplished their "immediate demands" and they rushed to take honorary degrees as forerunners. And with their incessant red-baiting they scrapped their integrity as quickly as the Communists did. Unlike the Communists, however, the SPA tacitly admitted the end: the organization ceased to exist as a political party and redefined itself as an educational and propaganda organization through, naturally, a newspaper, *New America*.

The only issue for Socialists, Communists, and Trotskyists in the 1950s was civil liberties, a necessary self-interest in the cases of the Communists and Trotskyists and a belated point of principle for the Socialists. In this issue they represented some of the few sensible elements remaining in a decade first marked by repression and semihysteria and later by quiet acquiescence in political conformity. But inevitable as this emphasis was, it was not radicalism. The Old Left was dead.

The periodical publications during the last days of the Old Left were few, concerned heavily with civil liberties and peace. Only the *National Guardian* maintained a respectable number of subscribers. Moreover the few substantial publications were not affiliated with the old parties. (Even the *National Guardian*, which cleaved closely to the American

Communist party line, was genuinely independent.) Rather, like the skirmishers of an army in indecorous retreat, the journals of the Left in the 1950s issued from independent individuals and small groups whose only affiliations were loose and personal. Interestingly, in this period of decline, many of them were quite good as journalism and as analysis. If disintegration was an unfortunate end, the independence which that disintegration fostered was exactly what had been so sorely wanting in the radical press for a full generation.

New Trends

NEW YORK, 1945-1946

ROBERT SOBEL

THE victory over Japan in 1945 brought a close not only to World War II, but also to a thirteen-year period of crusading in America, which began with the election of Franklin Roosevelt in 1932, passed through the various phases of the New Deal, was then transformed into the fight against the Axis, and finally ended with the signing of peace terms. In 1945 several groups attempted to channel this energy into support for the new United Nations Organization, while others hoped America would sponsor a worldwide development program to "internationalize the New Deal." There were demands for a renewal of prewar isolationism, and many thought the reform phase of the New Deal might be revived. A few relatively unimportant splinter groups tried to return to the issue of the 1930s and the great debates over technocracy, socialism, domestic fascism, etc. Most of these demands and hopes were ignored; by 1946 the outlines of the Cold War were visible, and new problems evoked new groups and ideas to meet them.

New Trends was founded by a small group of men who believed the philosophies of the 1930s might be applied to the problems of the mid-1940s and that the crusades of the earlier period were still worth fighting. There is no way of knowing how many people participated in the establishment of this small magazine, how it operated, or even its circulation. Several facts are clear, however. For the most part, the magazine was written by anarchists and syndicalists ("libertarians") who had been visible in radical circles in New York during the New Deal. Jack White, a minor novelist, wrote several pieces for the first issue. He was an active supporter of the Loyalists in the Spanish Civil War, and had been an organizer for the Lincoln Brigade. He remained the dominant figure at the magazine for the rest of its short life, usually contributing literary essays under the signatures of "Jack," "J. S. White," or simply "J. W." Pierre Besnard and George Michel were regulars; neither was mentioned in other magazines nor did either contribute to the larger journals of the period.

By all standards, *New Trends* was a failure. It had few subscribers at the yearly rate of $1.50, and virtually no newsstand sales. It began to skip issues early in its life and was obliged to publish filler material to pad the pages. The magazine had no "Letters to the Editor" column, a feature ubiquitous in most journals of the *genre*, and there is no evidence of careful, professional editing in its pages. Its articles tended to be on such themes as the Spanish Civil War, betrayal of the Russian Revolution by the Communists, the futility of the UNO, socialized medicine, and other crusades which had no major followings in the immediate postwar period. The journal ended in August 1946, with its tenth number. There is no evidence that many missed it in September.

Despite its short life and obvious lack of support, *New Trends* should not be ignored by students of American radicalism. Its very failure, in fact, indicates that the would-be readers of 1945-1946 were busy elsewhere and occupied with other movements in the postwar world. *New Trends* contained several articles on anarchism and syndicalism which show the direction these movements were taking after the war. There are pieces on the Spanish Civil War which reveal that the Loyalist movement was still alive in New York, and the articles on European affairs show clearly that the small band of American syndicalists had not changed their attitudes toward social democracy and communism as a result of the war. *New Trends* illuminates a small corner of postwar history, but one which should not be ignored. Furthermore, it is an historically interesting relic of the once-vital anarchosyndicalist movement of the first half of the twentieth century.

Hempstead, New York, 1968

Modern Review

NEW YORK, 1947-1950

DANIEL BELL

THE publication of the *Modern Review* was an effort to bring together leading figures of the international labor and Socialist movements to rethink the problems of Socialist theory in the post-World War II world. The decade of fascism and the half-decade of war had all but shattered the international Socialist movement. The leadership of the major Socialist parties—German, French, Spanish, Dutch, Belgian, and Scandinavian—had been driven into exile, either in London or New York; the "delegations" of an earlier emigration—the Russian, Italian, East European, and Baltic parties—which had spent the 1920s and 1930s in Berlin or Paris, had followed these men into a second exile. Now, in the first flush of the postwar "reconstruction," it seemed as if the old capitalist order had itself been smashed and that Western Europe, at least, would be rebuilt on democratic Socialist lines while the East European countries might be able to establish their own political independence on a Socialist basis. In England, France, Italy, Holland, Belgium, the Scandinavian countries, and in Poland, Czechoslovakia, Hungary, and Rumania, men who had plied petty occupations in exile were now sitting as ministers over the destiny of nations. Within this context, the *Modern Review* had high hopes of becoming an international forum for the discussion of Socialist problems.

The nominal editors of the *Modern Review* were Travers Clement, Lewis A. Coser, and George Denicke. One says "nominal" because even though these men carried out the editorial tasks of producing a monthly magazine, the moving spirit—in its conception and in raising funds—was Raphael Abramovitch, the leader in exile of the Russian Social Democratic Labor party, known popularly as the Mensheviks. A small, trim, erect man, with a well-shaped head and neat chin beard, Abramovitch (at that time sixty-seven years old) was one of that marvelous generation of Russian idealists who had suffered jail in their youth, brief glory as revolutionary leaders, and privation in exile, yet who continued to dedicate themselves selflessly—after thirty years of wandering it was all they had!—to ideas. History for them was not the history of the victors—how could it be, since they were the defeated—but of the "correct" interpretation of theory; and it was to that end that the *Modern Review* was dedicated.

The first group of active editors were themselves a mixed breed. Travers Clement, of old Yankee stock, was a veteran journalist who had been editor of the *Socialist Call*, and co-author (with his wife Lillian Symes) of the book *Rebel America* (New York: Harper and Brothers, 1934), which was a widely read and successful history of radicalism in America. Lewis Coser was a young Socialist, German-born, who had been active in left-wing groups first in Germany and later as an emigré in Paris, and who had come to the United States, after a year of hiding in southern France, in the fall of 1941. Russian-born George Denicke (who also wrote under the name of George Decker) had left Russia in 1921 with the Menshevik delegation, and had been the assistant editor in Berlin of *Die Gesellschaft*, a German Socialist theoretical magazine edited by Rudolf Hilferding.

The first editorial board served to identify the sponsors, organizational and intellectual, of the magazine. These included Abramovitch, Max Danish, the editor of *Justice*, the weekly newspaper of the International Ladies Garment Workers Union, which contributed most of the funds; John L. Childs, professor of education at Teachers College, Columbia University, and state chairman of the Liberal party; Sidney Hook, professor of philosophy at New York University and the best known expositor of Marxist thought in the United States; and Robert M. MacIver, Lieber Professor of Political Philosophy and Sociology at Columbia University.

Although the magazine was edited in New York, its focus, clearly, was international and the overwhelming number of contributors, in the first two years at least, were either Europeans or European Socialists living in the United States. The bulk of the articles, as can be readily seen, were devoted to Russia, to Socialist economic problems in Europe, the Middle East, and Asia, and to theoretical questions such as the nature of totalitarianism and bureaucracy. But there were difficulties from the start. Two of the editors, Clement and Coser, were of left-wing Socialist persuasion, while Abramovitch was a right-winger.

The blowup came in December 1947, at the end of the first year of publication, when Clement and Coser printed an article by Harold Isaacs, "South Asia's Opportunity," which called on the Socialist movements of those countries to take a "Third World" position lining up neither with the "capitalist anarchy" of the West nor the "totalitarian thralldom" of the Communist world. Abramovitch was appalled. For him, as he replied in the same issue, these were "obsolete Marxist formulations." The issue could only be between the democratic West and the Communist world, and no third position was possible. In consequence, Clement and Coser resigned, and in March 1948, *Modern Review* was reorganized as a bimonthly with Abramovitch as editor.

This task, however, was quite difficult for him: he was, at that time, deeply engaged in political work because of the ferment among the Russian emigrés as to possible social changes in the Soviet Union; he was responsible for the direction of the *Sozialistische Vestnik (Socialist Courier)*, the official organ of the Menshevik group, which had been published regularly since 1921; he was a regular contributor to the *Jewish Daily Forward*, and the active editor of the *Jewish Encyclopedia*, the two activities which gave him a regular income; and he suffered, cruelly, from blinding migraine headaches which often incapacitated him for days at a time. He engaged as managing editor Julien Steinberg, who was also an associate editor of *The New Leader*, but Steinberg, a brilliant but mercurial young man, was of procrastinating habits and the magazine encountered publishing delays. By January 1949, it ceased publication temporarily.

In the spring of 1949, Abramovitch asked me to join him as co-editor. I had known him for more than eight years, from the time I was managing editor of *The New Leader*, beginning in 1941. Jokingly, among our friends, I had been called America's youngest Menshevik because of my political affiliation with the group, going back to my teens. I had been teaching for three years at the University of Chicago and had just returned to New York, as a writer for *Fortune* magazine, and I welcomed the opportunity to remain active in intellectual journalism.

In our conversations, Abramovitch and I decided to convert the magazine into a quarterly, to seek for "weightier" articles, to invite younger writers, particularly academics, and to explore some of the philosophical and sociological currents which were becoming manifest at the time. Abramovitch was indulgent, but skeptical. "What is it that you want to write about?" he asked me on one occasion. I told him that as a result of the holocaust and the frightening aspects of human nature revealed by the war and the concentration camps, my friends had become interested in such thinkers as Niebuhr, Tillich, Barth, Kierkegaard, as well as in nineteenth-century historians such as Burckhardt, Acton, Tocqueville, and the like. I remarked that it might be interesting to go back to the old debates among Russian thinkers at the turn of the century, and run some articles on such interesting men—mystics and religious writers to be sure—as Vladimir Soloviev and Leo Shestov. "Soloviev and Shestov!" he asked in surprise, "Why, we *defeated* them in 1902!" (1902 was the year Abramovitch became active in the Russian Jewish Labor Bund, after being expelled from the Riga Polytechnical Institute for revolutionary activities.) Such was the unswerving political faith of the Russian Menshevik!

The *Modern Review* appeared for only two numbers in its new dress. There were now a number of more academically inclined contributors such as the philosopher Hannah Arendt, the historian Gertrude Himmelfarb, and the sociologists Philip Rieff and Philip Selznick. The shift in focus to reflective rather than topical articles was evident as well. But a number of other difficulties had become apparent. Abramovitch had conceived of the magazine as providing a platform for himself and his group in international Socialist affairs, particularly if a reconstituted Labor and Socialist International would ever achieve importance, and he was less interested in a sociophilosophical journal. At my end, I found it hard to interest my friends in a Socialist journal. A noncommercial, "cultural" magazine, in the last analysis, can only be the product of a like-minded group of individuals who want a place to express their ideas. At the time most of my friends were engaged in starting their academic careers, and in writing for the professional and academic journals. The 1950s was not a decade of vigorous political discussion. The demise of the *Modern Review* was an early signal of that fact.

New York City, 1968

New Foundations

NEW YORK, 1947-1954

ALAN TRACHTENBERG

THE title *New Foundations* is from a line in the Socialist hymn, "The Internationale": "The earth shall rise on new foundations." The image implies a hope linked to a program, a vision of a future embodied in an ideology. In its credo the magazine proclaimed itself "devoted to the political, cultural and intellectual problems of American students" (the list is slightly misleading, for cultural and intellectual were clearly subsumed under political), with the purpose of stimulating "clear thinking and progressive social action." The inseparability of thought and action is an essential feature of the world view projected in *New Foundations*: not to have served as an instrument of political action would have been a betrayal of the magazine's principles. The principles were Marxist, of the variety now identified as Stalinist—that is, Marxism as interpreted by the Communist party (an editorial refers scornfully to the fact that in universities "Sidney Hook, Koestler and even Trotsky are offered as 'authorities' " of Marxism).

The distinction between serving as an instrument of a potential mass movement and as an organ for a party—the distinction between a stimulant and a dogma—is sometimes impossible to detect in the magazine. The editors openly expressed their sympathy with American Youth for Democracy (AYD) and Labor Youth League (LYL)—both tied to the Communist party. With a revised format introduced in 1951 ("a more popular appearance in order to better reach the vast numbers of students who can be won to act for Peace"), the magazine revised and expanded its credo to make more explicit its commitment to "the philosophy of Marxism-Leninism, the philosophy of Socialism," and to "affirm our friendship with the Labor Youth League." In part the magazine may indeed have originated, as the first issue declared, "in the imagination of a group of overseas Marines who foresaw that student America would need a channel of expression after the war," but more consequential foundations seem to have been within established Marxist groups. The magazine's explicit effort was to cultivate an interest in Marxism among students. The tone and style of the effort reflect the intimidating political climate of the late 1940s and early 1950s—the opening years of the Cold War and of McCarthyism. "*New Foundations* actively combats reactionary and fascist ideologies in all their manifestations," announced the credo which appeared in every issue. The magazine made its attempts at persuasion and conversion and stimulation to political action against a background of increasing public and government hostility to the Communist party and suspected radicals. These were years of rapid decline in membership in the CP and its affiliates, and virtual expulsion from the main avenues of political life in the United States. Like the CP itself, *New Foundations* tried to explain the attacks upon radical and Marxist groups as part of a concerted drive by American capitalism toward suppression of dissent at home and domination abroad. The atmosphere of hostility and fear and suppression of Communists unavoidably set the tone of the magazine as defensive and polemical.

It directed its appeal to students, especially veterans, who were troubled by the signs of reaction in postwar America—the widely publicized investigations of the House Un-American Activities Committee, the blacklists, universal military training, what seemed to be the increasingly aggressive stance of American foreign policy, discrimination and lynchings, the arrest and imprisonment of Communists, the firing of professors, and finally, the Korean War. Articles frequently concluded with slogans for action: Defeat the Mundt-Nixon Bill! Halt the drive for a third world war! Stop the drive towards fascism! Implicit as a *leitmotif* throughout was the warning: "Act Today! Tomorrow you may be silenced." And running as a major theme concurrently was the magazine's central assertion: "Marxism shines as a beacon-light to a ship-wrecked world."

The distinctive features of the magazine, including its rhetoric, derive from its foundation in a theory which was also a party doctrine. It aimed to cultivate not merely political awareness and action, but "a sound Marxist approach": not enough to think and act, but to think and act *correctly*. Soundness was apparently a matter of conformance to a position or a line hammered out somewhere behind the scenes, for controversy as to what constituted sound Marxism rarely appeared in the pages of *New Foundations* (there were some exceptions, usually on cultural matters; but the pages did not seem open to any criticism of Marxism as such). The reader was presented with the assumption, expressed by the magazine's style and tone as well as its content, that "soundness" had already been achieved. Titles of articles, such as "Against the Equilibrists," or "Tito—Menace to Peace and Socialism," are one indication of what was considered "sound." The tone of editorial rhetoric (and frequently it is difficult to distinguish either by tone or substance an essay on art or a book review from an editorial) also conveyed a sense of conviction of correctness.

It is not, of course, surprising to find doctrinal correctness as a prominent aspect of the magazine's political policy. It implies an attitude more innocent than naive, a belief in an essentially simple world, in which historical truth is always self-evident to the person properly equipped to detect it. Accompanying innocence was an unmistakable passion, if not always for truth then certainly for justice. The world view of *New Foundations* politicised all of reality, or at least assumed rather blandly that all of reality was capable of political interpretation, and required it. Not that the assumption is itself invalid; but the singleminded attempt to see everything through the lens of a "sound Marxist approach" resulted in a number of distortions.

One extreme instance occurs in Volume 2. A rather favorable appraisal of William Faulkner appeared in an essay by Jack Kroner, identified as a veteran, a graduate student of English, and a member of the editorial board. The essay argued for Faulkner's importance as a writer whose world "contains a very important section of objective and subjective reality." "Although Faulkner's solution can hardly be recommended as a progressive one," Kroner writes, "his picture of the world is hostile in that it will provoke numerous doubts in the reader's mind. He has captured and refined an aspect of the contradictions of bourgeois life, previously unreached in American letters."

Two issues later (Vol. 2, No. 3), an editorial supported by two letters appeared under the heading, "Against White Supremacist Attitudes." The title was directed against Kroner. In his essay, we learn, he had failed "to fulfill the primary function of a Marxist: to combat chauvinistic (bourgeois) ideology." The crux of the criticism was that Kroner had neglected to attack and condemn Faulkner for fascism (as well as for his "abominable obscurantist style"). This failure in turn "produces the same result as if he himself had expressed chauvinistic beliefs and indicates that he himself has accepted them." In consequence Kroner was suspended from the editorial board: "first, because the board cannot have as a member anyone who has expressed openly chauvinistic attitudes [although he was accused only of failing openly to express anti-racist attitudes] until he has shown that he has overcome them; and second, because the members feel that he should devote his full attention to his own further struggle to overcome these attitudes."

Literary criticism can become a harrowing affair under these conditions. The editors concluded that "there can be no fundamental disagreement among Marxists concerning the criticism of the chauvinistic content of Kroner's article." And apparently they were right, for in the next issue, Kroner agreed entirely, and even attacked his defenders (whose letters never appeared in print). He confessed to "having been taken in, along with Faulkner, by the restricted realm of bourgeois categories," recognized that "chauvinism, today, is the foremost weapon of bourgeois ideology," and admitted that "my tacit acceptance of chauvinistic concepts was a 'concession to imperialism and fascism.'" And in a sentence which raises issues only to evade them, Kroner wrote, "If we enjoy Faulkner and are, at times, moved by him, it is not out of health but out of sickness. He appeals to that in us which is utterly sick and bourgeois." Kroner was, we learn from an editorial note to his reply, reinstated on the board out of respect for his "willingness and ability to struggle against white chauvinism."

This incident dramatizes a dilemma at the heart of *New Foundations*—one which remained unresolved, indeed unarticulated, in its seven years of publication. The dilemma is the desire on the part of many student and intellectual radicals to serve two impulses at once: the impulse toward a life of art and ideas, and an impulse toward a life of political action. In a curiously distorted way, the editors' attack and Kroner's submission may have expressed a desire to act responsibly in the face of a politically sick world—a desire to do and say the right thing to improve the world. The young people who wrote for *New Foundations* seemed convinced of the world-historical importance of their words, convinced that every word was an action, and needed to be judged in light of the "sound Marxist approach." The hope was that such judgments would in the end serve art and culture by creating a world in which they might flourish.

Almost as an ironic prophecy, the opening editorial in Vol. 1, No. 1, began by citing these words of the British scientist Hyman Levy regarding a young mathematician who had died fighting for the Loyalists in Spain:

> I could see in him the eternal conflict that tears asunder the soul of all that is best in the younger generation—the desire to enjoy the fruits of culture and the necessity to sacrifice oneself for its preservation.

Sacrifice can take other forms than physical death. The idea of a historical *necessity* runs like a deep flood in the pages of *New Foundations*—especially notable perhaps because the journal is addressed to students, who stand on the threshold of lasting commitments. One of the appeals of Marxism in the twentieth century, especially in America, has been its apparent ability to bridge the awesome chasm between culture and politics—to provide intellectuals with a ready-made synthesis of thought and action. The editorial continues to claim that Marxism is more than "a scientific, ethical and cooperative solution" to exploitation and oppression—more than a "political and economic system"; it is also "an all-embracing philosophical synthesis whose principles are derived from the critical evaluation of all practical and intellectual pursuits; and its principles and methods are richly applicable to every field of study and activity." It seemed capable of accommodating the most divergent desires and interests.

The early numbers of *New Foundations* devoted a remarkable amount of space to "cultural" matters: graphics, poems, stories, criticism (an editorial note at the end of Vol. 1 complains that almost 90 percent of all submitted material was literary: not enough history, science, and politics). Later, in response to increasing government pressure against Communists and the perilous state of academic and other freedoms, topical issues came to predominate in the magazine, though not exclusively. But whether the magazine made a convincing case for the "all-embracing philosophical synthesis" of Marxism, or whether it submitted the crucial question of how a "sound Marxist approach" is arrived at to honest discussion, is another matter. The desire for soundness itself seemed often to obliterate any promising dialectical exchange of ideas which might lead to synthesis. Antitheses were rare indeed.

The impact of Marxist thought—and the influence of the Communist party—upon student and labor radicalism in the postwar period is a separate matter. It is clear that an examination of *New Foundations* will be essential to any historian who undertakes that project. In the late 1960s the language of *New Foundations* seems already dated, echoes from another era. The revelations about Stalin at the twientieth congress of the Communist party of the Soviet Union was a great divide, and what may have seemed "sound" before that event seemed shattered and confused and false afterwards. But a historian will no doubt be able to reconstruct a continuity which does not now seem to exist between the efforts to form a Marxist student movement in the late 1940s and 1950s, and the apparently spontaneous outburst of student radicalism in the middle 1960s.

The historical interest of *New Foundations* may lie in its attempt to serve a perhaps premature purpose. The Stalinist rhetoric and the links with specific organizations were surely barriers to any genuine mass appeal. And the tone of humorless self-righteousness must indeed have interfered with the message. But the intention of the journal, to provide a major national periodical to deal with culture as well as politics, particularly from the point of view of students, has a strong appeal. The stress on a particular theoretical framework may have resulted in harmful exclusions and distortions. But the insistence on the importance of theory for radical political action is a positive note.

State College, Pennsylvania, 1968

National Guardian

NEW YORK, 1948—

HARVEY A. LEVENSTEIN

IT was a rather romantic place for a newspaper to be conceived: in the belly of a lumbering B-17 bomber as it trundled over recently liberated Germany in 1945, carrying two professional newspapermen who were to help "denazify" and democratize the press of Germany. One of them, a New Yorker, James Aronson, and the other, an Englishman, Cedric Belfrage, soon set to talking about the obvious: If they could show the Germans how to set up a "free" press in their country, why not try the same back in the states? Belfrage had been a theater and drama critic for the London *Daily Express*. He was a world-traveler and the author of a number of books. In the 1930s he had settled in Hollywood, writing movie scripts. He now planned to return to the United States after the war, to live with his American wife and children. Aronson, after his stint on General Eisenhower's staff, was to return to his job on the *New York Times*. Both were "progressive" and both thought that the time was ripe for founding a radical newspaper.

Like many similarly conceived ideas, the radical newspaper fell into limbo when the two dreamers returned to the United States and normal civilian life. Three years later, though, its time seemed to have arrived. Then, in mid-1948, a number of circumstances combined to create a propitious moment for the birth of the new paper. A "progressive" political movement was being mobilized behind the figure of Henry Wallace. It was gathering under its wing a multifarious coalition of people united by a common feeling that the Truman administration had betrayed the heritage of Franklin D. Roosevelt, that it was provoking a needless, aggressive Cold War against the Soviet Union abroad and abandoning the social justice aims of the New Deal at home. At the same time, *PM*, the one New York newspaper that was at all sympathetic to the new movement (and only in the freedom it gave some of its columnists and reporters to support it) folded.

As the nominating convention of the newly formed Progressive party approached, Belfrage and Aronson revived their old idea. They enlisted on their side the newly unemployed James T. McManus, a *PM* staffer who had also been the head of the left-wing Newspaper Guild in New York, and Josiah Gitt, publisher of the liberal York (Pennsylvania) *Gazette and Daily*, who was interested in starting a national Left-liberal weekly. The four decided to turn out an experimental preview edition of a new weekly, and distribute it at the Progressive Convention.

Thus, in late July 1948, delegates to the convention were treated to the first issue of the *National Gazette*, with Gitt listed as publisher and Aronson, Belfrage, and McManus as editors. The response of the delegates was enthusiastic enough to convince the three editors that there was a future for the journal. Gitt, pleading lack of time to devote to the venture, dropped out.

Armed with a few hundred pledges to subscribe to the yet-unborn paper, and considerable optimism about the future of the Left in the United States, the three editors set out to produce the new weekly. On October 18, 1948, barely three weeks before Wallace and their movement would meet its disastrous election setback, the *National Guardian* made its first appearance. The first issue labeled itself a "progressive weekly" and pledged that its point of view would be "a continuation and development of the progressive tradition set in our time by Franklin D. Roosevelt and overwhelmingly supported by the American people in the last four Presidential elections." But there was either some dissimulation in this pledge, or a grave misreading of what the American people had voted for in the last four elections, for the editors were also Socialists and made few bones about it. Unimpressed, *Time* magazine took one look at the first edition and opined that the new paper's complexion would vary "from pink to rosy red."

Time had more than ideological reasons for being unimpressed, for the new weekly showed presumptuous signs of becoming a left-wing version of *Time*. Its initial editions owed not a little to the zippy newsmagazine format pioneered by *Time* and imitated by *Newsweek, U.S. News and World Report*, and others. There were the now-familiar departments:

"The Nation," "The World," "Leisure," "Sports," "Better Living," and the "People"-like "Characters." Instead of "Business," Progressive readers were treated to "Labor's Week." As in *Time* magazine, much of the news content consisted of rewrites of material from the wire services and New York dailies, with the newsweekly's editorial slant injected into the selection and writing of the material. Unlike *Time*, the *Guardian* freely acknowledged that this was its policy. It would not have an editorial page, it said, but it would have an editorial point of view. Also, unlike *Time*, it did not force its writers into anonymity. Indeed, its first issue trumpeted forth pieces by some of the biggest names on the Left. There was Henry Wallace himself, writing of his being pelted with eggs in the South for his insistence on speaking only at integrated political rallies and his refusal to eat at segregated restaurants. Handsome young Norman Mailer, the highly acclaimed author of the best-seller *The Naked and the Dead*, gazed out from a center page, over an article outlining his political "Credo"—"an ignorant Marxist. . . . to the left of the Progressive Party and to the right of the Communist Party"—seeing hope for halting the rising tide of war and fascism in the United States among the millions of people who were going to vote for Wallace. Along with Wallace and Mailer, Louis Adamic, W. E. B. Dubois, John Lardner, Ring Lardner, Jr., Anna Louise Strong, Paul Sweezy, Frederick L. Schuman, and Ella Winter were listed among the regular contributors.

Clearly, something had to give. The magazine could not continue to combine the approaches of both *Time* and the *New Republic*. The *Time*-like features were gradually abandoned. "Sports," for example, did not last very long, perhaps because of the problem of reporting things such as the Yankees-Giants-Dodgers rivalry in a radical fashion. Soon, the articles were longer and fewer, the coverage more selective, more "political." Only the "Better Living" section survived into the 1950s, and then only in the form of a weekly cooking column, whose recipes for salmon loaf were hardly radical, and a "Dollar Stretcher" column. The latter, which lasted the longest, was a compendium of consumer information on such items as when shoe prices should be rising or falling, the advantages and disadvantages of laying linoleum, and occasional summaries of some of the ratings of *Consumer Reports*.

Success seemed to come quickly to the *Guardian*. Within a year, circulation had climbed from an initial 5,000 to nearly 100,000 and it continued to move upward. The editors talked cautiously but optimistically about their ultimate goal, a penny mass-circulation newspaper with a readership of over half a million. There were grounds for seeing a rosy future. The paper was a good one. The professional journalistic experience of the founding editors showed through on every page. The articles were well-written in a clear yet punchy style. There was a uniformity about them, a consistency of style and format, that bespoke of experienced editors' blue pencils. It was very likely the best-edited journal, in the journalistic sense, that the Left had ever produced.

Despite Wallace's disappointing showing in the election of 1948, the editors saw a ray of hope for their paper and for the Left, in the million people who did vote for him. Throughout 1949 they talked of those million as their prime potential market, as the first rung in their climb to mass-circulation status. They saw as their political goal the continuation and expansion of the Wallace movement.

But the high hopes soon waned. The Wallace movement began to disintegrate. The American Labor party, which the paper supported in New York, met setback after setback. Finally, in 1950, its standard-bearer and prime vote-getter, Vito Marcantonio, died at a street corner rally in New York at the age of 51. The Left was on the decline, or rather, on the run. Antiradical witch-hunts were mounted everywhere. People who read journals such as the *Guardian* were objects of suspicion and persecution. Readers began to fade away. Typical of many who stopped subscribing out of fear was the lady who at the end of 1949 wrote:

Please take my name from the Guardian mailing lists at once. You see, I live in a rather typical small New England town made up of good folks who not long ago put many well-meaning souls to death for witchcraft. Times have changed a lot, but many of these people unfortunately have not. I have no desire to spend the little life I have left being ridden out on a rail by well-meaning nitwits.

As the political fortunes of the Left declined, so did the economic fortunes of the paper. In February 1949, it received a subsidy, lasting a year, to help get it off the ground. Now, in early 1950, as the subsidy (apparently from Anita McCormick Blaine, cousin of right-wing publisher Robert McCormick of the Chicago *Tribune*, and, like him, an heir of the McCormick reaper fortune) ran out, the paper teetered on the verge of extinction. It was costing 12 cents a copy to produce a paper that sold for 5 cents, and there was no sign of relief anywhere. A switch was made to fortnightly publication; staffers went on half pay or less. Miraculously, the paper pulled through. Other sources of support were developed, and in March it returned to weekly publication.

But another major blow was about to fall. The war in Korea sounded the death knell for the Left in the United States in the 1950s. At first, this was not apparent at the *Guardian*. It greeted the war with a special issue analyzing its origins, placing the blame for it on the aggressive designs of Syngman Rhee, John Foster Dulles, General Douglas MacArthur, and their ilk. The issue, reprinted, sold 250,000 copies. But this was just a temporary pause, as the decline in the Left and the paper's readership continued. By 1951, readership was down to 50,000. Thereafter, the slide was steady, but less precipitous. In 1953, circulation stood at 45,000, by 1957 it had dropped to 35,000, and in 1961 it was down to 29,000. What is remarkable, however, is not the paper's decline in readership, but the fact that it managed to survive at all. Many of its competitors or allies on the Left, papers such as the *New York Daily Compass* and the *Daily Worker*, did not.

The demise of the other papers did not bring the upsurge in *Guardian* circulation that one would normally expect. The *Guardian* tried to capitalize on the death of the *Daily Compass* in 1953 by instituting a special eight-page New York edition, wrapped around the national edition, and by putting on a more moderate face for the liberal ex-readers of the *Compass*. It now called itself "an independent progressive newsweekly devoted to the interests and activities of New York liberals who mean business." But the *Daily Compass* readers switched to the *New York Post*, and the New York edition was soon abandoned.

The paper was more successful in attracting readers from the daily and weekly *Worker*, the organs of the Communist party. If it was uncomfortable to be seen in public with the *Guardian*, it was downright dangerous to be seen reading the *Worker*. Many Communists and fellow-travelers switched to the *Guardian* as the safer, and more readable, of the two. This aroused mixed feelings in the Communist party, which was always ambivalent about the *Guardian* anyway. On the one hand, party leaders saw the *Guardian* as a valuable organ for rallying support among fellow-travelers and non-Communist Socialists and radicals for their causes. On the other hand, they saw it as competing for the same market, both politically and in terms of readership.

In its politics, the *Guardian* tended to follow a line that sometimes, but not too often, ran counter to that of the CP. CP luminaries such as Herbert Aptheker would write for it occasionally. The magazine supported CP political candidates such as Benjamin Davis in New York, CP causes such as the defense of the Rosenbergs, and the CP leadership in their various trials. It backed Stalin and his successors in most of the conflicts of the Cold War. Articles on the great advances in living standards and well-being in the Soviet Union, the "New China," and the other Socialist countries were a regular feature of the paper. In the Third World, it praised and supported the emerging anticolonial movements virtually everywhere.

At home, its reporting tended to reflect the growing persecution of the Left in the 1950s. The early emphasis on labor and conventional political reporting gave way to depressing stories of trials, firings, hearings, and witch-hunts. The "Trenton Six," the Rosenbergs, the "Smith Act Ten," the "Martinsville Ten," Morton Sobell, blacks and radicals facing prosecution for specious reasons, became the stuff of the weekly headlines. From the *Guardian*'s own office, in 1953, the three editors were hauled before Senator Joseph McCarthy's ubcommittee and the House Un-American Activities Committee. After a long series of hearings, Belfrage was deported in 1955 for allegedly having been a member of the Communist party in 1937, under a false name. Thereafter, he resumed his world travels and became editor-in-exile, based first in England, and a number of years later in Mexico City.

On the most divisive issues on the Left in the 1950s the *Guardian* tried to walk a thin line between the views of the CP and the anti-Communist Left. Although it had supported Stalin rather uncritically until his death—defending his regime against charges of anti-Semitism, for example, in 1953, when he was in the midst of an anti-Semitic binge—it seemed to welcome Khrushchev's indictment of him at the twentieth party congress with something approaching relief. It supported the movements for the liberalization of the regimes in Eastern Europe and the Western Communist parties that subsequently surfaced. This did not please the faction that controlled the American CP.

The Soviet invasion of Hungary and the Israeli invasion of Sinai in 1956 found the *Guardian* treading on very thin ice. It tried to please all sides of the terribly divided Left, reporting at first that the Poles and Hungarians were injecting healthy reforms in the system; then that the

Hungarians had fallen prey to foreign and right-wing fascism; then that the Russian intervention had been unnecessarily brutal and perhaps uncalled for, but that the mass of the Hungarian people still retained their affection for the Soviet people. In short, the magazine published a confusing and confused series of articles that reflected the confusion and despair felt by many radicals. Although it was not sufficiently pro-Soviet to please the CP or sufficiently anti-Soviet to satisfy those who were revolted by the suppression of the Hungarian movement, the *Guardian* did manage to avoid a mass defection of either segment, while pleasing virtually nobody.

Similarly, on the sensitive question of Israel, the *Guardian* managed to tread the thin line. On the one hand, its reports tended to be sympathetic to Israel's complaints regarding the unyielding hostility of the Arabs to its continued existence. On the other hand, it clucked disapprovingly over Israel's joining with the neanderthal imperialists, Britain and France, in the Suez and Sinai venture.

The crises of 1956 did expose some of the strengths of the *Guardian*. Because it did not have an editorial page, it did not have to stick its neck out on everydivisive issue on the Left. Its line on particular issues, if it had one, was expressed in its reporting. One was never sure whether to blame the editors or the foreign editor or the reporter in the field for what may have been its outrageous stand on a given event. In addition, during the crises in Eastern Europe and Suez it had its own reporters in each of these places, sending first-hand reports from Poland, Hungary, France, Israel, and Egypt: an amazing achievement, especially for a weekly of that size. Supplied, usually, with a minimum of three articles from its own overseas correspondents, readers of the *Guardian* did not have to rely solely on the staples of left-wing reporting: hortatory editorials masquerading as news, sly rewrites of American wire service reports, or the propaganda of official spokesmen of sympathetic governments.

Not that the *Guardian* did not rely with some frequency on all of the above alternatives. It was best at the rewrites of information in the capitalist press; again, the professional experience of the editors paid off. Though its resources were limited, it had a staff librarian and a newspaper-style clipping and filing program. As was done on *I. F. Stone's Weekly*, it gave added weight to its radical interpretations of the news by quoting information provided by its opponents in support of its analyses. The *New York Times* and the *Wall Street Journal* were the usual sources, along with papers such as the *Christian Science Monitor*, *Le Monde*, and *L'Observateur*. Indeed, at times, it tried to sell itself as a left-wing clipping service. "The *Guardian*'s staff does the publication-reading job you don't have time to do," it said in 1950: "it digs out the nuggets of truth in the press of this and other countries, and pieces them together with its own correspondents' reports into running summary of the vital news."

Funds were always a problem, and desperate pleas for them were a regular feature of the magazine. During the 1950s, a number of rather imaginative fundraising schemes were invented. Aside from the usual appeals for direct subsidies from readers through devices such as the "Buck of the Month Club," groups of *Guardian* financial supporters were organized in various large cities. In Los Angeles, they held an annual "Guardian Angels Ball." In New York, the *Guardian* picnic became a regular feature. *Guardian* editors and reporters found themselves spending a considerable amount of time making public relations appearances at coffee klatsches across the country. On the tenth anniversary of the death of FDR, the paper, still desperate for any of the sheenhhat might reflect from his image, cut and sold a record in his memory. Called the "Unforgotten Man," it was produced by the *Guardian* staff and "performed by celebrated actors, singers, and chorus." Although it listed for $3.95, *Guardian* readers could have it for only $3.00.

The appeal of a bargain formed the basis for perhaps the strangest, but apparently the most successful, of the weekly's fundraising devices: "The *Guardian* Buying Service." Begun in the mid-1950s, it offered readers Zippo lighters, electric shavers, luggage, and numerous other articles at discount prices, with the profits going to support the paper. Although some of the items such as the Hungarian hand-embroidered peasant blouses and Pete Seeger records could, by stretching the imagination, be considered to have some radical connection, the large majority of items, the vitamin pills and the like, could not. By the later 1950s, the Christmas shopping season would find four, six, or eight pages of the paper devoted to ads for the Service.

The heavy emphasis on sales of vitamin pills symbolized one of the growing weaknesses of the *Guardian* as the decade drew to a close. It had become very much identified with a fellow-traveling readership, a readership that appeared to be getting old and, especially after the disasters of the mid-1950s, very tired. In a desperate move, the *Guardian* tried to make inroads among the new generation of college students. It supported all the right old causes—peace, nuclear disarmament, and freedom of speech—and all the right new causes—Martin Luther King, Jr., Fidel Castro, Sukarno, Kwame Nkrumah, Tom Mboya, and the whole new generation of Third World anticolonialists. For a while, at the end of the 1950s, it appeared to be pleasing nearly everyone on the Left. Editor James McManus wrote an ecstatic series of articles on Castro's Cuba that warmed the hearts of the slowly emerging "New Left" searching for a non-Stalinist road to socialism. Cuba, it appeared, had found that road. The old fellow-travelers were pleased by the continuing support of the Soviet position in the Cold War.

But all was not so well. The new young leftists found the paper's seemingly uncritical admiration for the Soviet Union oldfashioned and vaguely Stalinist. The older fellow-travelers were not overjoyed by its uncritical support of Castro and, more importantly perhaps, of the divisive, liberalizing, polycentric forces within the Communist world. Of the two, it was the alienation of the new generation of leftists that would prove most explosive in the 1950s. Then, the two tendencies, embodied in two factions on the staff, split the paper wide open, creating two rival papers, the *Guardian* and the *Liberated Guardian*. After some years of competition, only the *Guardian* survived, but it was a barely recognizable descendant of the well-edited, well-written, newsy paper of the 1950s.

The divisive tendencies, the centrifugal forces, were becoming apparent in 1960. In retrospect, it is clear that the paper would have great difficulty supporting all of the different groups, movements, tendencies, and countries it was backing, especially once conflicts between them arose. Ironically, then, it was to be the very success of many of these movements, and of the polycentric forces that the journal supported, that would lead to its demise. Again in retrospect, perhaps one of the most important items it published in 1960 was another letter canceling a subscription, this time, significantly, from Berkeley, California: "I no longer wish to continue my subscription to the *Guardian*. Hoped you would make the break to a genuinely new left position, but see only a constant back-sliding toward 'pro-Soviet liberalism' characteristic of earlier years. Sorry." Whatever the writer meant by "pro-Soviet liberalism,'' one thing was becoming clear: the best-edited paper on the Left would be in for all sorts of trouble from the new generation of radical students in Berkeley, Madison, Ann Arbor, and Cambridge, even though in many cases they were the sons and daughters of its most faithful subscribers.

Hamilton, Ontario, 1973

Monthly Review

NEW YORK, 1949—

PETER CLECAK

DURING the 1950s, a combination of Cold War repression and prosperity made political survival the dominant issue confronting every segment of the American Left. The failure of the Progressive party in the 1948 elections shattered the fragile postwar leftist coalition and prefigured the subsequent decline of the Left in the next decade. In the absence of effective political organization, isolated radicals turned increasingly to small magazines for a sense of symbolic community. The openended form of the monthly magazine provided a continuous forum for developing radical theory and for assessing the progress of socialism in every area of the world. During this dormant decade of American radicalism, *Monthly Review*, an "Independent Socialist Magazine" edited by Leo Huberman and Paul Sweezy, played a significant role in preserving a historical and theoretical continuity between the crumbling Old Left and the new radicalism of the 1960s.

Huberman, a respected historian and social critic, and Sweezy, a distinguished Marxian economist, founded *Monthly Review* in May 1949. Despite political and financial obstacles, the magazine survived its infancy. Circulation rose from 500 to approximately 2,500 during the first year of publication. And, in contrast to most radical periodicals, which die as easily as they come into existence, *Monthly Review* has grown steadily into one of the most formidable Marxist journals published anywhere in the world: its scope, influence, and reputation are international. After nearly twenty years of continuous publication, the English edition has a circulation of about 8,600 and a readership probably three times as large. *Monthly Review: Selecciones en Castellano*, the Spanish edition which began in 1963, is circulated throughout Latin

America. And the first issue of *Monthly Review: Edizione Italiana* appeared in Rome in the spring of 1968. Thus, any preliminary assessment of the first twelve volumes reprinted in this series (May 1949-April 1961) is not a survey of the remains of an extinct radical magazine, but rather an attempt to understand a living organism through an examination of some of its earlier stages of growth.

During the early years of the Cold War, Huberman and Sweezy became the chief intellectual representatives of a rather unique position between the polarized elements of the American Left. Both the Communist and anti-Communist Left forged essentially *metaphysical* rather than *historical* views of the realities and potentialities of socialism in the various parts of the world: "communism" was either inherently good or it was inherently evil. The American Communist party generally adopted an uncritical attitude toward the Soviet Union and the nations of Eastern Europe, whereas the anti-Communist Left—a scattering of small groups and independent radicals—united in the belief that the Soviet Union was a permanently authoritarian regime with limited prospects for economic development and no chance at all for creating a genuinely human society and culture. Huberman and Sweezy chose to occupy the no-man's-land between, retaining their critical independence *and* their belief in socialism.

In their introductory editorial, "Where We Stand" (Vol. I, No. 1, May 1949), the editors outlined the principal aims and assumptions which have guided *MR* from its inception. In spite of the political decline of the American Left at midcentury, they predicted that "in the long run, socialism will prove to be the only solution to the increasingly serious economic and social problems that face the United States." But the widespread ignorance of the nature of socialism and capitalism convinced them that the most imperative political function of an American Socialist magazine was educational. *MR* was therefore to be "an independent magazine devoted to analyzing, from a socialist point of view, the most significant trends in domestic and foreign affairs."

Focusing on the decline of capitalism and the rise of socialism as the decisive historical transition of the twentieth century, Huberman and Sweezy defined socialism broadly as "a system of society with two fundamental characteristics; first, public ownership of the decisive sectors of the economy; and second, comprehensive planning of production for the benefit of the producers themselves." On the basis of this minimal definition, they argued that socialism had become "a reality with the introduction of the first Five Year Plan in Soviet Russia in 1928," and that "its power to survive was demonstrated by the subsequent economic achievements of the USSR during the 30s, and finally, once and for all, in the war against Nazi Germany." But the editors rejected "the view that the USSR is above criticism, simply because it is socialist," adopting instead the "principle that the cause of socialism has everything to gain and nothing to lose from a full and frank discussion of short-comings, as well as accomplishments, of socialist countries and socialist parties everywhere."

This distinctive combination of intellectual independence and moral commitment to the advancement of socialism helps to clarify the basic patterns of continuity and change in the first decade of *Monthly Review*. The chief continuity derives from the editors' comprehensive Marxist world view. *MR* has consistently adhered to the central principle of Marxist methodology: that to understand and participate in social change, one must cut through the observable phenomena to formulate and tentatively answer fundamental economic questions. Early in the century, Lenin examined international cartels because they

show to what point capitalist monopolies have developed, and they *reveal the object* of the struggle between the various capitalist groups. This last circumstance is the most important; it alone shows us the historic-economic significance of events; for the *forms* of the struggle may and do vary in accordance with varying, relatively particular and transitory causes, but the *essence* of this struggle, its class *content*, *cannot* change while classes exist.

To fail to arrive at this point means to accept history as an irrational and uncontrollable process. To stop here insures a crude and simplistic caricature of historical development. Huberman and Sweezy have sought to define the relationships between the economic essence and the social, political, and ideological structures of the two competing social systems—capitalism and socialism. Lenin summarizes the importance of the methodology succinctly: "I trust that this pamphlet ["Imperialism"] will help the reader to understand the fundamental economic question, *viz.*, the question of the economic essence of imperialism, for unless this is studied it will be impossible to appraise modern war and modern politics." Huberman and Sweezy have consistently analyzed immediate issues—"modern war and politics"—in terms of their deepening theoretical analysis of world systems in conflict.

The editors gradually developed a model of the structure of monopoly capitalism which illuminates the domestic and international consequences of its chronic inability to dispose of surplus capital profitably and rationally. In the inaugural issue of *MR*, Sweezy indicated that "American capitalism is coming increasingly under the domination of a few giant corporations which in turn are owned and controlled by a handful of extremely rich capitalists" (Vol. I, No. 1, p. 21). Throughout the 1950s, Huberman and Sweezy showed how monopoly capitalism maintains its economic vitality through waste, excess consumption, massive government military spending, and imperialism, while it largely avoids the major social problems of poverty, unemployment, and racism. An understanding of the economic essence of the American social order enabled the editors to anticipate the political and social problems which have become the standard fare of critics in the 1960s.

In the early years of the Cold War, liberal defenders of the status quo, such as John Kenneth Galbraith, took the position that if the external Communist threat were to diminish, government spending could be shifted from defense to social reconstruction without any permanent disorganization of the corporate sector of the American economy. As early as 1952, Sweezy and Huberman challenged this persistent view on the grounds that military spending constitutes the most "rational" solution to the chronic tendency toward stagnation. Massive governmental expenditures on armaments increase corporate profits by socializing the costs of production; and by sustaining the illusion of an external threat, the Garrison State justifies the enormous tax burden on nonowning classes and provides the cornerstone of an anti-Communist ideology which virtually paralyzed dissent in America during most of the 1950s. Thus, a growing military budget is a crucial economic, political, and ideological means of perpetuating the existing class structure with its enormously inequitable distribution of wealth, power, and privilege.

In their essays on American foreign policy, Huberman and Sweezy consistently cut through the Cold War rhetoric of "Democracy versus Communism" to expose the economic roots of global anticommunism as practiced in slightly different forms by the Truman, Eisenhower, and

Kennedy administrations. They argued that a growing military machine was crucial to the maintenance of a vast neo-imperialist empire which stimulated corporate production and profits by supplying cheap raw materials, expanding investment opportunities, and wider markets. They explained the changing *forms* of American foreign involvement during the 1950s—from nuclear confrontation with the USSR to counterinsurgency in the underdeveloped world—in terms of the relatively constant *content* of the struggle to preserve the ''free world'' and contain the expanding Socialist world. In 1954, for example, the editors charted the disastrous consequences of pursuing the special interests of American imperialism at the expense of the peoples of Southeast Asia:

> To the extent that we support France—and we are already paying about four-fifths of the French military effort in Indo-China—we support both colonialism and aggression. To the extent that we support Bao Dai, we claim the right to tell the Vietnamese people who should rule them. And if we send American forces into Indo-China, as Dulles and other high government spokesmen have repeatedly threatened to do . . . we shall be guilty of aggression ourselves. . . .
>
> Are we going to take the position that anti-Communism justifies anything, including colonialism, interference in the affairs of other countries, and aggression? That way, let us be perfectly clear about it, lies war and more war leading ultimately to full-scale national disaster (Vol. VI, No. 6, pp. 70-71).

The subsequent history of American involvement in Southeast Asia clearly answers the question and at least partially confirms the prediction.

A clear perception of American capitalism and imperialism as a world force not only requires an understanding of the essential characteristics of the system, but also a comprehension of the structure and potentialities of socialism in its various forms and stages of growth. For it is the interaction between socialist forces and the internally dictated requirements of an expansive, irrational monopoly capitalism which, according to Huberman and Sweezy, constitutes the central dialectic of contemporary world history. Throughout the 1950s, *MR* traced the development of socialism in the underdeveloped and overexploited areas of the world —Asia, Latin America, and Africa. In May 1949, the editors accurately prophesied the historical implications of the Chinese revolution: ''The impending victory of the Chinese Communists is a world-shaking event comparable in importance to the Russian Revolution of 1917. Then, one-sixth of the land surface of the globe; now, one-fifth of the human race'' (Vol. I, No. 1, p. 5).

And by the middle of the decade it was clear that the outward thrust of American imperialism made revolution the primary road to socialism throughout the underdeveloped world. In their examination of the North American suppression of the Guatemalan revolution in 1954, Huberman and Sweezy projected the main directions of the ''great Latin American Revolution of the twentieth century,'' predicting that

> much more of Mr. Dulles' brand of anti-Communism will split Latin America between extreme Right and extreme Left, and will force the Latin American revolution relatively quickly to take on the characteristics and forms which are so familiar to us from the events of the postwar years in Asia. And under such circumstances, the leadership of the revolution will fall into the hands of the Communists as certainly as it did in China and Indo-China (Vol. VI, No. 3, p. 101).

And at the end of the decade, Huberman and Sweezy published ''Cuba: Anatomy of a Revolution'' (July-August 1960), a brilliant book-length assessment of the achievements and aspirations of that revolution, as well as of the internal and external obstacles to Socialist development in Cuba and throughout Latin America.

The basic continuity of *MR*'s analysis of the interplay of capitalist and socialist forces is reflected not only in the consistency of the editors' position, but in the changes as well. The 1950s was a decade of profound and frequently unexpected change within and between parts of the capitalist and socialist worlds. For all its irrationality, monopoly capitalism in America exhibited a staying power which few Marxist critics were able to foresee. And despite its many defeats abroad, American foreign policy was successful in temporarily securing vast areas of its informal empire. Moreover, the secondary centers of capitalism—Japan and Western Europe—made substantial economic recoveries and achieved a greater measure of political stability than critics on the Left had believed possible in the years immediately following World War II. In the advanced Socialist countries the changes were even more dramatic.

After recovering from the widespread destruction of World War II, the Soviet Union continued its impressive economic and social reconstruction. But after the death of Stalin in 1953, the USSR entered a new and confusing period of its internal development which had profound effects on the shape of socialism in the Soviet Union and Eastern Europe, as well as in the underdeveloped world.

The interplay between rapidly changing objective conditions and the editors' subjective responses reveals the strengths of Marxist perspectives when employed by sensitive and intelligent critics. The basic pattern of the editors' response to major historical events of the decade is nowhere more clearly illustrated than in their changing attitude toward the progress of socialism in the USSR. In the early 1950s they concentrated on the spectacular postwar economic recovery and development in the Soviet Union. By the spring of 1955, after the fall of Malenkov, Huberman and Sweezy increasingly hoped that the solution to the most basic problems stemming from backwardness—poverty, hunger, illiteracy, and disease—would mark the end of the most politically repressive period of Soviet development: "There can be no doubt, we think, that the Russian Revolution has accomplished its work; from now on, progress depends on the expansion of the socialist economy *and* on the full development of socialist legality" (Vol. VI, No. 11. p. 404). Stalinism, they maintained, was an "extremely dynamic and profoundly self-contradictory phenomenon." Under Stalin, "the Soviet Union had become the world's second industrial power, with an educated citizenry and surrounded by friends and allies; on the other hand, it was governed by the methods of an oriental despotism rather than a modern civilized society" (Vol. VIII, Nos. 3 & 4, p. 70). According to Huberman and Sweezy, the achievements of Stalinism canceled its premises. Having liquidated backwardness through backward political methods, Stalinism would, or rather *could*, liquidate itself. But from the editors' point of view, the disparity between expectation and achievement remained depressingly wide.

Toward the end of the decade, they exhibited a growing disenchantment with the Soviet Union, arguing that while the excessive features of the dictatorship had been "moderated," the Soviet Union had nevertheless not moved to liquidate the dictatorship and form a Socialist democracy which would guarantee the degree of individual, political, and cultural freedom that Soviet economic and social development permitted.

On the fortieth anniversary of the Bolshevik Revolution, the editors observed that the material conditions "which produced the dictatorship *have* been overcome. The Soviet Union is no longer a backward country and is rapidly overtaking the most advanced. Internationally, it is at least as secure as any nation in the world. Our theory is being put to the crucial test of practice. And so far—let us face it frankly—there is precious little evidence to confirm it" (Vol. IX, No. 7, p. 212).

Disenchantment with the pace and direction of Soviet internal developments gradually deepened and extended to a critical attitude toward Soviet foreign policy. Huberman and Sweezy increasingly doubted the legitimacy of Soviet claims to moral leadership of revolutionary forces in the underdeveloped world. Soviet emphasis on peaceful coexistence and on "socialism in one country" helped the United States implement counterrevolutionary strategies, thus compounding the obstacles to national liberation in every part of the underdeveloped world. During the 1960s, especially after the Sino-Soviet split, Huberman and Sweezy came to view Peking rather than Moscow as the moral and symbolic center of world revolution. But even this major change can be understood as a part of a continuing effort to understand short-run historical developments in terms of the dominant historical pattern of this century —the decline of capitalism and imperialism and the rise of various forms of socialism.

From this brief historical distance, it is difficult to evaluate the first twelve years of *Monthly Review*. In retrospect, the confusing welter of historical detail disappears, and the major trends take on a deceptively regular appearance. But since the obstacles to clear analysis remain, it is important to try to explain mistakes and achievements of previous theoretical efforts. Both the central weaknesses and strengths of *Monthly Review* derive in large part from the ambitious theoretical aims of Marxism and from the difficulties of applying Marxist perspectives to the historical present.

I think the two principal (and interrelated) weaknesses of *Monthly Review* are a latent tendency to perceive changing historical realities in terms of partially outmoded theoretical formulations, and a tendency to overestimate the tempo of the historical transition from capitalism to socialism. Because of its ambitious aims, Marxism makes rigorous demands upon critics. Theorists operating in the Marxian tradition proceed from the basic Hegelian premise that the "truth" is the whole. Thus, they must develop a theoretical mode which helps to explain and relate parts of social organisms to their national and international wholes. And in addition to developing cross-sectional views, Marxist critics are committed to understanding the historical process in motion. These theoretical aims necessitate a high degree of abstraction, a continuous search to identify the key aspects of economic, social, and political reality which set the limitations and define the potentialities of revolutionary practice. The long-range focus often blurs the specific textures of immediate events. There is a further complication to this complex process—namely, that a changing reality constantly calls into question the validity of particular theoretical formulations. At its best, Marxism is a self-transcending set of propositions which must be continuously tested against a multitude of particular and concrete historical phenomena. But the very potency of basic Marxian formulations often delays recognition of their obsolescence. For Marxists committed to revolutionary change, however, these disparities between theoretical formulations and developing historical potentialities may constitute the difference between success and failure, as the tragic death of Che Guevara illustrates.

While Huberman and Sweezy always avoided sterile dogmatism—the most frequent perversion and distortion of the powerful analytic tools of Marxism—they occasionally tried to press changing historical patterns into partially obsolete Marxian formulas. For example, while the editors were gradually developing their model of monopoly capitalism, they occasionally viewed political developments in America through more traditional Marxian perspectives. As a consequence of underestimating the postwar economic potential of American capitalism, they overestimated the radical potentialities of American labor, the traditional Marxian agency of social change. Thus, even by the end of the 1950s, they did not fully appreciate the strength of the alliance between American business and labor, interpreting the major steel strike of 1959 as the beginning of "intensified class conflict in the United States" rather than as an interlude in class collaboration. The editors predicted that "from now on Big Business and organized labor, no longer able to collaborate at the expense of the third parties [*i.e.*, exploitation of foreign markets], will [each] try to improve its position at the expense of the other" (Vol. XI, No. 10, p. 361). They predicted that should this happen, the unions, representing only a small minority of the working class, might become conscious of the need for a larger, more militant organization and eventually "attempt to expand" their "political power." The editors remarked that "nothing could do more to shake this country out of the moral and political stagnation into which it has fallen during these years of the American celebration (which is essentially the ideological aspect of the Big Business-organized labor alliance)." And they conclude that "for two decades now, American society has been in a state of what the French call 'immobilism.' It has lasted so long, indeed, that many have come to believe that it must last forever. This is of course far from the truth, and the steel strike may be the first sign that we are even now emerging into the light of a new day of labor militancy and social struggle." Although Sweezy and Huberman were never misled by the generally calm social surface during the late 1950s, their outmoded assumptions about the specific role of organized labor temporarily prevented them from correctly identifying the principal agents of social conflict of the 1960s—the civil rights and black liberation movements.

The second and related weakness in *Monthly Review*'s analyses—the tendency to base predictions on an accelerated view of historical change—also derives from the abstract character of the editors' Marxism. If Huberman and Sweezy were prone to overestimate the rate of capitalist decline, they were even more apt to overestimate the rate of Socialist development. For instance, in evaluating the achievements and prospects of the Soviet Union on its fortieth anniversary, the editors declared that the USSR

already leads the world in natural resources and trained manpower, and it will be a matter of a few years only—say a couple of decades at the outside—before these "original factors of production," as the classical economists used to call them, will translate themselves into the world's highest level of per capita production. And the gap, once opened, will grow steadily wider—unless and until the erstwhile leading economic nations discard their crazy-quilt system in favor of rational socialist planning (Vol. IX, No. 7, p. 210).

Though partially based on Soviet experience, these projections were mainly predicated upon unrealistic theoretical assumptions about the efficiency of centralized economic planning. The editors did not give sufficient weight to their own speculations about the political implications of Soviet economic progress. Arguing that during the Stalin era the Soviet Communist party was "sensitive to public opinion" in order to "mold and manipulate it rather than to win its support," they correctly predicted that "public opinion would acquire a political weight which it has never yet possessed in the Soviet Union. . . ." But they did not foresee that increasing the relevance of public opinion would reduce the effectiveness of economic planning. Popular pressures for more consumer goods in the Soviet Union have (among other things) slowed its projected overall rate of growth: they have contributed to a formidable range of planning problems—from the sheer complexity of regulating production of millions of consumer items to the difficulties of conserving intellectual and material resources required for further growth. In short, the optimistic predictions have not been fulfilled. And as a consequence of overestimating the rate of Socialist development in the advanced countries, Huberman and Sweezy also overrated the tempo of capitalist decline. In their initial assessment of the 1960s, "For Whom the Bell Tolls" (January 1960), they asserted that "the largest, and in our judgment, the least uncertain of these foreseeable developments is the continued rise of socialism and decline of capitalism on the world-historical stage" (Vol. XI, No. 9, p. 305). In the 1960s, the competition between advanced capitalist and Socialist societies did not result in a standoff which would have enabled revolutionary forces to advance rapidly in the underdeveloped parts of the world. Instead, the United States was able to mount a sustained counterrevolutionary offensive which has transformed wars of national liberation into more bitter and protracted struggles of international scope.

On balance, however, the weaknesses of *MR* seem to be relatively minor flaws within the context of a major intellectual effort. The traces of obsolete Marxian formulations, the tendency to compress stages of the transition from capitalism to socialism, and the occasionally apocalyptic tone echo in a minor key the dominant strengths of *MR*—the development of powerful theoretical perspectives on capitalism and imperialism, and the generally accurate and often prophetic analyses of emerging historical trends throughout the 1950s. The most impressive quality of the magazine, in my opinion, is the durability of Huberman's and Sweezy's main perspectives. By avoiding the anti-Communist Left, the editors were not forced to divorce their Socialist vision from historical realities. And by avoiding the inflexible ideology of the Stalinists, they were able to advance Marxian theory in the process of their analyses and interpretations of "the most significant trends in domestic and foreign affairs." Moreover, in the early 1960s, the independence and flexibility which characterized *MR* in its formative years enabled Sweezy and Huberman to understand the shift in the main locus of the world revolution—from the competition between advanced forms of capitalism and socialism to the revolutionary struggle against imperialism throughout the underdeveloped world. They have never pushed a line; instead, they have consistently exercised honesty, flexibility, and intelligence in assessing the changing forms of the conflict between socialism and capitalism.

The high quality of *MR*'s continuing analyses of major world developments distinguishes it from most of the material published in left-wing journals during the Cold War. The devitalizing effects of this period on American radicals have been obvious from the outset: exclusion and self-imposed exile from intellectual life, frustration at the slow pace of social change, and government persecution all contributed to the indifferent quality of most radical critiques of American society.

The dramatic witch-hunts of the early 1950s tend to overshadow the more routine and cumulative impoverishment of the whole of American intellectual life—an impoverishment which has seriously crippled the efforts of nonradicals to understand the present as history. Throughout the 1950s, the respectable academics and intellectuals constantly reburied what they considered the dead horse of Marxism. John Kenneth Galbraith concluded that American poverty—as well as other major social problems—had been reduced to isolated and manageable "pockets." Daniel Bell recorded the end of innocence and ideology in America. And during this period, American-Soviet tensions eased somewhat. According to the most sophisticated intellectuals, a prosperous and comparatively harmonious postcapitalist social order was taking shape just beneath the visible surface of American life.

But the postcapitalist society has matured only in the imaginations of the critics. For, to understate matters, the 1960s have reduced the liberal analysis to a shambles. The turmoil of the inner cities, the persistence of poverty and racism, the revolt of the young at the hypocrisy and cant of American public and private life, reveal the liberal belief in orderly, gradual domestic progress as an untenable myth. Although still in an incipient stage, revolution has become visible on three continents. And Vietnam has clarified America's counterrevolutionary role to all but the sightless: the "welfare" and "warfare" states are more closely inter-twined than ever. In 1967, Andrew Kopkind inventoried the pieces of the shattered liberal consensus: "The civil war and the foreign one have contrived this summer to murder liberalism—in its official robes. There are few mourners. The urgent business is now for imaginations freed from the old myths to see what kind of society might be reconstructed that would have no need for imperialism and no cause for revolt" (*New York Review*, August 24, 1967, p. 6). Huberman and Sweezy began that task nearly two decades earlier when the pressures to conform were consider-ably more intense. Throughout the 1950s, *MR* was a strong and steady voice of reason in the United States. Nearly every major American radical critic of that period will be found in the pages of these first twelve volumes—Paul Baran, C. Wright Mills, William A. Williams.

In a recent appraisal of the Italian edition of *Monthly Review*, Vittorio Saltini remarked that "*Monthly Review* . . . is the best Marxist journal not only in the United States, but in the world." This assessment is perhaps hyperbolic, and somewhat premature. But with the evidence of more than a decade of *Monthly Review* before him, the reader may begin to formu-late his own conclusions.

Irvine, California, 1968

Alternative

NEW YORK, 1948-1951

WILLIAM APPLEMAN WILLIAMS

AS I read, and then reread, these issues of *Alternative*, I kept thinking of David Dellinger standing on the speaker's platform, and later being arrested, during the October 1967, anti-Vietnam War demonstrations at the Pentagon. The first thrust of my thoughts was very simple: "What a good and important man. How much he has given in order to create a better America in his own time."

In the narrow sense, of course, that thought was generated because back in April 1948 Dellinger (along with Robert Auerbach, Roy Finch, and a handful of others) launched *Alternative* as part of their effort to produce the kind of action represented by the Pentagon confrontation. When he said in October 1967 that the movement had shifted from protest to resistance, he was only partially correct. For, in truth, he and his associates called from the outset for men and women to "refuse" to support war and the draft. They advocated "civil disobedience" to achieve the "total abolition of the Army" in May 1948, and in February 1950 opened a campaign to accomplish the "social organization of conscientious objection."

From the first, *Alternative* concentrated on opposing the draft as the primary strategic move against war. It fought the draft as an institution (and system) practicing segregation and other forms of discrimination, and it encouraged all men to refuse to be drafted. Part of its support for the group advocating the nonpayment of taxes likewise stemmed from the same opposition to war. In a very real (and almost literal) sense, therefore, *Alternative* was the handwriting on the wall that preceded the antiwar and antidraft movement of the mid-1960s.

677

Alternative was also against many other things. It considered Henry Wallace "muddleheaded" in his 1948 presidential campaign, and it opposed both the Communists and those who launched militant, red-baiting campaigns against the Communists. The editors also stated flatly that "it is not possible to trust governments," and openly attempted on that and related grounds "to be dangerous . . . to the economic and political systems" of the capitalist West and the Communist East, and "to all dictatorships."

The simple truth, however, as the editors admitted at one point, is that *Alternative* was far better at saying NO! than it was at formulating relevant, viable, and creative alternatives to the existing system. Beyond stressing the individual's "obligation to lead an unfettered, responsible" life, the best the editors ever did was to announce that they were at work on "thinking through a new social program and carrying it into action." The brief reports on a few tiny and scattered communal groups offered little hard information and hardly any inspiration.

There was one article that purported to give significant examples of how to live differently as a radical, but the proposals were mundane if not trite. Radicals should offer "new ideas in design of clothing" and practice nudism (at least in the summer), should "invent new recipes" as part of abandoning frugality and simplicity in their diet, and of course be freer in sexual behavior (including simultaneous use by both sexes of the bathroom).

The two principles stated most clearly and forcefully by the editors as bases for an alternate organization of society involved individual responsibility and the lack of coercion. The "secret of conscience," they asserted, was "individual responsibility above and beyond any authority." "The true notion of democracy," they explained, "is that no one shall be on top, no one shall have power over others." "Administration and coordination," they amplified, "are the only legitimate functions of politics." And those were to be exercised only through persuasion.

Several thoughts come to mind in connection with those axioms for radical reconstruction. First of all, the emphasis on personal conscience can lead very easily to a privatizing, hedonizing, and self-centered individualism that is at best anarchistic and at worst selfish, arrogant, and delusive. The anarchism implicit in such an approach, moreover, is not only utopian in an escapist sense in the middle of the twentieth century, but it would operate to subvert the very improvement in man's life it is supposed to produce. There is far too much to be done by and with and for millions of people to talk about alternatives in terms of loosely associated quasi-anarchistic communities. The poor at home and abroad have become poorer under American capitalism, but they would suffer even more if American radicals abandoned the nation's economic strength to achieve their individual salvation.

The proposition that "no one shall have power over others" is not much more than grand rhetoric unless it is amplified far more carefully and extensively than was ever done by the editors of *Alternative*. No individual or group can persuade everyone, even everyone in a small community, all the time. When that approach fails, moreover, someone either exercises power over other people or the original community cracks open into two or more dissident communities. It is not simply imaginary to suggest that people acting on the two axioms offered by the editors of *Alternative* might very well practice more violence than the majority of citizens in other, less idealistic societies.

Encouraging individuals to do what they believe to be right (or good), while at the same time telling them that no one else should have power over them beyond the limits of persuasion, is a dangerous course of action if the object is to create a peaceful, cooperative community capable of producing enough material wealth to succor other societies and enough leisure for individuals to live a fully human life. Those two propositions come closer to being a definition of the millennium, and in a significant sense *Alternative* did fall back on a kind of midtwentieth century millennarianism.

Since Dellinger and the other creators of *Alternative* are perceptive and honest men, it may very well be that they recognized and wondered about the ambiguous legacy of *Alternative* as they looked out across the thousands of young people massed in Washington in October 1967. On the one hand, *Alternative* undoubtedly played an indirect but nevertheless significant role in the long effort to mobilize such a movement of protest and resistance. On the other hand, the failure of *Alternative* to offer any significant creative options beyond protest and resistance also influenced the character of that movement.

For to be against something bad is to be for something good only in a limited sense. The possibilities for greater and more sustained improvement remain nothing more than possibilities unless they are first formulated as intellectual guidelines for action by a social movement. Unfortunately, *Alternative* never met and discharged that responsibility.

Madison, Wisconsin, 1968

Liberation

NEW YORK, 1956—

THOMAS WAGSTAFF

THE American political phenomenon known as the New Left enjoyed its meteoric heyday in the turbulent decade and a half between its birth in the civil rights demonstrations of the late 1950s and its last major manifestation in the "Cambodian Spring" of 1969. During that period no American political journal better expressed, or more completely identified with, the animating principles of the movement than *Liberation*.

Founded in 1956 by a group of veteran independent radical activists and pacifists, *Liberation*'s birth coincided with a series of propitious events. The revelations of Stalin's crimes at the twentieth congress of the Communist party of the Soviet Union and the brutal suppression of the Hungarian uprising obliterated the last vestiges of the moral authority of the splintered and harried orthodox Marxist Left. In America, the seemingly still complacent atmosphere of the late Eisenhower Era crackled with the ominous energies of a gathering storm. There were ample manifestations of a renewed and more urgent concern with the traditional concrete problems of racism, economic exploitation, and militarism. Also being felt were the first broad stirrings of concern with what would come to be amorphously defined as the "dehumanizing" aspects of plastic technology and prefabricated mass culture. Martin Luther King's Montgomery, Alabama, bus boycott drew to a successful conclusion and introduced the first hopeful prospect for meaningful mass direct-protest action since the end of the CIO's unionizing drives in the 1930s.

The *Liberation* group was uniquely suited by conviction and experience to the situation created by those developments. The aged and aging veterans of a variety of movements and causes who made up this group had retained a passionate belief in the need for immediate radical change and in the efficacy of immediate direct action to achieve it. They were untainted by Stalinism and were committed to the development of a "politics of the future" that would incorporate the values and transcend the limitations of both liberalism and Marxism.

The spiritual father of *Liberation*, and, until his death in 1967, the most prominent figure on its editorial board, was Abraham Johannes (A. J.) Muste, one of the most active, durable, and appealing individuals in the history of twentieth-century American radicalism. The other key editors were Bayard Rustin and David Dellinger, both long-time associates of Muste in the Fellowship of Reconciliation and its subsidiaries, the Congress of Racial Equality and the Committee for Non-Violent Action. They were joined by Staughton Lynd, the young scholar-evangelist; Paul Goodman, the social critic and libertarian philosopher; Sidney Lens, a prolific radical journalist and labor movement activist; and Barbara Deming, an indefatigible participant in and eloquent reporter of numerous peace and civil rights actions.

Muste provided the principles and inspiration that formed and guided *Liberation*. His ideas had been shaped during fifty years of intense and dedicated participation in radical causes. Born in Holland, raised in midwestern America, and ordained as a Dutch Reformed minister, Muste early found in his religious convictions a compelling urge to social activism. "The eternal unrest of humanity and the discontent of the soul urge men to action," he wrote at the age of twenty in his first published essay, "and in action is the principle of all progress on the part of the race."

While minister of a small Massachusetts congregation during World War I, Muste embraced the pacifist cause. Forced to abandon his pastorate in 1916, he joined the Quakers and quickly became a leading figure in the Fellowship for Reconciliation. In 1919 he became involved in the Lawrence Textile Strike and began an association with the left wing of the American labor movement that lasted until the eve of World War II. He served as general secretary of the Socialist Amalgamated Textile Workers of America and helped to found and operate the radical Brookwood Labor College. During the 1930s he was largely responsible for the development of the sit-down tactics that would later figure so prominently in the early career of the New Left.

During this period, Muste also moved increasingly away from his original religious orientation. With the onset of the depression, convinced of the primacy of social revolution, he abandoned Christianity entirely, declared himself a Marxist-Leninist, and joined the Trotskyist wing of the Communist movement. He also renounced his pacifist convictions. "I chose revolution," he later wrote in his autobiography, "recognizing that it might involve violence."

In the late 1930s, as the threatening clouds of war again hovered over the world, Muste returned to religion and nonviolence. He denounced the organized Left, declaring that its dogmatic commitment to theory led inevitably to efforts to "overcome violence by violence, [to] establish democracy by dictatorship," and to share responsibility with the Right for the growth of the modern Leviathan State and the ultimate horror of war. Returning to his Quaker faith and ties, he re-entered and assumed the leadership of the Fellowship for Reconciliation. At the end of the war, as the nuclear age dawned, Muste—his passion for justice undiminished and his energies unflagging—campaigned vigorously for the development of "a strong and moral non-Communist Left," without which, he warned "we shall not escape nuclear war." Finding fresh inspiration in the ideas of Albert Camus and the example of Gandhi, he called for a movement that would be revolutionary in its radical and immediate assault on injustice anywhere and everywhere, pacifist in opposition to violence and coercion in any form, and capable of avoiding the traditional political drift toward centralization and authoritarianism—a movement that would "enable us, in a phrase of Camus' to be 'neither victims nor executioners!' "

Muste's seemingly incongruous intellectual swings from evangelical Christianity through atheist Marxism to existentialism and back again become explicable once we recognize that the animating principle of his entire career was a romantic, ultimately nonrational concept of a transcendental impulse, triggered by whatever immediate issues were subjectively felt to be paramount at the moment. The "discontent of the soul," urging to action, as he had early described it, was superior to any "scientific" social analysis. "I have to experience ideas rather than think them," Muste wrote. In describing his conversion to Marxism, he confessed that "I never became in any sense a scholar in Marxist and Leninist literature. . . . In any event, I turned to these books and periodicals in the late Twenties as I had turned to the mystics and early Quakers a dozen years earlier, not out of academic interest, but because I faced conditions and problems about which I *felt* I had to make decisions.

The result of the reading was in each case *acted out* rather than written about.''

This same sense of the primacy of emotions over ideas, of issues over analysis, was also the only unifying force in the New Left of the 1960s and the only principle that gives any coherence to the confused and contradictory history of what was essentially more a religious than a political movement. (During the 1930s Muste stated, ''it was on the Left . . . that one found people who were truly religious. Here . . . was the true church.'')

The editorial, ''A Tract For the Times,'' that formally announced the origin of *Liberation* in 1956 stated that ''many people are fed up with 'politics' '' and called for a return to ''ethical foundations and dynamic.'' Proclaiming the goal of ''the transformation of society by human decision and action,'' *Liberation* announced an effort to create a ''synthesis of the individual ethical insights of the great religious leaders and the collective social concern of the great revolutionists.'' As the ''creative imagination'' becomes the paramount political force, the journal prophesied, ''the outmoded 'scientific' aspect of Nineteenth Century Marxism will begin to disappear, and Marx will then appear in his true light as one of the great visionaries and utopian thinkers.''

In the 1960s, *Liberation* became deeply embroiled in the rapidly swelling waves of protest that swept through American society. It provided excellent first-hand reports on every aspect of the burgeoning black protest movement, covered the Cuban Revolution and the domestic reaction to it, and reported and analyzed every aspect of the Left and antiwar movements in America and abroad. It also published numerous pieces of social and cultural analysis, many of them by first-rate critics, artists, and scholars. Bertrand Russell, James Baldwin, Kenneth Boulding, Albert Camus, Lewis Mumford, Robert Theobald, and Theodore Roszak were among *Liberation*'s early contributors.

The editors and staff participated prominently in, indeed often led, the events they reported. *Liberation* is the ''house organ'' of those who ''put their bodies on the line for justice,'' wrote Paul Goodman in 1964. Staughton Lynd became a central figure in the campus revolts. Rustin organized and led the 1963 March on Washington. Barbara Deming participated in and reported on (often from a prison cell) a seemingly continuous series of peace and civil rights marches and demonstrations. Muste, at the age of eighty, scuffled with South Vietnamese government agents in Saigon and, in 1967, only weeks before his death, played a prominent role in the huge and hectic spring antiwar confrontation in Washington. Even David Dellinger, the undramatic workhorse of the *Liberation* staff, totally lacking the charismatic presence of his colleagues, found himself a central figure in a national drama. Dellinger stood in the dock at the tragicomic show trial of the Chicago Eight, resembling, in his drab suit and narrow tie, amidst his bearded and costumed co-defendants, a balding alumnus who had wandered innocently into a fraternity orgy only seconds before the police raid swooped down.

As the public protests spawned by the Vietnam War grew to massive proportions in the mid-1960s, *Liberation*'s editors, intoxicated by their own emotional zeal and the giddy effect of ceaseless activity, began to sense and proclaim a genuine revolutionary situation. They optimistically identified the inchoate and disparate groups involved in the protests as a unified and purposeful force, and editorially elevated the "Movement" to the status of proper noun. Lynd, in a 1967 article, defined the "Movement" as a "mood rather than a strategy" and a few sentences later advocated "choosing the Movement as a vocation" without pausing to consider the implications of choosing a mood (or even a strategy) as a vocation.

Liberation had at that point made no serious effort to define either itself or its "Movement" in coherent political terms. An attempt by the editors and leading contributors to offer a "What Is to Be Done" forum in 1967 produced a mélange of wildly optimistic but hopelessly confused and contradictory manifestoes. "The New Left . . . stands bewildered before the imperatives of ideology," Sidney Lens admitted. "Is it Marxist or non-Marxist, socialist or non-socialist, violent or non-violent, capitalist or anarchist?" Lynd confessed that "there has not been during these decades a book, or even a group of essays, to which you could point and say: Here you have what we believe." Goodman exulted in the fact that "there is no party platform."

With its inability to define itself politically and its lack of consistent theory or strategy, *Liberation* also became increasingly bewildered by the question of tactics. The absolute commitment to nonviolent resistance, the determination to be "neither victims nor executioners," had been the only firm doctrine shared by its founders. Originally warmly embraced by the early black and student movements, the nonviolent position was overwhelmed and submerged by the events of the mid-1960s. The bloody urban riots and the battle cry of "Black Power" dominated the thinking of the most revolutionary of the young black radicals and the militant images of the indomitable Cuban and Viet Cong guerrillas superseded Gandhi and Thoreau as the symbols of the revolution.

Faced with these developments and unwilling to accept the necessity for a break with large and growing elements of the "Movement," *Liberation* began to hedge on the issue of violence. Dellinger, musing on the future of pacifism in 1965, came close to flashing a green light for armed insurrection in the ghettos. "Can we," he asked, "urge the Negroes of Harlem . . . to refrain from violence if we offer them no positive method of breaking out of the slums, poverty and cultural privation that blight their lives. . . ? It is contrary to the best traditions of non-violence to do so." (Dellinger had spent all of World War II in a federal prison for urging refusal to fight against fascism.)

Although *Liberation* never entirely abandoned its pacifist philosophy, it began to publish contributions that openly called for the barricades. Carl Oglesby, the SDS leader, authored a 1968 piece on violent tactics in the black movement and declared a "fundamental obligation to support what they choose in pursuit of their own liberation." After the 1967 Pentagon confrontation, historian Arthur Waskow considered the issue of violence. "There are a few of us," he states, "who feel July 6, 1775 has already arrived and a 'Declaration of the Causes and Necessity of Taking Up Arms' well justified. A few of us feel . . . the taking up arms is never wholly justified." Admitting that "more of us are not certain what to think," Waskow concluded with the inane proposition that "we examine the rough guerilla-Gandhi mixture and try to develop a true synthesis of the two approaches."

Liberation did criticize the more obviously deranged insurrectionary proposals issued by some factions on the Left. It did so, however, in extremely gentle terms throughout 1967 and 1968 when the issue was live and immediate, and, in stern and strident tones, only after 1969 when, with its proponents dead, exiled, or engaged in calmer pursuits, the issue of revolutionary violence again became an academic one.

The romantic revolutionary illusions fostered by *Liberation* had in fact much to do with creating the emotional and intellectual climate in which obviously absurd and demented propositions (for urban guerrilla warfare by a hopelessly outnumbered and defenseless black minority, or kamikaze raids on military installations that would strip the United States of its defenses and leave world capitalism prostrate before the avenging missiles of the Red Chinese) could be seriously entertained and debated.

Lynd described that emotional state perfectly in his description of his own euphoria during the 1965 peace demonstrations in Washington:

> It was unbearably moving to watch the sea of banners and signs move out . . . toward the Capitol as Joan Baez sang ''We Shall Overcome.'' Still more poignant was the perception—and I checked my reaction with many many others who felt as I did—that as the crowd moved down the Mall toward the seat of government . . . toward the waiting policemen, it seemed that the great mass of people would simply flow on through and over marble buildings, that our forward movement was irresistibly strong, that even had some been shot or arrested, nothing could have stopped that crowd from taking possession of its government. Perhaps next time we should keep going. . . .

At the San Francisco State campus strike, Dellinger reproved Abbie Hoffman's insanely extravagant statement that ''Black Panthers and even White Panthers wait on the rooftop ready to shoot if the administration calls the police onto the campus.'' Dellinger sounded more like an indulgent father rebuking a spoiled child than a responsible revolutionary denouncing a hopelessly and dangerously adventurist cohort: ''I am sure that Abbie has no intention of going up onto a college roof with a gun himself, but what of the kids who might take him seriously.'' The parental tones (Hoffman was thirty-three years of age) perhaps reflected a subconscious understanding that, in the irrational and irresponsible Panthers, Yippies, and Weathermen, the brand of mystical revolutionary romanticism represented by *Liberation* faced its own badly deformed, but clearly recognizable, offspring.

By 1969, *Liberation* was printing the juvenile vulgarities of Jerry Rubin (our ''political program is rock and roll, dope and fucking in the streets'') presumably as part of its continuing quest for a ''synthesis of the individual ethical insights of the great religious leaders and the collective social concern of the great revolutionists.'' By the summer of 1969 the debacle of the New Left was complete. A quick reaction easily swept the putschist elements out of control of the campus demonstrations in the spring. By the fall the campuses had returned almost entirely to their traditional torpor. The vision of black revolution dissipated as the Panthers immolated themselves in ludicrous and murderous internecine brawls. The large young and middle-aged alienated white elements that had sought spiritual release in the "Movement" turned to the safer mystical comforts provided by the wave of occultism, the religious revival, nature worship, and the instant ecstasies of drugs. The idea that it was possible to build a genuine revolutionary movement without a coherent political platform or an identifiable class constituency was revealed as the ephemeral illusion it had always been.

Liberation quietly returned the "movement" to the lower case. Dellinger called for a clear understanding that there was no "way of getting rid of repressive institutions without immense sacrifice, dedication and responsibility." Julius Lester, himself a veteran of SNCC's Commando phase, wrote an excellent set of sober, self-critical articles. The New Left revolutionaries, he said, were "victims of our own illusions." They had created a "politics of romanticism which enshrines the dead and does little for the living." Instead of planting the "tiny seeds of the New Man," the New Left had "degenerated into a movement of emotional totalitarianism."

William Appleman Williams incisively pointed out that the radical movement of the 1960s had produced, as its conception of the meaning of the "Beloved Community," only a "collection of disjointed notes on what it does not mean and a vague assertion that all things will be beautiful come the revolution." It seemed an apt summary of the first fifteen years of *Liberation*.

Chico, California, 1973

Contributors

DANIEL AARON, professor of English at Harvard University, is best known for his *Men of Good Hope* (1951) and *Writers on the Left* (1961). His most recent book is *The Unwritten War: American Writers and the Civil War* (1973).

HANNAH ARENDT has written numerous essays and books on the problems of radicalism, including *The Origins of Totalitarianism* (1951, 1968) and *On Revolution* (1963). She has lectured throughout Europe and America and is presently university professor of the graduate faculty at the New School of Social Research.

DANIEL BELL is professor of sociology at Harvard and vice-president of the American Academy of Arts and Sciences. His best known works on radicalism include his *Marxian Socialism in the United States* (1961) and *The End of Ideology* (1960).

ALFRED M. BINGHAM was a member of the Connecticut State Senate in 1941-1942 and chairman of the Board of Trustees of Mitchell College, New London, Connecticut, between 1956 and 1970. He has written *Insurgent America: Revolt of the Middle Classes* (1935), *Techniques of Democracy* (1942), and *Violence and Democracy*, with Jonathan B. Bingham (1970). He is presently an attorney and a judge of probate.

RUSSELL BLACKWELL was active among American partisans of the Spanish Loyalists and a leading force in the issuance of *Spanish Revolution*.

ALAN BLOCK is chairman of the Department of History at Essex County College, Newark. He is associate editor of *Revival of American Socialism* (1971).

DAVID BRODY has taught at Columbia and Ohio State universities and was visiting professor at the University of Warwick, United Kingdom, during 1972-1973. He is now professor of history at the University of California at Davis and has written numerous books on the subject of American labor, including *Steelworkers in America* (1960), *The Butcher Workmen* (1964), and *Labor in Crisis* (1965).

DAVID E. BROWN received his Ph.D. from Ohio State University and is at present chairman of the Department of Political Science at the State University of New York at Potsdam.

MARI JO BUHLE was visiting lecturer in American Civilization at Brown University during 1972-1973. She has written extensively on American feminism and socialism, and has contributed on that subject to Edith Altbach, *From Feminism to Liberation* (1971). She is also co-editor of a new edition of the Stanton, Gage, Anthony *History of Woman Suffrage*.

PAUL M. BUHLE was founder of *Radical America* and editor from 1967 until 1973. He has written numerous essays on American radicalism, Marxist theory, and popular culture in a wide range of periodicals. He is co-editor of *Woman Suffrage in America*.

MILTON CANTOR is managing editor of *Labor History* and professor of history at the University of Massachusetts, Amherst. He has written on numerous subjects relating to labor, black history, and American radicalism.

JOSEPH CLARK is at this time press director for the American Cancer Society and a contributor to and editor of *Dissent*. He was secretary of the National Student League in 1934.

PETER CLECAK is director of the Program in Comparative Culture at the University of California at Irvine. He is the author of *Radical Paradoxes: Dilemmas of the Postwar American Left* (1973), and has contributed to numerous periodicals including *Saturday Review, The Nation*, the *American Scholar*, and the *Massachusetts Review*.

JOSEPH R. CONLIN, editor of this volume, presently teaches at California State University at Chico. He was formerly visiting professor of history at the University of California at Davis and at the Centre for the Study of Social History at the University of Warwick, England. His books on radical history include *Big Bill Haywood and the Radical Union Movement* (1969) and *Bread and Roses Too: Studies of the Wobblies* (1970).

DOROTHY DAY is editor of the *Catholic Worker* and has long been the guiding spirit of the Catholic Worker Movement.

RICHARD DRINNON is professor of history and chairman of the

Department of History at Bucknell University. His best-known work in radical history is *Rebel in Paradise: A Biography of Emma Goldman* (1961, 1970).

MELVYN DUBOFSKY has taught at Northern Illinois University, and the University of Warwick in England. He has written numerous works in American labor history, including *We Shall Be All: A History of the I.W.W.* (1969) and *When Workers Organize: New York City in the Progressive Era* (1968). His most recent book is *American Labor Since the New Deal* (1971), of which he is editor.

GUY ENDORE of Los Angeles was editor of *Black and White* and *Clipper: A Western Review*.

RICHARD FITZGERALD, presently of Laney College, Oakland, California, formerly taught at Long Beach and San Francisco State universities. He is an expert on the political cartoon and has lectured on the subject in numerous places, including the National Gallery of Art. He has recently published *Art and Politics: Cartoonists of the Masses and Liberator* (1973).

JAMES B. GILBERT is professor of history at the University of Maryland. He was formerly an associate editor of *Studies on the Left* and has authored *Writers and Partisans* (1968) and *Designing the Industrial State* (1972). He was Visiting Lecturer-Reader at the University of Warwick in 1972.

MARTIN GLABERMAN is currently instructor at Wayne State University after some twenty years experience in the labor movement. He is the author of *Union Committeemen and Wildcat Strikes* (1955) and the *American Working Class in The Sixties* (1966) among other books and articles.

WALTER GOLDWATER is the proprietor of the University Place Book Shop in New York City and a member of the Board of Governors of the Antiquarian Booksellers Association of America. As a bibliographer, he has compiled *Radical Periodicals in America 1890-1950* (1964).

HERBERT G. GUTMAN is president of the Labor Historians Association, associate editor of *Labor History*, and chairman of the Department of History at the City College of New York. He is the author of several important articles and papers on the development of American labor and radicalism.

ALLEN GUTTMANN is professor of English and American Studies at

Amherst College. He has held several distinguished fellowships and lectureships abroad, and served on the editorial board of *American Literature* between 1970 and 1973. Among books on several subjects he has written *The Wound in the Heart: America and the Spanish Civil War* (1962).

JOSEPH HANSEN was formerly a secretary to Leon Trotsky and has been active in work for the Socialist Workers party since its early days. He was the principal editor of *The Militant* several times.

MICHAEL HARRINGTON is by profession an author and professor of political science at Queens College, New York. He is a former chairman of the Socialist party, and is presently an editor of *Dissent* and of the *Newsletter of the Democratic Left*. Among his books are *The Other America* (1962) and *The Accidental Century* (1965).

DAVID HERRESHOFF is associate professor of English and American Studies at Wayne State University. He is the author of *American Disciples of Marx: From the Age of Jackson to the Progressive Era* (1967), and has contributed essays to Harvey Goldberg, *American Radicals* and to Bert Cochran, *American Labor in Midpassage*.

JEFFREY HEYNEN is a former editor of Greenwood Press. He is presently executive vice-president and director of operations for Redgrave Information Resources Corporation.

DONALD CLARK HODGES is professor of philosophy and past chairman of the department at Florida State University. He has been director of the Florida Center for Social Philosophy and president of the Missouri State Philosophical Association, and has served on the editorial boards of *Social Theory and Practice* and *Philosophy and Phenomenological Research*. In addition to contributing over 100 articles to several anthologies and professional journals, Professor Hodges has written *Socialist Humanism: The Outcome of Classical European Morality* (1973).

SIDNEY HOOK has been professor and chairman of the Department of Political Science at New York University. He is the author of numerous books on political philosophy, including *Religion in a Free Society* (1967), *Reason, Social Myths, and Democracy* (1940), *From Hegel to Marx* (1962), and *Political Power and Personal Freedom* (1959).

PHILLIP J. JAFFE was editor of *China Today* and editor and publisher of *Amerasia*. In addition to several books on the subject of East Asia, he has recently written *The Rise and Fall of Earl Browder: The Inner History of the American Communist Party* (1973).

FREDERIC C. JAHER teaches at the University of Chicago in the Department of History.

OAKLEY C. JOHNSON was managing editor of the *Monthly Review*. He was a teacher for fifty years and an editor of several other journals. He has written for many periodicals and his books include *The Day is Coming: Life and Work of Charles Ruthenberg* (1957), and *An American Century: Recollections of Bertha W. Howe* (1966).

IRVING KATZ, associate professor of history at Indiana University, has contributed articles to *The New England Quarterly, The Historian*, and *Mid-America*. He is the author of *August Belmont: A Political Biography* (1968).

GEORGE HARMON KNOLES, presently Margaret Byrne Professor Emeritus of Stanford University, was formerly chairman of the Department of History at the university. He has served on the executive committee of the Organization of American Historians and is the author of *The Presidential Campaign and Election of 1892* (1942) and *The Jazz Age Revisited* (1955) among other titles.

JOSEPH P. LASH, formerly United Nations correspondent for the *New York Post*, is a past winner of the National Book Award and the Francis Parkman Prize. For his books on Eleanor Roosevelt (*Eleanor and Franklin* and *Eleanor: The Years Alone*) he was awarded a Pulitzer Prize in 1972. He is also author of *Dag Hammarskjold: Custodian of the Brushfire Peace* (1961) and *A Friend's Memoir* (1964).

CHARLES LEINENWEBER has taught at the California State University at Long Beach and at the University of Essex, England. He presently lives in Florida.

HARVEY A. LEVENSTEIN is presently assistant professor of history at McMaster University, Ontario, after having taught at Brooklyn College and Teachers College, Columbia University. He has written various articles for scholarly journals as well as *Labor Organizations in the United States and Mexico: A History of Their Relations* (1971).

DWIGHT MACDONALD is staff writer for *The New Yorker* magazine, and during 1972-1973 was visiting professor of English at the State University of New York, Buffalo. He has been movie critic for *Esquire*, editor of the *Partisan Review*, and staff writer for *Fortune*.

Briefly a member of the Socialist Workers' party, MacDonald's radicalism is best known through his journal, *Politics*, which he edited and published between 1944 and 1949.

ROBERT D. MARCUS is associate professor of history at the State University of New York at Stony Brook. He has written *Grand Old Party: Political Structure in the Gilded Age* (1971) and, in collaboration with David Burner and Thomas H. West, *A Giant's Strength: America in the 1960s* (1971).

PAUL MATTICK is the author of a number of books, including *Marx and Keynes: The Limits of the Mixed Economy* (1969), *Arbeitslosigkeit und Arbeitslosenbewegung in den U.S.A.* (1969), *Der Leninismus und die Arbeiterbewegung des Westens* (1970), and *Critique of Marcuse* (1972).

DONALD J. MURPHY has taught at Cleveland State University and at the California State University at Chico. He was Fulbright Scholar at the University of Turin, Italy, during 1972-1973 and presently lectures for the University of Maryland in Europe.

GEORGE NOVACK is at present associate editor of the *International Socialist Review*. A former research associate for the Fund for the Republic, he has written on a variety of philosophical and social subjects. His most recent book is *Democracy and Revolution* (1971).

HOWARD H. QUINT, professor of history at the University of Massachusetts, was Fulbright Lecturer in Mexico during 1956 and, during 1961-1962, Fulbright Lecturer in Italy. He is the author of *The Forging of American Socialism* (1953). With Robert Ferrell, he edited *The Talkative President: The Press Conferences of Calvin Coolidge* (1964).

GEORGE P. RAWICK has written widely on the subjects of American labor, radicalism, and Negroes. He has taught at several colleges and is presently professor of sociology at the Empire State University of the State University of New York at Saratoga Springs. His most recent work is *The American Slave: A Composite Autobiography* (1972), of which Volume I is *From Sundown to Sunup: The Making of the Black Community*.

DALE RIEPE has taught in several American universities and in India and Japan. He is now professor of philosophy at the State University of New York at Buffalo. He has written several books on Eastern philosophy and also *Radical Currents in Contemporary Philosophy* (1970), *Reflections on Revolution* (1971), and *Philosophy at the*

Barricade (1971). His most recent book is *Phenomenology and Natural Existence* (1973).

STANLEY K. SCHULTZ teaches history at the University of Wisconsin and is chairman of the American Institutions Program there. He has edited *Cities in American History* with Kenneth T. Jackson (1972) and has written *The Culture Factory: Boston Public Schools 1789-1860* (1973).

STANLEY SHAPIRO is assistant professor of history at Wayne State University and secretary-treasurer of the Labor Historians. He has contributed several articles on liberalism and labor in the World War I period to *Labor History* and *The Historian*.

STEPHEN SITEMAN is assistant to the president at the State University of New York at Stony Brook. Formerly, he was secretary to Norman Thomas (1951-1967) and was a member of the National Committee of the Central Committee for Conscientious Objectors.

ROBERT SOBEL, professor of history at New College, Hofstra University, is author of several books on the American Stock Exchange. Among them are *The Big Board: A History of the New York Stock Market* (1965) and *The Great Bull Market: Wall Street in the 1920s* (1968).

MADELEINE B. STERN is a partner of Leona Rostenberg Rare Books in New York City. She is the author of numerous studies in nineteenth-century Americana, including *The Life of Margaret Fuller* (1968), *Louisa May Alcott* (1950), *Purple Passage: The Life of Mrs. Frank Leslie* (1953), and *We The Women: Career Firsts of 19th Century America* (1963). Most recently she has edited *Women on the Move*, a series of reprints.

WITOLD S. SWORAKOWSKI is a consultant to the director of the Hoover Institution, Stanford, and Professor Emeritus of Stanford University. A former member of the Polish Diplomatic Service, he is the author of *The Poles in Olsa Silesia* (in Polish, 1937), and *The Communist International and its Front Organizations: A Research Guide* (1965).

PHILIP TAFT, Professor Emeritus of Brown University, is past president of the Industrial Relations Research Association and of the Labor Historians Association. Among his many works on labor history are *The AFL in the Time of Gompers* (1957), and *Organized Labor in American History* (1964). Professor Taft also contributed to the John R. Commons *History of Labor in the United States from 1896-1932* (1926-35).

ALAN TRACHTENBERG is professor of American Studies and English at Yale University. His publications include *Brooklyn Bridge, Fact and Symbol* (1965), *Democratic Vistas, 1865 to 1880* (1970), and *The City: American Experience* (1972).

THOMAS WAGSTAFF is associate professor of history at California State University at Chico. He has contributed to several professional journals, including *Labor History* and *Civil War History*, and is the editor of *Black Power: The Radical Response* (1969).

DANIEL WALDEN, associate professor of American Studies at the Pennsylvania State University, has written or edited *American Reform: The Ambiguous Legacy* (1967), *On Being Black* (1970) with Charles Davis, and *W.E.B. DuBois: The Crisis Writings* (1972).

JAMES WEINSTEIN, editor of *Studies on the Left* between 1960 and 1967, is presently editor of *Socialist Revolution*. He is the author of *Decline of Socialism in America* (1969) and *The Corporate Ideal in the Liberal State* (1968). With David Eakins, he edited *For a New America* (1970), a collection of writings from *Studies on the Left*.

WILLIAM APPLEMAN WILLIAMS, formerly professor at the University of Wisconsin, now teaches at Oregon State University. He is the author of many books, the best-known of which are probably *The Tragedy of American Diplomacy* (1962, revised edition) and the *Contours of American History* (1961).

INDEX

Fabians, 40, 43; part in forming SPA of, 47, 61, 117; leaves IWW, 96, 101, 132; weakness of, 100; outpolling SPA, 178

Socialist Literature Company, 436

Socialist party of America, 142, 214, 372; as apex of American radicalism, 7, 82, 533; as unsectarian before 1919, 9, 47, 48, 87, 534-535; criticized by communists, 11-12, 284; as "wing" of reform movement, 21; strength in Oklahoma, 24; founding of, 44, 47, 62, 303; early structure of, 47-48; presidential campaigns of, 48, 61, 68, 87, 177, 178, 180, 181, 182, 447, 540; relationship with IWW, 48, 68, 95, 96; appeals to reformism, 49; factionalism within, 49, 84, 136, 159, 171, 533; electoral failures of, 49; recovers during First World War, 49; periodicals of, 6, 15, 49; distaste for official organ of, 62; electoral successes of, 60, 69, 135; reaction to world war, 92-93, 145, 579; 1919 split of, 145, 154, 159, 161, 171-172, 181; decline of, 162, 177, 178-179, 180, 186, 640; and communists, 170; and World War II, 179; after World War II, 639

Socialist Party Monthly Bulletin, article on, 87-90

Socialist Review, article on, 191-197

Socialist Spirit, article on, 43-46

Socialist Trades and Labor Alliance, 95

Socialist Union party, 322, 323, 324

Socialist Woman, article on, 442-449

Socialist Workers party, 7, 205, 209, 304, 518; founded, 331; splits within, 338, 523; "French Turn" of, 339

Socialist World, 181, 187, 188

Socialists, American, periodicals of, 6, 11, 24, 49; origins in America, 21-24; characteristics of, 55, 85, 89; hostility to Roman Catholic Church, 66; attitudes toward war, 92; factionalism a characteristic of, 117; effects of World War I on, 135, 145; development compared to European experience, 145-147; resistance to Comintern, 147-148

Solidarity, 101

Solow, Herbert, 523

Sombart, Werner, 356

Soul of the Russian Revolution (Olgin), 173

South Slav Federation (SPA), 137

Sozialistische Vestnik, 646

SP. *See* Socialist party of America

SPA. *See* Socialist party of America

Spanish Civil War, radicals and, 229, 230, 257, 275, 284, 330, 343, 398, 415-416, 421, 481-486, 546, 643

Spanish Revolution. (United Libertarian Organizations), article on, 481-486

Spanish Revolution (Workers' party of Marxist Unification), article on, 481-486

Spargo, John, as journalist, 46, 194, 530, 575; leaves SPA, 135, 567

Spartacus Youth League, 338

Spector, Maurice, 327-328

Spencer, Frederick. *See* Bisson, T. A.

Spencer, Herbert, 21

Spero, Sterling, 514

Spies, August, 381, 388

Spooner, Lysander, 377

Springfield Republican, 37

Stachel, Jack, 238

St. John, Vincent, 96, 100, 101, 118, 127

Stalin, Joseph, 114, 148, 207, 221, 288